WALTER B. GIBSON AND THE SHADOW

WALTER B. GIBSON AND THE SHADOW

Thomas J. Shimeld

Foreword by *Robert W. Gibson*

McFarland & Company, Inc., Publishers
Jefferson, North Carolina, and London

The present work is a reprint of the illustrated case bound edition of Walter B. Gibson and The Shadow, *first published in 2003 by McFarland.*

LIBRARY OF CONGRESS CATALOGUING-IN-PUBLICATION DATA

Shimeld, Thomas J. 1977–
Walter B. Gibson and the Shadow / Thomas J.
Shimeld ; foreword by Robert W. Gibson
p.   cm.
Includes bibliographical references and index.

ISBN 0-7864-2361-7 (softcover : 50# alkaline paper)

1. Gibson, Walter Brown, 1897– — Characters — Shadow.
2. Detective and mystery stories, American — History and criticism.
3. Detective and mystery plays, American — History and criticism.
4. Radio plays, American — History and criticism.
5. Authors, American — 20th century — Biography.
6. Private investigators in literature.
7. Gibson, Walter Brown, 1897–
8. Shadow (Fictitious character)
I. Title.
PS3513.I2823Z87   2005   813'.52 — dc21   2003000003

British Library cataloguing data are available

On the cover: photograph of Walter B. Gibson (collection of
William V. Rauscher); The Shadow illustration by Annushka Sonek

Manufactured in the United States of America

McFarland & Company, Inc., Publishers
Box 611, Jefferson, North Carolina 28640
www.mcfarlandpub.com

To Wendel W. Gibson:
Though your eyes never read this story,
your heart knew it all along,
and your spirit set it to prevail.

Contents

Foreword

by Robert W. Gibson, M.D.

Growing up with a father who created the Shadow and was the most published author of magic was unusual and exciting.

In the first grade my teacher asked that we all make some sort of presentation to the class. Most of the kids read a poem, sang a song, showed a family heirloom, or whatever. I performed magic. My father had taught me a trick when I was only six years old. I displayed a metal cylinder, showed with my wand that it was empty, put cotton in the top, and then covered it with a lid. I next covered the cylinder with a cardboard tube, took off the lid, and withdrew a dozen silk handkerchiefs. Not only were my fellow students amazed, but the teacher called my parents to ask if they knew what I was doing.

I became acquainted with many famous magicians— Howard Thurston, Harry Blackstone, Sr., Joseph Dunninger and many more. Over the years, I have also met many amateur magicians. Whenever I have mentioned that my father was Walter B. Gibson, they have said, "Walter Gibson, the author of magic books? My first book on magic was by Walter Gibson. He hooked me on magic!"

My father first wrote of the Shadow in 1931 when I was just six years old. His workroom was next to my bedroom. The writing schedule demanded almost round-the-clock writing; I can still remember the typing as I went to sleep. It was pleasant to know he was nearby.

My bedtime stories were the plots of Shadow novels in their embryonic stage. Of course, there were other stories that poured from my father's fertile, creative mind. Among them were the adventures of a remarkable family of fish, which should have been published.

Most people know of the Shadow through the Blue Coal radio programs of the 1930s. These programs were taken from the Street & Smith Shadow novels, which often involved collaboration with my father. Repeatedly I have been told: "The

Shadow! Our family always listened to the Shadow on Sunday afternoons at four o'clock. It was the time we all got together." The Shadow seemed to transcend all generations. I like to think that possibly millions of people associate the Shadow with those enjoyable family Sunday afternoons.

My father knew every famous magician and had personal contact with many prominent writers, but their prestige or prominence never drew him. He could spend an hour talking with the bellman of a hotel. He simply enjoyed people.

I am deeply grateful to Thomas J. Shimeld for bringing together this biography. Few people other than magicians have heard about Walter B. Gibson. Virtually everyone over the age of 50 has heard of the Shadow. This biography should help the world know Walter B. Gibson, the creator and author of the Shadow.

Preface

A young boy enters the local library and rushes to the corner of the building. He sits on the floor and looks at the bottom shelf of books. Various titles of books on magic as a hobby and as a form of entertainment intrigue the young reader. He chooses one which details the workings of close-up miracles. It is presented in an easy to follow language and illustrated by handfuls of pictures. He reclines back into the corner and begins reading his first book on magic…

A family gathers in front of the radio in the late 1930s on Sunday night. They eagerly watch the amber glow of the dial as they await the laugh that fills the hearts of evildoers with terror and sends chills down everyone else's spine…

At the end of a long, hard week at work and school, there is a sigh of relief, the weekend is here. And there is a hint of joy and anticipation to leave the building so each individual can head straight for the newsstand. Twice a month at the end of the week adults and children alike rush to their local newsstand for a single purpose: they must follow the further adventures of their hero in the pulp magazines…

A couple move slowly through the dark theatre. In the shadows they spy two seats in the center of the theatre — a perfect spot to view the huge screen in front of them. With popcorn and drinks carefully balanced in their hands, they excuse themselves as they inch between people's knees and the backs of the chairs in the row in front of them, careful not to step on any toes in this row, or not to knock into any heads in the front row. The two finally claim their seats just before the lights begin to dim and the rectangular screen facing them begins to shine…

A boy grips the loose boards and hoists himself up into the tree. A comic book delicately rests under his arm. He scrapes his hand on the rough tree bark as he reaches for the next board. He glances down at the colorful book under his arm. He scampers up the rest of the tree into the safety of the rickety struc-

1

*ture which the tree supports with its powerful arms. The cover of the thin book
is opened and the boy is transported to a world filled with adventure…*

Their stories are different but their feelings of joy through escapism remain the same. These people, from different times and different places, share in the excitement of the creations of one individual: Walter B. Gibson. From magic, to dance, to occult, to true crime, to judo, to hypnosis, to the Shadow, Walter Gibson wrote about it all, and more. But after writing 187 books, contributing 668 articles to periodicals, inventing 283 full-length novels of *The Shadow Magazine*, creating 48 separate syndicated feature columns (running from one article to 2,000 numbers), reporting adventures of the Shadow and Blackstone the magician in 394 comic books and newspaper strips, and aiding in the development of 147 radio scripts and numerous other works, not to mention inventing many widely used magic tricks and traveling with and befriending the great performers in magic history — Harry Houdini, Howard Thurston, Harry Blackstone, Sr., Joseph Dunninger among others — Walter Gibson is still relatively unknown. Yet he has touched almost everybody's life in one way or another. No matter who you are, where you live, or how old you are, the aura of Walter Gibson's creations have touched your life.

I never really knew how much Walter Gibson had influenced my life until I started researching his works. In fact, that young boy in the opening paragraph was me. I was enthralled with magic after seeing a beautiful magic show, Le Grand David and his own Spectacular Magic Company, in Beverly, Massachusetts. I was seven years old and desperately wanted to learn everything I could about the world of magic. I had to know how the tricks were done. I wanted to become a magician. But how? Where does one go to learn the secrets of this mysterious world? My first destination was the library.

When I arrived at the library, I found a small section devoted to magic. I chose the largest, most attractive book to read. Its pages fully described many of the wonders of magic. Jammed full of pictures, it was an easy task to understand each trick.

I learned a few standard tricks and wanted to learn more. I revisited the library and borrowed a book on Houdini. I learned how to walk through a wall (although I've never attempted such a miracle), and how Houdini escaped from handcuffs and locked trunks.

When I opened the covers of these two books I unlocked the world of magic. I also, unbeknownst to me at the time, opened my life up to the influence of Walter Gibson.

I have now memorized the exact position of the magic books in all the local libraries. And all these collections have something in common: at least one magic book written by Walter Gibson. In fact, I can say with some confidence that every library around the country has at least one book (magic or otherwise) written by Walter Gibson. It may not be authored in his own name, for he ghostwrote for others and created many pseudonyms, but I can almost guarantee that there is one there.

Gibson's indirect influence over me continued through the years. By the time I was eleven, I wanted to purchase a real magic trick like the ones I had witnessed on stage four years previously. I had numerous magic sets which were bought at local toy stores, but I felt I was ready for the big time. My friend Ronald Goldberg and I scoured the yellow pages, looking for some clue of the location of a magic shop; there was none. In exhaustion we attempted our search one last time, and, as if by magic, the telephone number and address for Don Paul's Magic Shop appeared in the phone book. We went to visit as soon as we could. Little did I know as I opened up the door on that blue building that my life would be changed forever.

Inside the shop we met a magician, James Lantiegne, who introduced us into a young magician's club called the Society of Young Magicians. It was Assembly #1 sponsored by the local Society of American Magicians, Assembly #118, the Walter B. Gibson Assembly. We were lucky enough to have the founder of the SYM, Wendel W. Gibson, become our magic instructor.

After a few years in magic, learning all sorts of fascinating tricks from Wendel Gibson, I found out that Wendel was actually the nephew of Walter Gibson, and many of the tricks I was learning from Wendel were taught to him by his Uncle Walter. Wendel told me of his uncle's prolific writing career, and his involvement with the creation of the Shadow, but I was too young then to realize the significance of all he told me.

In fact, it wasn't until years later when I found a collection of tapes of the old Shadow radio broadcasts in a bookstore that I began to realize the importance of my magic instructor's uncle.

Furthermore, when I returned to the library to check out magic books, I noticed that many were written by Walter Gibson. I began to feel privileged to know the nephew of such a great writer, yet I have now found that Walter Gibson was even greater than I thought back then.

As the years moved on I became friends with another young magician, John Fleischer. He came to me with the idea of creating a magic magazine for the advancing young magician. I was sixteen at the time and John was a year or so younger. Three years of planning went into this project and finally *FizBin* was born.

Our first regular column was the "Blackstone Roadshow" reprinted with Wendel's permission. It tells of his exploits with Harry Blackstone, Sr. when he traveled with the show. Walter Gibson and Blackstone were good friends and Wendel was becoming interested in magic at this time and was lucky enough to secure a job with this large traveling stage show thanks to his uncle's influence.

Once *FizBin* was a year old, Wendel suggested a new column entitled, "Tricks My Uncle Taught Me." This column demonstrates the fertile mind of Walter Gibson. Wendel recalls the times he spent with his uncle learning various card tricks that have a powerful presentation, but are virtually self-working. This column gave me an opportunity to take a further look into the creative mind of Walter Gibson.

Wendel eventually approached me about the vast materials he had collected about his uncle through the years. He spoke about never having the time to sort through the boxes of diaries, newspaper articles, and other such memorabilia. I offered to sort through it for him, figuring it would be a wonderful way to gain some more knowledge about Walter Gibson and about magic history; yet it became more than this, it soon became the opportunity for me to lead the life of this active writer and magician.

I sorted through boxes and boxes of papers. I methodically put each paper in chronological order and made piles according to decades of Walter Gibson's life: the 1900s through the 1980s. It took a summer to sort through this vast array of materials, and this didn't even include reading them. I was intrigued by the wealth of knowledge that lay in front of me; piles of material that only I had access to. Because the information before me was so wide-ranging, I approached Wendel with the idea of putting together a book. He enthusiastically agreed, and at the age of nineteen, I began reading through the materials.

I was lucky enough to have access to all of Walter Gibson's personal diaries that he kept as a child. This opened his world to me. I was quickly transported back in time to the beginning of the twentieth century. The creative mind of Walter Gibson was open for me to inspect. I began to make connections between the two of us. I then surpassed my age in my readings and took a look into the future. It was as if I was Walter Gibson, living his life, sensing his thoughts, feeling his emotions.

Events, people, places all whirled by me. I lived an entire life in just a single year. It was simply amazing. I felt such a strong connection with this man of words that I did not want to see his life end. I knew the last pile from the 1980s contained his obituaries. I had borrowed the pile from Wendel and brought it home. It lay on my desk, beckoning me to read it. It contained the death of a hero. I couldn't bear to read it. It was too personal, it would mean that the adventure was over.

I finally got enough courage to begin reading. The first paper was an essay by Will Murray remembering his good friend Walter Gibson. As I began to read a sick feeling squeezed my stomach. My eyes began to water. A quiver of my lips indicated my attempt to hold the emotions back, but it was too late. I began to cry. I cried for the truth I learned. This great man whom I admired was dead. I cried for the realization that I could never meet him, never speak to him. I cried because, along with him, it seemed I had died too. I was his playmate as a boy, his college chum at Colgate University, a fellow writer with the newspapers. I was there when he received the job of fleshing out the Shadow character in a magazine. I reveled in his joy of its success. I met all the great magicians with him. I knew his mind, I understood his thinking. I virtually became him. And to be there with him through his last days, see his death, and not die too created a feeling of loss. A piece of who I was died.

It took me twice as long to get through this last pile. It was sad to see such a great person die. Yet it motivated me even more to complete this work.

Walter Gibson's goal in life was never to become rich or famous, just simply to keep busy; and with such a prolific writing career he certainly accomplished this. During his younger years he wrote his life experiences in diaries, and during his older years he wrote about the mysteries of life in his books. Much of Walter Gibson's work goes unappreciated for he never desired the fame of being an author. He obviously did not want name recognition, evident by his use of seventy-nine pseudonyms. Walter Gibson, in fact, did the work of seventy-nine people in his lifetime. Never before has his entire life story been put together in one book. In turning the page you, the reader, will open yourself to the life of Walter B. Gibson, just like I opened myself to his life as a boy sitting in the corner of the library reading my first book on magic.

1

Setting the Scene of
an Extraordinary Life

*The family lived in the city [of Philadelphia] which was fashionable in
those days, especially for business owners. Then came the movement where
everybody was moving out to the suburbs, and Grandfather liked that idea,
so he went up and bought a house [in Germantown]....*
— *interview with Wendel Gibson, 26 June 1996.*

A shadow. People's shadows stand beside them throughout life as a reminder of
where they have been and as a hope that there will be more to come. Shadows melt
and bend, develop, if you will, with the inspiring light of day: the more intense this
light shines, the more clearly one sees his shadow. The shadow is always there, waiting to be seen. The moment one enters the world he receives the gift of a shadow. It
may be years before one notices this constant companion. Everyone knew his shadow
as a child, but where is it now? One may intellectually know of its existence yet never
stop to see it. Does the shadow merely follow, or rather guide? Can the shadow see
into the future? What can one learn from it? Only the shadow knows....

Like the magic posters of old in which devilish spirits whispered knowledge in
the conjurer's ears, so too did Walter B. Gibson have a guiding spirit. Pictured more
as a cherub than a devil or nymph, this spirit guided Gibson on a wonderful road of
wonderment, self-discovery and imagination in which he thoroughly enjoyed what
he did.

Throughout Gibson's entire life this cherub was beside him, as a shadow, urg-
ing him forward. It possessed his entire being to write. He could not do anything
else. Gibson was obsessed with being productive, and he viewed writing as the most
productive thing he could do. His writing carried him far in life. It may have contributed to some difficult happenings, but on the whole writing was a source of enjoyment for Gibson. He embraced life's mysteries and reveled in sharing them with the
world.

7

Walter B. Gibson's vast array of creations came from his extraordinary capacity for knowledge. The genius of Gibson's mind can be attributed in part to his upbringing in an extraordinary family. The Gibsons encase a rather unique drive to succeed and harbor a strong emphasis on education.

Gibson's literary creations are due to the fact that he had the unique ability to tell a story well. His full life gave him an ample supply of anecdotes to relate on any subject. The ability to spin a good yarn is well woven into the talented genes of Gibson's family. Gibson's mother, May Whidden Gibson, was a very reserved, religious woman. (Due to her moralistic views she was against alcohol. Nevertheless she was tolerant of others drinking. Gibson and his second wife, Julia, use to enjoy a White Horse Scotch now and then and they liked to collect the little plastic white horses that adorned the bottle. Gibson always had a good laugh remembering his mother's affection for these mysterious white horses that he collected. She acquired some from Gibson so that she may decorate her plants and house with them "not knowing that each one of them represented a bottle of scotch!"[1]) Gibson's mother had a family tree that sprouted fascinating stories of bygone years. Her lineage can be traced as far back as the flight of the pilgrims to America on the *Mayflower* with a possible branch devoted to the famed John Smith who sailed this well-known voyage. Ms. Whidden's family was noted to be well versed in storytelling and sharing anecdotes of their lives. Her great-grandfather Captain Noah Smith was well noted for his anecdotes and ability to captivate an audience with such stories. In the town chronicle of his home town of Reading, Massachusetts, it is said that Captain Smith was "always social and cheerful, had a keen relish for 'Attic salt,' and possessed an unfailing supply of it himself. His memory contained an inexhaustible fund of anecdote and story, and it was ever his delight to entertain his friends with a relation of them."[2] A family of wonderful storytellers and witty humorists fortunately had its influence on its nearest of kin.

Ms. Whidden's cousin, Gibson's first cousin once removed, was a well-known American writer, Kate Douglas Smith Wiggin. Ms. Wiggin was born on September 28, 1856. Her parents, Helen Elizabeth (Dyer) and Robert Noah Smith, a lawyer, educated at Brown University and Harvard, brought Wiggin up in Philadelphia, Pennsylvania: Gibson's own hometown. After her father's death, Wiggin's mother remarried a physician and the family moved to Hollis, Maine.

Wiggin was primarily educated in Hollis. At the age of seventeen, she moved to Santa Barbara, California, with her family. It was in California that Wiggin became involved in a kindergarten teaching training course in Los Angeles in 1877. She enrolled in the first class of this new, novel teaching course conducted by Emma Marwedel.

Marwedel prepared Wiggin well enough for her to be selected to organize the Silver Street Kindergarten in San Francisco. This kindergarten is noted to be the first kindergarten west of the Rocky Mountains in which parents could enroll their young children free of charge.

A year later Wiggin married and quit her profession. But she was a woman who could just not lounge around; she had to remain active, as did many of the members of her family. She began writing children's books, and later novels, a venture in which she often collaborated with her sister, Nora Archibald Smith. One of Wiggin's most popular books was *Rebecca of Sunnybrook Farm*. Published in 1903, this children's book became one of the most widely sold books of its day.

Along with writing books and pieces for magazines, Wiggin had a keen interest in music and the stage. She traveled in Europe and befriended many popular names in the various trades she was fascinated by.

After her first husband's death in 1889, Wiggin remarried in 1895. The two spent much time together. They purchased a farmhouse in Wiggin's childhood town of Hollis, Maine. "Quillcote" became an important place for Wiggin to write her books. The two also lived in New York City, and planned annual trips of approximately three months out of the year to spend time in the British Isles.

When Wiggin died on August 24, 1923, the twenty-five-year-old Walter Gibson had wished to acquire her estate, "Quillcote," in Hollis, Maine. "'There was a little theater there that would have been great for practicing my magic tricks,'" states Gibson to Jim Haviland in *MaineLife*.[3] But unfortunately, things did not work as Gibson had hoped. But little did Gibson know that in less than ten years his life would take an interesting turn which would parallel his cousin's life. For as Wiggin was a pioneer as a writer and kindergarten worker, so too would Gibson be a pioneer as a writer and magician.

Inspired by the calm and important ancestry he had in Maine, Gibson spent an important portion of his life writing the Shadow in the small town of Gray, Maine. Gibson's mother grew up in Calais, Maine, which is located at the northeastern most tip of the state. Ms. Whidden's grandfather Noah Smith, Jr. was one of the better-known political leaders of Maine. As a lawyer, Smith moved his family to Calais, Maine, in 1830. He soon became very involved in the state's politics. For a number of years he was an active member of the Maine Legislature which opened the door for him to become Speaker of the Maine House of Representatives in 1854. In 1858, Smith became the Secretary of State. When a dear friend, the Honorable Hannibal Hamlin, was elected as vice-president, he secured Smith in the seat of secretary of the United States Senate in Washington. Later Smith would become the legislative clerk of the Senate.

With such an interesting and extensive heritage it is no wonder that Gibson could speak on any subject and relate it to a personal story of his life. Yet this is only half his heritage.

Gibson's father, Alfred Cornelius Gibson (April 24, 1849–February 1, 1931), was a young teenager at the time of the Lincoln assassination. Alfred Gibson recalls in a newspaper article that "The facts of the trial remain vivid in my memory. I was a boy at the time and the episode was big, because of my inexperience rather than from any sense of the vast importance of the trial. I did not realize, as I do now, the historical importance of the occasion. It has taken the intervening years with myself as with others to orient this period in the history of our country." In the late 1920s,

Alfred Gibson was noted as the last surviving person who was present during the conspiracy trials. (For a full account of Alfred Gibson's reminiscences of the trials see Appendix I.) Prior to his sixteenth birthday, Alfred enlisted in the 215th Regiment Pennsylvania Volunteers as a fifer. Alfred first served as an orderly for Colonel Francis B. Jones and was later reassigned to serve as a clerk to Major General John F. Hartranft. General Hartranft was ordered to Washington after Lincoln's assassination to serve as provost marshal general in the trial of the conspirators. It was the duty of the clerk to give daily accounts of the prisoners to General Hartranft. Alfred's spare time enabled him to be with the prisoners, pitching quoits and playing the fife. He also got the opportunity to sit in on the trial, which commenced May 12, 1865, and concluded on June 14, 1865. On July 5, President Johnson approved the verdict of the trial commission and chose July 7 to be the date of the hanging of the four sentenced to death. The arsenal penitentiary building in which the trial was held was the site of the hangings. General Hancock protected the arsenal with 10,000 troops, in fear that the guilty parties would be rescued. Only a few were admitted to witness the hangings, one of which was young Alfred Gibson.

Mrs. Surratt's daughter, her mother being one of the guilty, lay sobbing on Alfred's bed in the arsenal, as just outside the window, her mother stood on the scaffold. Alfred stood directly in front of Atzerodt, who was to attempt to murder Vice President Johnson. His close proximity to the convicted allowed him to hear Atzerodt's broken English exclamation, "Shentlemens, take ware." This account of "Gentleman, beware" was not recorded in any of the accounts of the hangings, but it left a great impression on Alfred, "both because of the peculiar way of saying 'beware' and because I was so close to the speaker," recalls Alfred in a newspaper article, years later.

Because of Alfred's position as clerk to the provost marshal general, it was his duty to write the names of each of the condemned and seal them in vials in order to identify the bodies in the future. The four conspirators were buried, with the vials, in a corner of the arsenal yard. "Several years later, when relatives obtained the bodies, I read in the newspapers that identifications were made possible through the discovery of these vials" states Alfred proudly in his article, "The Lincoln Conspirators."

Alfred Gibson received a few mementos from his involvement with the trial of the conspirators. The four ropes that were used to hang the four guilty parties were cut up into small pieces and distributed to the witnesses; Alfred obtained a piece of each of the four ropes. Three of the ropes Alfred gave away to friends, but retained one of the ropes, the one that hanged Mrs. Surratt. Alfred, in his later years, donated it to Ellis Post, Grand Army of the Republic, and it resides in the post's museum. Furthermore, the pine uprights used to support the trapdoors in the scaffolds were crafted into eight canes, one of which was given to Alfred. He later gave the cane to his father, Joseph Gibson, who had served as a soldier in the Civil War in the Seventy-first Pennsylvania Infantry. The cane was then lost and never recovered by the Gibsons.

Alfred Gibson also received a letter of recommendation from General Hartranft in 1866, who, at the time, was auditor general of Pennsylvania. Alfred used this letter after his graduation from Central High School in 1867 to secure a job with a gas fixture firm.

September 12, 1897, 2:00 P.M. A newly acquired shadow falls for the first time on the floor of the southeast corner room of the Gibson home at 703 W. Philellena Street as Dr. Donlon and nurse Susan Appleton bring Walter Brown Gibson into the world. The newborn Gibson could not realize his fortune to be born into such a nurturing family who would encourage his yet-to-be-discovered talents. The gene pool had just the right ingredients and Alfred and May Gibson had just the proper knowledge to bestow upon their children. Such a combination could only produce something special and thus Walter Gibson was born. He was the middle of three sons, between Theodore and Anthony, mothered by May Whidden Gibson. Alfred Gibson had been married previously and had a son, Arthur, and two daughters, Helen and Alice, in this first marriage. When Alfred Gibson's first wife died he spent some time in Europe on a business and pleasure trip. Traveling by ship in those days would make this tour months long, so May Whidden, the first cousin of Alfred's recently deceased wife, accompanied the family to act as a nanny for the children. Spending over three months together overseas brought Alfred and May closer together. Upon the family's return to the United States the new couple married. Together they had Theodore, Walter, and Anthony which made the children not only the half brothers of the first three Gibson children, but also second cousins. This fact brought about some interesting circumstances, for Arthur, Helen and Alice each had children that were around Walter's age, so Walter was technically these children's uncle. This made for great fun when the children were out on the town and needed parental consent to participate in some activity: "Will my uncle's permission be all right?" and the person demanding the permission was directed to the twelve-year-old Walter Gibson.[4]

The Gibson children grew up in a section of Philadelphia, Pennsylvania, called Germantown. This wonderfully rich and historic town must have been a true inspiration for Gibson. According to Edward B. Phillips in his articles "Germantown, PA," and "The Battle of Germantown," found in the *150th Anniversary of the Battle of Germantown* booklet, the town of Germantown lived up to its establishing goals of being a land of political and religious freedom. The first formal protests against slavery were held here in 1688.

Just like the Gibsons the early settlers were cultured and valued education. The first schools were taught by Francis Daniel Pastorius, a scholar and prolific writer. F.D. Pastorius was actually the author of the first school book published in 1698, titled "A New Primer." He had great interest in the town and developing it further. The settlers quickly began this development.

Germantown became famous for its stockings, thanks to the weavers and knitters of the town. Through the years shops were built, and mills which ran on water-power were constructed. Germantown opened the first paper mill in 1690, and in Philly County as early as 1683, a mill was erected for grinding grain. For a period,

Walter B. Gibson's birthplace in Germantown, Pennsylvania. Photograph by Thomas J. Shimeld.

Germantown became the leading industrial center of the nation due to its large factories.

To further increase the population of Germantown, and to better extend its products to other parts of the country, a railroad was built in 1832. This was where the first locomotive was built in the United States, called "Old Iron Sides." This inevitably increased the business end of this section of Philadelphia. The commercial business and banking industries increased, and the population grew.

Germantown is of great political importance as well. The American Army under General George Washington camped in Germantown before and after the Battle of Brandywine. On October 4, 1777, Washington's Army surprised Howe's army in the Battle of Germantown which took place up the street from Gibson's birthplace and childhood homes. It is said to have been "one of the most bitterly fought battles of the Revolutionary struggle, when its [Germantown's] streets and fields were strewn with the dead and wounded of both armies." The British reported that 535 of their men were killed, wounded or missing as a result of this battle, but Washington received reliable word that their damage was well over 800 men. The American loss as stated by the Board of War was 152 men killed, 521 wounded and 400 missing.

After the end of the Revolutionary War, Germantown still remained in the political light. Germantown was the first to send in a signed petition to adopt the federal Constitution. In 1793, Germantown became the state and national capital for a short time due to a fever epidemic in the city. President Washington spent the summer of

1794 in the "Morris House" in Germantown, thus making it the "summer White House." This house still stands around the corner and a few blocks up the street from Gibson's childhood homes. The people of this section of Philadelphia further exercised their political views on religion when they petitioned the Legislature of the State in 1795 to grant religious freedom to all creeds. William Penn and the Rhinelanders, the original settlers, got their wish for Germantown by establishing it as having true political and religious freedom.

Today, Germantown is still very popular. It is one of the leading centers of arborculture and horticulture. It is also a great educational center, having a couple of theological seminaries, several colleges, a large number of public and parochial schools, and a number of private schools.

The Gibsons lived first in the city of Philadelphia. The trendy movement of living in the suburbs soon took hold of the family, and they bought a house in Germantown, at 703 W. Philellena Street, where Walter Gibson was born and lived the first few years of his life. Gibson spent the remaining years of his childhood in a much larger house just up the street. The Gibsons were fortunate enough to be able to construct this second grand house due to the income received from the Gibson Gas Fixture Works. Alfred Gibson, in his later years, opened this company at 1426 Callowhill Street in Philadelphia, Pennsylvania.* The Gibson Gas Fixture Works sold and produced gas fixtures, and later produced electrical fixtures. It was an easy conversion from gas to electric for all one had to do was run the electrical wires through the gas pipes and to the fixture. Alfred Gibson came across this knowledge on a trip to New York one day. He was crossing the water on a ferryboat when he noticed that the ferry was running electrical lights. He wondered how this was accomplished. He eventually got in contact with the ferry owner to ask him how he had run electricity to the lights. The owner said that he had bought a generator that was connected to the steam engine, and that's where the electricity was supplied from. But to get the electricity

Logo of the Gibson Gas Fixture Works owned by Gibson's father, Arthur C. Gibson, and operated out of 1426 Callowhill Street, Philadelphia, Pennsylvania. Reproduced with permission from Robert Gibson.

*The company brought much money to the Gibson family by offering the public such an important service. The company's Album No. 18, published in 1901, lists electrical fixtures for as little as $.40 for a Colonial Style, 6 inch projection bulb, with satin gold finish, or as much as $225.00 for an "Electrolier," a 56 inch hanging fixture, with a spread of 20 inches, including 13 lights, finished in old brass ($10.00 extra for gold fringe).

to the light fixtures was easy: he simply ran the wires through the gas pipes! Alfred Gibson found out all the important information: when the man thought it up, whether it was an original idea, if anyone else was doing it (no one was) and if he had patented it (he had not). This became crucial evidence in later years when Alfred Gibson took it upon himself to fight a patent awarded to an individual who claimed he had invented the idea of running the electrical wires through the pipes. This was a huge trial at the time for it was so important to the future of electricity. Alfred Gibson left the gas fixture business under the supervision of someone else so he could devote all his time to the trial. Thanks to Alfred Gibson's research the patent office eventually revoked the patent that they had given to the other party.

Thanks to the profits of the Gibson Gas Fixture Works, things were going well financially for the Gibsons, so Alfred Gibson decided to build a bigger home for his family. Around the corner and down the street from their home on W. Philellena Street, Alfred Gibson bought half a city block at 707 Westview Avenue. An enormous three-story brick mansion with distinctive white pillars was constructed on this land by Wilson, Harris & Richards Architects. Completed in 1909, this home was where the Gibsons lived in a very formal fashion. After walking across a tile vestibule guests are greeted by the open arms of a dark, grand hall with a staircase to the upper floors. The hall acts as the head of an octopus with tentacles leading to the huge rooms around it: the reception room to the immediate right is complete with a cozy corner fireplace; this room opens into a formal dining room, also accessed from the hall with its own fireplace. At dinnertime in the Gibson home the family would sit in a formal fashion around the table with Alfred at the head. The dinner was prepared by a cook and would be served to them. Everything had to be perfect: sitting in a rigid way with good table manners. The children often got a good laugh reminiscing about the youngest brother's antics. Anthony used to play with the metal napkin ring by turning it on its side and pushing it off with his finger to provide a backspin so it would return to him. Anthony once directed the ring at his father, but instead of coming back, it cracked right into his father's plate, and "…this was virtually a crisis within the family."[5]

Off the dining room to the back of the house is the pantry, kitchen, and out-kitchen with a private staircase and back door for the help; to the left of the hall one finds a vast living room with a fireplace; two covered wooden floor porches act as the ears to this grand rectangle of the living room, hall, dining and reception rooms; a smoking room with a fireplace proudly displaying the initials ACG (Alfred Cornelius Gibson) and date 1909 complete the main rooms on the first floor.

The second floor contains six bedrooms, including the master bedroom along with three bathrooms. The third floor, where Gibson's room was, has an additional four bedrooms along with two servants' rooms in the back half of the house. On top of all this rests a spacious attic. There is also a full basement. Wendel Gibson, Walter Gibson's nephew, who also lived in this house most of his childhood, recalls that his grandfather "…built this huge, red brick, three-story, beautiful home, [with] big white pillars in the front…. A stable, with living quarters for help, so it was like a

In 1909, the Gibson family moved just up the street to this mansion where Gibson spent the later years of his youth. Photograph by Thomas J. Shimeld.

house, ... set there [behind the home] with a nice driveway going up to it. I remember they always had a horse when I was a kid. Grandfather finally got a car. He took us for a ride in it when he first got it. His chauffeur was the fellow who used to drive the horse and buggy."

Wendel described the inside of the house: "When you come in [the house], after the vestibule, you're in this hall with a beautiful chandelier — that was a work of art for the Gibson Gas Fixture Works — it filled that whole area. To give you an idea of the size of the house: You're in that [hall] where that chandelier is coming down and the stairway goes up ... and it goes across so it's like a balcony.... Half-way up [there's another one], half-way up to the next one and you're up at the top, that's where this [chandelier] comes down from; the same as they used to have in the theatres."

Alfred Gibson was obviously very proud of his home. He spared no expense. Wendel estimates that the house cost $100,000 in those days which would be roughly equivalent to $1,000,000 today. The house has become a treasured part of the family, a home with great memories that the family, even today, goes back to visit every now and then with the permission of the current owners. Though the house today is divided up into apartments, and some of the land has been sold off, it is still a strikingly beautiful home of which its owners are rightly proud.

Wendel Gibson had many fond memories of times spent at the house. Around the age of five, Wendel, his sister and father went to live in the home after Wendel's mother died. They spent approximately a year there. Wendel grew very close to his uncle Walter during this time. Wendel recalls him playing games with the kids and performing magic tricks. One of the most interesting would be a type of hide-and-seek magic trick. Gibson would go upstairs with the kids and enter a room. He told the kids to count to thirty before entering the room and then they were to try to find him. Wendel recalls entering the room with others and searching every single possible hiding spot, yet they could never find Uncle Walter. He had simply disappeared, as if by magic! Gibson would then reappear in another room of the house, or in the hallway, and enter through the door of the room laughing. It turns out that Gibson would actually sneak out the window of the room onto a small ledge that ran around the house. He would then scoot his way along until he reached another window that he had left unlocked for the purpose of reentering the house. This was certainly a house of great memories and a wonderful history.

Around the time of the conversion from gas to electricity trusts were being formed in the world. The large one in the electrical fixtures industry was General Electric, and it bought out small outfits like Gibson Gas Fixture Works. Alfred Gibson had thought that what he developed was his and no one but his family should have it. He offered the factory to his boys, an offer which would guarantee them continued wealth. But they wanted to find their own adventures away from the nest. Alfred Gibson never sold out to a big corporation, but was forced to sell his factory piece by piece, until it was totally liquidated because of his sons' need to separate themselves from the family in pursuit of their own dreams.*

This Gibson ambition and adventure certainly was well established in Walter B. Gibson's mind. Gibson's generation were in conflict with their family, for they were attempting to break away from the Victorian era. Gibson's father pressured his sons into being successful, expecting them all to live up to the Gibson name, a family full of scholars and lawyers. They did not want to do what their family had always insisted that they do. They wanted to live their own lives, in their world of the 1920s and 1930s. Walter Gibson was no different. He entered the world to establish himself and do something productive, but the lessons of his youth would always stand by him on every avenue he ventured down. Walter B. Gibson refused to live in the shadow of his father's creation, yet rather desired to fulfill his destiny by creating his own Shadow.

Today a parking lot occupies the space at 1426 Callowhill Street in Philadelphia where the works once stood.

2

The Magical Years
of Youth

Manchester, Vermont. A small boy is playing a game in which he is handed one end of a long string. The object of the game is to follow the string to its other end to collect the prize which will be there. At the other end of Walter Gibson's string is a box of simple magic tricks. Of such are the ways of Fate.

— J. Randolph Cox, The Man of Magic and Mystery:
A Guide to the Work of Walter B. Gibson,
Scarecrow Press, 1988.

In gliding back through the years of Walter Gibson's full life, one sees that from a very early age Gibson was learning the necessary skills that would aid him in his career in later life. From simple play, to family trips, every small detail of Gibson's early life was slowly molding his mind and turning his thoughts towards the linguistical, the mystical and the magical.

The Gibson family enjoyed traveling during the summer. Each summer they vacationed in various spots throughout the United States and often in Canada. It was during these trips that Gibson became inspired to pursue various interests in later life. One of the most important discoveries occurred just prior to Gibson's tenth birthday in Manchester, Vermont, during the summer of 1906. The Gibson family rented a house on Main Street, just south of the St. John's Episcopal Church. Gibson spent the summer making friends and playing with the neighborhood children. During this summer one of Gibson's new friends had a birthday party, which, of course, Gibson eagerly attended. The party must have been a typical birthday bash, with friends, family, and food, but at this party the children played a special game. A game that would change Gibson's life forever. To begin the game, each child was given a different colored ribbon. It was the child's mission to follow the ribbon throughout the house and it would lead him to a present. With a laugh and a smile, the children received their individual colored ribbons. Gibson began to follow his.

17

The ribbons slithered around furniture, in and out of doors, up and down stairs. Children scattered throughout the house, holding onto their precious ribbons which gave them claim to their surprise present at the other end, just as a leash tells all passersby on the street that the pup at one end belongs to the person at the other. The laughter came to a crescendo when the present appeared in view. A twinkle in Gibson's eye showed his thrill at finding his prize at the end of this adventure. At the end of Gibson's ribbon lay a magic game box. This German trick box had standard tricks of the day. This small adventure in a new friend's house would lead Gibson on a lifetime pursuit in the mystical world of magic, as if the ribbon were his life-line that gave Gibson a glimpse into his future.

This box of tricks soon led Gibson to claim magic as his hobby, and anything to do with the strange, weird, and unusual also fit into his interests. He was wide-eyed in his search for anything having to do with magic. A frequent reader of the *St. Nicholas Magazine*, Gibson was delighted when it began running a series on magic. The series, "Magicians' Tricks and How They Are Done," was written by Henry Hatton and Adrian Plate; both were magicians affiliated with the Society of American Magicians. (The S.A.M. is a club in which, in later life, Gibson would become very involved). In 1910, these two magicians also had authored an excellent book entitled *Magicians' Tricks: How They Are Done* (New York: Century Company). Hatton and Plate's work exposed many young people of the day to magic. At an earlier time the only book that taught magic in a straightforward manner with easy to follow directions was Professor Hoffmann's *Modern Magic*. In reflecting back on this time of his life, Gibson considered the former book to be *Modern Magic's* equivalent. Gibson enjoyed Hatton and Plate's book so much that he later had it republished in 1979 and supplied the introduction. The clarity, no-nonsense approach in these writings would also characterize Gibson's future works.

A product that further fed Gibson's magic bug magically appeared in 1911. The Mr. Quick boxes of magic were introduced by A.C. Gilbert, a medical student at Yale at the time, in conjunction with Petrie-Lewis, who had a factory in New Haven, Connecticut. A box had such tricks as the multiplying wheel, which had never been in a trick box set before. It also had such things as the shell coin and the passing coin. These box sets were sold in department stores through demonstrations.

Many children had magic sets in their youth. After all, who has not been interested to some extent in magic as a child? Yet there is a time in every budding magician's life when they want more from the magic world. It is at such a time that a person begins to pass through the invisible door which holds the secrets of magic locked inside. This is the time when these people start frequenting magic shops. And once a person purchases his first magic trick here, there is no turning back, for the magic bug finally has a secure hold. Its magical needs are impossible to cure, and lead to a life filled with fantasy, mystery and magic!

There were a few magic shops in the Philadelphia area that Gibson frequented. One such shop, owned by Carlton who had worked at Martinka's, was a small one which was virtually just a show window in an inexpensive hotel. Eventually the proprietor of the shop went broke and the man who owned the hotel took it over.

Another shop in Philadelphia called Yost's was very difficult for Gibson to get into at this stage of his interest in magic. This was an exclusive magic shop for professional, accredited magicians. It was almost an "invitation only" type shop: if you weren't invited, you didn't go in.

Such magic shops gave Gibson a perspective not many children got. But Walter Gibson's childhood was not unlike many other boys' of the era: playing war games, sleeping outside in tents, building forts, playing with friends, going to Sunday school and church, enjoying the occasional auto ride, and of course baseball. But there was a slight difference that foreshadowed the genius of Walter Gibson's mind.

Throughout Gibson's life, he always had a particular fascination with reading, games, magic and puzzles. He was enthralled with the details of life, and thought a little bit differently than his peers. At the age of four, Gibson liked to join his family in a game of hearts. His kindergarten teacher actually had a special pack of cards for Gibson so he could make up his own games and puzzles with them. At the age of seven, Gibson entered the Chestnut Hill Academy, not far from his home. His interest in literature became more apparent at this time with his first published work. In October 1905, a puzzle Gibson had submitted to the St. Nicholas League section of the famous *St. Nicholas Magazine* was published. It read: "(4) Change this figure to another system of notation and it will give the name of a rare old plant." Answer: If one changes the 4 into the Roman Numeral IV which can be pronounced i v or ivy, one arrives at the name of the delicate green leaf climbing plant. The inspiration for this mind-boggling puzzle came from young Gibson's favorite book at the time, L. Frank Baum's *Queen Ziki of Ix*. Just as Baum had used the Roman numeral IX as the name of a fictitious land, so too did Gibson see the Roman numeral IV as a possible word.

In 1908, at ten years old, Gibson took it upon himself to begin a diary. This diary was the stepping stone for many to come. The busy life of a ten-year-old did not allow much time to write in such a journal, but Gibson, every now and then throughout the year, would largely scroll in cursive a day's events. He paid particular detail to such incidentals as the weather, a trend that would continue in the volumes of diaries to come. He also listed such things as baseball and football scores. There were even pages devoted to a specific local baseball game in which he illustrated the action moments of the game through roughly drawn cartoon characters. Baseball would become a favorite of Gibson's, probably sparked by his father's interest in the game. (It seems Alfred Gibson even played baseball for a time, as Gibson notes in his 1984 diary on November 13: "Checked baseball cyclopedia for data on Al Reach — yrs. 1871–76 when my father subbed for him. Good anecdotes from that.") Walter Gibson could spout off anybody's average. His father would also follow baseball religiously. In a distinguished stroll Alfred Gibson would enter the room to see his family anxious for details on the day's game. He would announce, "The A's won." After a brief pause to build suspense, a moment in which nobody dared to breath, he would say, "Yankees 5."

Gibson's diaries would further illustrate his other loves. He paid close attention to detail in drawing maps of favorite adventure areas, making sure to label all the important parts. Often he simply stated that the day's adventures were "piles of fun." Although rough, this first diary gave a glimpse at what was to come, and it gave a glimpse into Gibson's own mind.

This boy grew up to be a man with many creative ideas running through his head. And as a child and young man, his mind also whirled and he would jump from subject to subject; not having space on one page of a diary, he would use another in the beginning or at the end, jotting down numbers and symbols to follow to make sure the reader read it all in the correct sequence. Gibson attempted to aid the reader in this process by providing a table of contents, or beginning notes that describe his process of thinking. Even in his first diary, Gibson included such a helpful page entitled "Directions":

> direction —1— Go to 112. Read back to 110 then go to 113 read ahead come back to 103 after reading 116 Awlays [sic] read the dates read to 109 then skip to 117 Now your [sic] all right aren't you?
> Directions— 2 — read 122 skip back to 99 read then go to 94 read back to 90 skip to 125 That wasn't very hard was it? Now your [sic] all right.
> See 45 now

This page was typical in the earlier years of his diaries. As he progressed in years he organized the system more, and made his directions more coherent. In his 1916 diary's introduction, Gibson admitted that, "while other [notes] outgrew their territories with the result that all the notes are jumbled in a hap-hazard, conglomeration; the numbering is misleading, and the entire system is most perplexing." Reading through his earlier diaries, gives one the feeling that one is reading a "choose your own adventure" novel, for one is constantly turning pages forward and back to keep up with the day-to-day adventures. A man enthralled with puzzles has produced a most interesting puzzle out of his early diaries.

As Gibson grew older, his interest in literature and language grew with him. At age fifteen, he still had the not so unusual interests in stamps, baseball, football, and skating ("My skates are nice & new," states Gibson in his 1913 diary on February 8, "cause I skate on my neck..."), but he also enjoyed learning about magic, was on the debating team, and thoroughly enjoyed language. Gibson had some interest in foreign languages at this time for he frequently wrote in his diaries in French and sometimes Latin. His writing interest in English also escalated.

Gibson's interest in the spoken and written word gave him much to say on various subjects, especially in debating various matters. One hot topic of debate at the time was women's suffrage. Gibson was sixteen years old when the Legislature in Pennsylvania accepted women's right to vote. Gibson had strong convictions regarding this subject and argued for it. He briefly recalls in his diary on February 3, 1913, "Had an argument with Bill K. on Women's Suffrage.... He's against it. I'm for it. He says it's a bunch [of] rotten women that'll vote. I say they're good women. Women have more of a right to vote. He says they'll come around disgracing the polls. I say they'd better 'em. Well we had some argument, and we almost got mad."

Gibson's diaries from now on become much more detailed, and written in consistently. His interest in writing in general took effect then. On February 4, 1913, Gibson states in his diary that he, "handed in a story for the *Wissahicken* [the school paper] last Wednesday. It was called the 'Hidden Will.' It's a peach. I don't know if they'll take it though." But to Gibson's amazement, he did get this mystery story published on February 20. He exclaims that day, "I'm going to write some more," and he certainly did! A niece of Gibson's, Libby Figner, remembers (in a personal letter to the author of August 10, 1998) visiting her grandfather's house as a young girl. Gibson was eight years older than she and in grade school. He was in his third-floor bedroom writing a mystery story during her visit. "Figs" (as Ms. Figner was affectionately called) was shocked to see Gibson bolt down the stairs crying. The family nurse, Ms. Wright, consoled him. Walter Gibson had frightened himself with his own story.

On June 11, 1914, one sees that Gibson had furthered his magical career. He writes:

> Last Spring I had become interested in magic, & I met a fellow at Keewaydin [a summer camp Gibson attended], who gave me pointers & advised me to go in the Retail Business. The result is that now I am in partnership with one Howard Rippey; firm of *Gibson & Rippey*, & we are making good coin. I have given several performances, taken a course of Sleight of Hand at the "Magic Shop," am acquainted with the "Mysterious Dunninger," one of New York's best magicians.

His performances increased too. He recalls performing a larger show with a friend of his named Howard Kenner. Together they put on a show at William Temple around the Thanksgiving of 1914.

Gibson had a little more free time now to pursue his magic career for his father wanted him to transfer from Chestnut Hill Academy to the public Northeast High School in Philadelphia, even though Gibson had been happy and progressing rapidly at Chestnut Hill. He entered the junior class in 1913 and graduated in 1914.

Gibson continued his education at Peddie Institute (now called Peddie School) at Hightstown, New Jersey. This was a preparatory school for Colgate University. At Peddie Institute, Gibson immersed himself in learning — physically and mentally. He was involved with the YMCA, enjoying tennis, baseball and swimming; and academically he had classes in French, trigonometry, Latin, the Bible, public speaking and gym. Gibson was also on the debate team and wrote for the school paper, the *Chronicle*. Gibson managed to entertain with his magical miracles at every opportunity he received. He performed a "side show" at the local Strawberry Festival on Friday, June 13. "I hauled in $1.85...," he reports. He would also perform for friends and family. When visiting his older sister, Alice, in Princeton, Massachusetts, in August 1916, Gibson received an engagement at the town hall. He immediately sent word home for them to ship him his trunk of magic. A week later, on Thursday night August 17 Gibson gave his performance. He writes: "Fixed up my paraphernalia today ... and gave my performance. It went fine. I don't remember one that I 'got away with' better. I was somewhat hampered by the lack of an assistant and forgetting some of my things, but … all went well."

He often performed at parties for his younger brother Anthony. The two siblings had a wonderful, close relationship. Gibson often hung around with his brother and his friends. They often attended movies together. Gibson was what every child would want a big brother to be. He was caring and giving, and always thinking of his younger brother. He would often purchase toys and whatnots for Anthony. But of course they wouldn't be brothers without a few pranks between the two. Anthony was always the victim of Gibson's playful April Fool jokes.

Gibson's writing interest skyrocketed during the school year of 1915–16 at Peddie Institute. His first article, describing a magic trick, was called "A New Rising Card;" it was published in the magic magazine the *Sphinx* in 1915. Three more articles were published in this popular magic magazine that year, and two more in 1916. Later Gibson wrote for a magician from whom he often bought magic, Collins Pence, who owned The Eagle Magic Company. Pence had a falling out with the *Sphinx* over advertising, so he decided to publish his own periodical, the *Eagle Magician*. Gibson agreed to write promotional material and later articles for this new publication. Walter Gibson furthered his writing career when he became a member of the *Chronicle*'s staff on Friday, February 11, 1916. He wrote articles for this school paper and a few short stories. On March 9, 1916, Gibson writes that he had to "write a story for the *Chronicle*. I wrote home for them to fish up my 'Romuda' the story I wrote for the *Archive* last year." Gibson describes the story entitled "The Romuda" (there has been some discussion on whether this story's title is spelled *Remuda* or *Romuda* but one can clearly see in Gibson's diary that he spelled it with an "o") as a mystery "about a Russian who came to America, and joined a secret society against his will etc. etc. etc. and finally blew up the society with him in it." This story was originally written for the school paper at Northeast High, but found its true success in the *Chronicle*. On Monday, May 1, 1916, "The *Chronicle* came out, 'The Romuda' winning 1st prize and 'The M. of T.H.' also being published," boasts Gibson in his diary. The "M. of T.H." was a parody that Gibson wrote on *The Merchant of Venice*, properly titled, "The Merchant of Trask House." Gibson seemed to enjoy writing some silliness, for he wrote another parody of *Julius Caesar* on May 14, entitled "Baldy Swetland," which illustrated many phases of school life, and was to become the senior play. An example of his humorous writing appeared in his 1916 diary on January 4 and 5:

> My spirit is filled with sadness
>   As around this place I fool
> And I long with fervored madness—
>   For my dear old school!
> Some Poetry! A new style I just invented. "Ironical
> Lyric" is its name.

But after all he wrote, "The Romuda" gave him the chance to meet former President William Howard Taft.

At the 1916 graduation ceremonies of Peddie Institute on Wednesday, June 7, former President Taft spoke on preparedness, and after various other speeches he presented the graduates with their well-deserved diplomas. Taft presented Walter B. Gibson with his diploma and rewarded him with his prize from the *Chronicle* for his mystery story "The Romuda." Upon presenting this prize, former President Taft said that he hoped this would be the beginning of a long, and great, literary career for Gibson. And so it was.

3

Shaping the Future

Jan. 1st 1918; 1 A.M. A strange feeling grips me as I write. I do not feel tired; I seem filled with a strong vigor. The past seems vague and far away, while the future spreads before me, full of mystery.
— Walter B. Gibson, foreword to 1918 diary.

As college is meant to do, Colgate University greatly prepared Walter Gibson for his life and career. It is here that his interests became more focused, and one can see that he was well on the path to a fascinating future. It is in these years that his interests molded him into the person who would become a prolific writer.

After graduating from Peddie Institute, Gibson was enrolled in Plattsburg Military Training Camp, in Plattsburg, New York, for the summer. And in the fall he entered Colgate University, where his uncle, Frank, was treasurer and professor of Greek. Gibson's brother Theodore also attended Colgate University and became a member of the teaching staff as a mathematics instructor. Theodore also wrote the Colgate song, "Fight for the Team."

Gibson's life gradually became more magical while at Colgate. Five articles about magic appeared in the *Eagle Magician* that year. By the finish of college, Gibson had contributed 217 articles to various magical publications.

In addition to Gibson's writings about magic, he actively searched for magic shops in the area where he could collect some more tricks of the trade, and meet more magicians. A favorite shop was Thayer's. Gibson used these tricks he learned to entertain friends and family. He especially liked the "Four Ace Trick" in which four aces are magically found in a shuffled deck of cards. This trick intrigued him so much that in later years he invented his own version. Gibson did perform some larger-scale shows for hire, but these were less frequent during his years at Colgate, probably because of the workload. On Thursday, May 3, 1917, Gibson presented such a show. He writes that, "I worked the 'Miser's Dream,' 'Patriotic Rockets,' 'Water from Pocket,' & coin from glass to ball of wool. Everything went neatly." Some other magic that Gibson enjoyed performing at this time was card flourishes, the Svengali Deck (a trick deck of cards that allows the magician to perform astounding card tricks with no sleight of hand), coin effects and mind-reading acts.

Magic was truly part of his life at this point, but college life came first. Gibson took classes in Greek, Latin, rhetoric, French, public speaking and biology. He was also elected assistant editor of the school paper, the *Echo,* and was appointed to the social committee.[1] The Christian Endeavor group, basketball with friends, and frequent trips to the library took up some more of Gibson's spare time. But there was one event that pulled Gibson's interest like a magnet. He feared to get pulled in, but had a fascination with it: war.

In Gibson's 1917 diary on Saturday, February 3, he writes about the foreshadowed war:

> The United States has severed diplomatic relations with Germany. Torpedo boat destroyers are patrolling the coast. All interned German ships under guard. Affairs have taken an exceedingly serious turn.

Over the next few days, and in sprinkles throughout the next following months, Gibson reports on the world happenings:

> — *Sunday, February 4, 1917* — German ships interned at Philadelphia have been seized — same at Boston. Militia are being ordered out; American wheat ship sunk. Roosevelt "on the warpath."
> — *Monday, February 5, 1917* — Issue with Germany still as serious as ever, & war is very probable. Something should develop very soon.
> — *Monday, March 26, 1917* — 20,000 Militia called out.
> — *Wednesday, March 28, 1917* — 15,000 more Militia called out.
> — *Thursday, April 5, 1917* — Senate passes War Measure 82–6.... THE HOUSE PASSED WAR BILL — THE NATION IS VIRTUALLY AT WAR NOW.
> — *Friday, April 6, 1917 at top of page* — FRIDAY APRIL 6TH U.S.A. DECLARES WAR ON GERMANY
> — *Friday, April 6, 1917* — BILL PASSED 136–50. PRESIDENT SIGNS MEASURE. WAR IS ON.
> — *Wednesday, May 16, 1917* — That reminds me that it was tres froid au jourd'hui (I might as well practice my French — I may need it soon).
> — *Saturday, May 19, 1917* — Pershing and 25,000 Regulars to France at once.

As one can see, Gibson was fascinated by the idea of war. Like many people, he enjoyed playing war games when he was young; this fascination with such games carried over to his college years when the real thing arrived. He used the top and bottom margins of his diaries after this to indicate world happenings and the development of the war. The war had changed Gibson's day-to-day life and his thinking. At Colgate, after war was declared, there were frequent drills to get the students ready for any military action needed.

One can see how tightly the war wound its grasp around Gibson once one has read the foreword to his 1918 diary:

Jan. 1st 1918; 1 A.M. A strange feeling grips me as I write. I do not feel tired; I seem filled with a strong vigor. The past seems vague and far away, while the future spreads before me, full of mystery. What is in store for me in this coming year? What is in store for the world? Will the dawn of peace be clear a year from now; will 1919 [see] its entrance grim and foreboding, or will it greet this tired earth with a blessing of cheer and good will? Great things have happened during the past year. I little thought, as I listened to the whistles and bells just twelve months ago, that we would be engaged in the great conflict; that we should be standing as the latest and greatest champions of Democracy and Humanity when those whistles ushered in the next infant year. Yes, great things occurred in 1917 and great things will occur in 1918. Perhaps this Diary will never be filled, but will end abruptly, with the marginal reference reading, "Somewhere in France." Yes, 1918 is a year of hope and promise: yet; at the same time; a year of foreboding. Hopes will be realized; ambitions will be crushed; reputations will be made; careers will be ended. And may my hopes; my ambitions; my reputation; my career, be remembered among those —for better or —for worse.

Gibson follows these touching hopes with a poem of the future:

The Future

The past is but a memory, the present but a dream,
The future lies beyond, a narrow silent stream,
And down its winding, rippling course one's life flows
    swiftly on,
The shoals of sorrow quickly pass, the pools of joy
    are gone.
Until at length the race is run, the placid lake the
    gain.
Where gladness, calm and happiness, in peace triumphant
    reign.

The future is greatly anticipated by Gibson, but only time shall tell its final course.

The year 1918 was not much different from any other year of school for Gibson. He continued his interest in public speaking and conversational French. He developed a great interest also for his psychology and biology classes. In fact, he enjoyed biology so much that he joined the Biological Society. Gibson was also involved in the Outing Club, frequently participating in its adventurous hikes, which brought back memories of his early teenage years spent hiking and camping at Keewaydin. He also enjoyed watching movies; in fact, almost every night he went to see a different one. Magic became more integrated into his life. Indeed Gibson toured with the Music Club, performing his magic act before the concert.[2] Gibson and his best friend, Truman, were both signed up to join the Music Club after mystifying Professor Hoermen on Friday, February 1, 1918. The concert trips occurred during April. Gibson writes that his program as of Sunday, April 7, 1918, included, "Paper tearing; handkerchief frame; Linking Rings; Wonder Cabinet, with Billiard Balls and Dyeing Handkerchiefs for encores." This small tour went well for Gibson. For Thursday, April 11, 1918, he writes, "The concert went great and my act perfectly, especially the linking rings, which made a great hit." Furthermore, for Sunday, April 14, Gibson excitedly scribes that he "had quite a write up in one of the Bri[d]g[e]hampton papers. It told of the concert, and said I had a most pleasing act which mystified everyone, and that I was a 'real artist.'" Gibson's interest in magic greatly increased this year. He practiced much more, and his engagements increased vastly in number.

Yet, all of these magical escapes were overshadowed by the prospect of entering the Great War. Gibson's involvement in military training increased greatly during this school year. At Colgate, military training was taken as if a school course. Gibson would have frequent tests in map work, trench digging, and shooting. Gibson seemed to enjoy this training, or at least he never complained about it.

The summer of 1918 saw Gibson in the role of camp counselor. He left Saturday, June 29, and returned on Monday, September 2. He enjoyed his time with the children at this New York camp. In addition to running baseball games, as well as his daily duties and activities, he was in charge of the evening entertainment. He filled this time with mind-reading acts, magical sketches, storytelling, a high-dive act (in which a friend was going to dive into a small bucket of water, until the skit was conveniently interrupted), and a play. This seemed to be a relaxing summer, and a needed break from the stresses of school life.

For September 12, 1918, Gibson writes, "21. Today was my birthday and I celebrated by registering." The war was still on and soon to become a greater part of Gibson's life. On Tuesday, October 1, 1918, he was inducted into the army. In the entry for this day, he writes:

> "You're in the Army Now." This noon we had formation after chapel, and we all took the oath; after which various speeches from the President and Thero [*sic*] were read. Mess today at noon — and it was a wild affair. I was made Right Guide, this morning, but have no status as yet. Brief elementary drill in afternoon.

Gibson eventually made the grade of private. He enjoyed his time with the Army in Wawfssville, New York. He called it "Utopia" and the "good life" because he did not have to deal with classes and schoolwork. But the "good life" didn't last long. The Germans signed an armistice on Monday, November 11, 1918. And the war was finally won on Wednesday, December 4, 1918, after 21 months of fighting. Gibson was honorably discharged on December 18, 1918, due to the expiration of his term of service. He concludes his diary, and this year, with the following words in the Epilogue:

> Nearly a year has passed since I penned the Foreword to this volume; and such a year! Little did one dream of the great events which were to mark 1918 as the year of years! The fears and trials of the Spring, when the great German hordes pushed on so dangerously — and then the hopefulness of the summer, followed by the terrible scourge of the early Autumn, which seemed to blight all our hopes— and then that joy of that November day — the 11th — and the greatest Thanksgiving Day in the history of mankind…. The sun of peace has risen above the horizon, and is flooding us with its blessed light.

The obvious joy Gibson felt at America's achievement of peace also filled the hearts of many Americans.

The era of reconstruction had begun, not only for America, but for Gibson as well. He finished the semester at Colgate, taking classes in economics, psychology, five hours of experimental psychology, history, and international law. Extracurricularly, Gibson found himself on the Prom Committee, associate editor of the *Sal,* a member of the Biological Society and Outing Club, and he found a strong interest in astronomical observation. Walter Gibson has always been known for his wonderful mind and his creative projects; because of such gifts, many people have labeled him unique, having never met a man quite like him. Gibson may have experienced some discomfort in college from being so different. This could have influenced his choice toward the end of his junior year to leave Colgate; Gibson felt that he had gained all the knowledge he could and decided to leave college to reconstruct his life into, what he felt to be, something more beneficial.

On Tuesday, July 1, 1919, Gibson got his first job in the working world with a newspaper, the *Record.* He originally saw the managing editor, a Mr. Dwyer, about a reporter's job, but Gibson started out on the lower end of the pole. He earned $50.00 a month stamping checks, filing them, and running an adding machine. He eventually tried ad writing, but he was told he would have to wait for reporting. Seemingly dissatisfied with this, he left the paper to get a job at an insurance company, Penn Mutual. He started here on Wednesday, September 10, 1919. His job was mostly to write up insurance policies.

After the summer of 1919, Gibson's interest in magic grew enormously. He had more free time on his hands so he was able to satisfy his magical bug more properly. His continued contributions to magic magazines won him the recognition of the *Sphinx* editor, Dr. A. M. Wilson, who wrote a letter of commendation to Gibson for his fine work. He also included an application to join the Society of American Magicians. Gibson immediately filled out the form, included the $7.00 check for payment of dues, and sent it in on Monday, January 20, 1919. Gibson's membership card is #586 signed by the then president of the Society of American Magicians, Harry Houdini, and the Secretary, Oscar S. Teale. Gibson also became a member of the Mystic Circle of Philadelphia, and the National Conjurers' Association. The Yogi Club was another magic club in the Philadelphia area and was for professionals only; Gibson would have to wait. Gibson, as a member of the Mystic Circle, eventually instigated the founding of the Philadelphia Assembly of the Society of American Magicians. Gibson and his old-time friend and Germantown neighbor James Wobensmith, the only members of the Society of American Magicians who also attended this group, were strongly in favor of establishing it. They finally made an application to the parent assembly in New York. The Philadelphia Assembly was established by February 24, 1920, as Assembly #4. Around this time, it grew to thirty members. The president of the assembly was James Wobensmith, Samuel O. Paul was installed as vice president, Walter Gibson became the secretary, the treasurer was Howard F. Kenna, and Carl Brema, Oscar Thomson, and Guernsey Moore were trustees. Later in life, Gibson became vice president, and then president of the assembly from 1926 until 1927. He later became a trustee of the assembly. Edward T. Hollins, a more recent member of Assembly #4, reported on the history of his assembly. In this report he includes excerpts from the *Sphinx* magic magazine in order to illustrate "the flavor and thought behind the formation of our assembly" to his fellow magicians. These excerpts deal with the formation meeting, initiation and the first elected officers. The November 1919 *Sphinx* states:

> The evening of October 28 marked one of the greatest steps for the advancement of magic ever taken in Philadelphia. A few days before, letters had been sent out to a great number of Philadelphia magicians inviting them all to a meeting in the Grand Fraternity Building on the night of October 28. Owing to the short notice, a great number of enthusiasts were unable to respond. Nevertheless, the turn out was quite large, over twenty being present, and the meeting was full of interest and enthusiasm.
>
> The purpose was the formation of one strong, united Philadelphia society, and Mr. James Wobensmith was elected temporary president, with Mr. Sam Paul as secretary pro tempore. The President was empowered to appoint a committee to take up the matters of bylaws, entertainment, etc.
>
> Then came the question of affiliation. A long discussion was held, considering every possible course that the society might take. The result was the unanimous decision of all present to apply for a charter as a branch assembly of the Society of American Magicians. The officers and committee were directed to take this matter up with the S.A.M. so that definite application or similar action might be made at the next meeting of the club.
>
> The next meeting was set for some time in the later half of November. By that time all magicians who were not notified will be sent word, so that they may join with us in the movement. Correspondence should be addressed to Mr. Sam Paul, 5535 Girard Avenue, Philadelphia, PA.
>
> The meeting adjourned at 10:30 and was followed by a brief entertainment.
>
> Magic has been very active during the past month or two. La Temple has been busy in Philadelphia and vicinity with his new illusion act. Nate Leipzig and Roland Travers both played the Nixon with two exceptionally fine acts. The Asahi Troupe were in town for a few days with an excellent show. Adelaide Herrmann, Wallace Gavin and the Al Golem Troupe also appeared. Magic is evidently alive here, and the boys are going to make it even more so.

The March 1920 *Sphinx,* as reported by Walter Gibson, stated:

> On Tuesday, February 24th a party of fifteen members of the Parent Assembly came to Philadelphia and formally installed the Philadelphia Assembly. The party arrived at 7 P.M. and a meeting was called at 8 P.M. at the Grand Fraternity Building where the mysteries were conferred....

Gibson made numerous connections in 1919 in the magic world, and performed many shows. Magic became an ever- growing part of Gibson's life. Every day Gibson mentioned something about magic in his diary. The magic bug had completely taken over.

Gibson's diary became much more detailed in this year than in years past. In February 1918, Gibson had read an article by Arnold Bennet about what diaries should be. The article stated that they should be (1) Truthful, (2) Extremely Personal, (3)

Not a half-hearted attempt, but a first-rate effort. Gibson had to agree with this article, but he felt that his diaries fell short of these goals. Gibson paid much attention to detail, always noting the weather conditions and temperature, and highlighting the interesting facets of the day in the small area in which the Wanamaker diaries allowed for writing. He also enjoyed noting the number of days he spent in various towns around the country, and occasionally the exact time spent on the train in traveling to these towns. But Gibson thought his diaries often lacked the personal touch. He surrenders to this idea and writes on Wednesday, February 13, 1918, "I will confine the incidentals to the brief spaces allotted to each day, but the heart of the tale will be in the 'appendix' which henceforth will be of utmost importance, and [not just] a continuation of the day's story — but an account of my spiritual or mental, rather [than] my bodily self." One finds that his past diaries are a wonderful log of what he did on specific days of a certain year. But in future diaries Gibson promises to write his feelings and thoughts on particular matters. Immediately after this new realization of what a diary should be, he confides in the allotted space at the bottom of the page his experiment with smoking a cigar and a cigarette. He seems ashamed at such experimentation and he attempts to excuse such an act as sheer defiance and as a means to look important. But he promises he will never do it again. Yet during his years writing the Shadow, the cigarette would become a good pal to Gibson in calming his nerves, an unfortunate side effect of the massive output of the Shadow novels.

Gibson's departure from college and commencement of his future was an education in itself. Gibson sums up the events of the year in the Epilogue in his 1919 Diary:

> Well, another year has gone, and with it many great things. In some ways it has been the most eventful year of my life — and the most interesting. 1919 has been a year of turbulency. But not the turbulency, I feel, of upheaval and unrest, but that produced by the peculiar settling of life back to its normal and natural conditions.
> Everyone has been affected by the changes which have occurred. But the experiences which I have undergone have also been the result of a settling down of my own life. 1919 has marked my entrance into the Game of Life — a sudden change from the peace and quiet of college into the more serious whirl of business. It has, in a sense, been a premature change — for it was one scheduled for the Spring of 1920. But I think that in reality it was not at all premature — but an extremely wise and important step. For I felt that I was ready for bigger things in life, and that another year of college would have retarded instead of advancing my interests. But the Future will decide.

And Walter B. Gibson certainly did take a step toward a wonderful, and exciting future.

Walter Gibson's true writing career began in the early twenties. He applied for a job as a reporter on the Philadelphia *North American*. There would be no job openings until the fall. In the meantime, Gibson quit his job at Penn Mutual in order to take a job with his brother Arthur at the Connecticut General Insurance

Company. His pay was $30 for two weeks of work. He would type policies, make collections and deliveries. He truly enjoyed his work and wrote on his first day on Monday, January 19, "…I liked it immediately. I went in with Art in time for the Agent's Meeting, and did considerable work on the typewriter. In fact, I got out at 5:45 and so interested was I in my work that I thought it was an hour earlier." This sense of loss of time would accompany his future passions of writing and magic.

Gibson's magical life continued to grow and he found himself amongst some of the top magicians in the field at that time. On Wednesday, January 28, 1920, Gibson and his magic pals arranged a party the following evening for magician Horace Goldin. The following evening, Gibson wrote in his diary, "…saw Goldin's act which was a fine one. We dropt around and saw him afterwards … and took him to Sam's where we had 'refreshments' and then descended to Sam's 'Magic Dept.' where we chatted and did Magic until 3 A.M. when we broke up." Gibson would often travel to neighboring states in order to meet other magicians. He went to New York in February and on Wednesday, the 18th, he wrote about the day there: "First we visited Martinka's, where we saw the theatre and D. Ellison's collection of wands, and met Carlton, the Herrmann's, and afterwards to see 'Zelo' … and then we called on Dunninger and had a nice chat." It seems in these years, Gibson would spend vast amounts of time with his magic pals.

Gibson's act had grown some from what magicians term "platform magic" into more "stage" tricks with the help of the S.A.M. On February 19, 1920, Gibson reflected on his day with his magic friends. He writes, "In the evening I went out to see Sam; he, Ed and I got the levitation in operation. It works fine. We were floating around on it, considerably, and they left me 5 ft. in the air, for several minutes." Gibson enjoyed all of his time with his magic friends, and his name was becoming well known in the magic world.

It was during these carefree days of his early years that Gibson made important connections and decisions that would effect his future writing career. In March, as Gibson was helping his friend Sam Paul set up his apparatus in St. James's Hall, he broke the news to him that he would be unable

Walter Gibson in his twenties around the time he created puzzles for newspapers. Reproduced with permission from Robert Gibson.

to "take the road" with him and his act. He was obligated to stay at his insurance job. Yet this decision was very important for it opened up his summer in order to work in other venues. Gibson ended up working at a traveling carnival known as "Ruppel's Greater Shows," which traveled throughout New Jersey and Long Island. Gibson became involved with the carnival and John Duffy, a man from Columbus, Ohio. Duffy wanted to build an illusion show and needed help. This is when Walter Gibson got involved with him and the carnival. Gibson had his own position in the show performing platform magic as Duffy did the large-scale illusions. Gibson also aided in the set-up and tear down of the show. They had a 22 × 12 foot portable stage which they would unpack from a truck and assemble under a tent.

It was at this carnival that Gibson learned the "behind the scenes" working of the games, material he would use in the future in syndicated features, and which would eventually result in a book. He wrote fifty numbers between 1923 and 1924 titled "Bunco Games to Beware Of." The articles described the workings of various carnival games and how they could be gimmicked in order to favor the operator. The articles were rewritten and published with essays about con-artists, the shell game, and the methods of card cheats, totaling sixty-six entries, in Gibson's eighth publication, *The Bunco Book,* published in 1927. It was reissued in 1946 with a new introduction by Sidney H. Radner, and was again republished in two volumes, *The Bunco Book* and *Carnival Gaffs.* The original articles were illustrated by Gibson's carnival pal John Duffy, who had a gift for beautiful scenic paintings. He was a very talented artist and his talent was recognized by the carnival. He would paint and design its banners, and work at concession stands when not performing: there was always work for him. Yet he was down on his luck at one point while he was in the Philadelphia area. Gibson knew he needed the money so he enlisted him to illustrate the articles and other series such as Gibson's "Miracles — Ancient and Modern." And many of the original drawings from the articles appeared in the published book. John Duffy would also provide the illustrations for some of Gibson's other syndicated newspaper features.[3]

Upon the original publication of *The Bunco Book,* an ad was put in *Variety* magazine and another one was sent to *Billboard.* Unfortunately, *Billboard* would not accept the advertisement. Gibson explains that, "A guy said that carnival games were never made up crooked, that there were reputable manufacturers of marked cards, and though some people did things like that — they [*Billboard*] refused to run the ad."[4] The publisher was upset, but figured there was nothing they could do. But Gibson had an idea. Along with the publisher, they wrote a letter of apology to *Variety* and requested their money back for they had been told that their book and advertisement were unethical, and they included a copy of the letter from *Billboard* magazine. Gibson states, "Our ad stayed, and *Variety* ran a front page story saying '*Billboard* refuses to run ad exposing crooked carnival games.' We got a front page story out of that."[5]

Gibson drew much attention from the magic world during 1920 by writing for many of the magic magazines published at that time. He had been contributing articles and tricks to such magazines since 1915, but 1920 was his most prolific year for writing. He wrote 59 different articles during this year, the most in one single year over his entire lifetime. Such contributions include a continuation of his "Up to Date Tricks," a nine-part series of tricks that appeared in the *Sphinx*; it began in the 17th volume of the magic magazine in October 1918 and ran until February 1920. He began another series this year, "Manipulative Magic," which first appeared in September 1920 and ran in ten parts until August 1921. Gibson's first professionally published fiction, "A Tale of Tomorrow," was published in the August 1920 issue of this magic magazine. He contributed other articles and tricks to this magazine during this year (and many others). He also began a couple of series in the *Magic World* magazine. The "Practical Card Tricks" series first appeared in the January 1920 issue of the *Magic World* and ran for fourteen parts through March 1921. Another series, "Tricks with Matches," started in this magazine in May and was a ten-part series that ended in March of the following year. "Special Secrets" was the third series that began in October and ran through February in three parts. He also contributed other tricks and articles to this magic magazine separate from these series. Gibson also contributed articles and tricks to other magic magazines including the *Magic Wand,* the *Magical Bulletin,* and *Felsman's Magical Review.*

Gibson further continued his magical development by performing more shows. Churches, clubs and rotary shows where all perfect places in Philadelphia to perform. Gibson states that "Philadelphia was honey-combed with lodges in those days, and people were very neighborhoodish, and Philadelphia was a closed place on Sunday nights; there'd be no theatres open, so they had lodge nights. I did [some] club dates; there were a lot of dates, but you had to hustle to get them."[6]

The year 1920 was not only the beginning of a new decade in the 20th century, but it was also the beginning of what would become a very busy life for Walter Gibson. His contributions to magic magazines, making business connections, and working for the insurance company took its toll. He was no longer able to continue writing his annual diaries. In his 1920 diary, Gibson states:

> Note: For the past few months the keeping of the Diary had become more or less burdensome, and finally, the last notation was made under the heading of Monday July 25 — a brief word simply to serve as a reminder when, at some future time, the record should be revised [it never was].
>
> After four and ½ years of uninterrupted record, the Diary, which had become almost an institution in the writer's life, gave one great gasp and passed out.
>
> The reason for this sudden collapse is very evident if one will but study the conditions that caused it.
>
> A Diary should be at once a Chronicle of Events, and a Record of Opinions. During its early years, this Diary faithfully held to those two fundamental requirements, but there came a time when the writer's opinions became more established and could not be set forth at length in this volume without misunderstanding by those who should read it; and certain events occurred which had better not be

recorded without a lengthy and even then incomplete explanation, which might be unfair to certain parties concerned.

In other words the Diary had reached a point where its existence was rapidly becoming a handicap rather than a help. There was no use in keeping up a cut and dried Daily record, largely bluff with little notes on the side to serve as mere reminders of something not mentioned. If the Diary is to be read by others, it should be complete and faithful; if not it's to be so read, description of events is unnecessary, for enough of them will remain in the author's mind to be written as reminiscences hereafter.

However, altho' the last few months of 1920 must be made up largely from memory, a brief record of some events of interest will be jotted down, and in future years a similar record will be kept, which, while it will not be of interest to a reader, may yet be of value as a future reference.

And the rest of the pages remain blank.

This was his last diary for many years. Gibson did use a 1921 and 1925 Wanamaker diary, but for a different use. The 1925 diary has ideas for tricks, one featured on almost every day of the year. The 1921 diary was used as a savings account book for the budget of the Philadelphia Assembly of the Society of American Magicians. It was also used as an address book. An entry that stands out is the address of one Harry Houdini, who apparently lived at 278 W. 113th St., New York, New York, at the time.

Gibson returned from traveling with the carnival around Labor Day of 1920, and he anxiously took his first newspaper job at the *North American*. He worked for around $15 a week. He was the "cub reporter" and mostly did the grunt work along with a story here and there. The newspapers in Philadelphia were highly competitive at the time for there were five morning papers and three evening papers. As a result of the pressure of this competition, Gibson's editor was very hard on them and did not appreciate his reporters trying to spice up their articles with flowery language, which was the custom of the day. In fact, when one reporter wired an article to the editor in regards to a tragic flood in Pennsylvania which destroyed many homes and even killed a number of citizens, he began his story something like, "'God sits in sadness above the town, pondering the tragedy that struck....'" "The editor was furious. He quickly wired a short response back to his reporter: "'Forget flood. Interview God.'"[7] Gibson was lucky enough to have the ability to find stories out of nowhere. He had once interviewed a newly elected governor of Pennsylvania who told him that he had celebrated his victory with "'two cups of Postum.'" The people of Philadelphia laughed for years.[8]

This was the heyday for the first women reporters. They were affectionately called "sob sisters," for they were the ones who contacted the families and friends of disaster victims and would write tales of their plights. The men reporters would receive the factual aspects of each story, and the women would get the leftover personal matters. It was thanks to this system that Gibson got his first opportunity to write a big story. That day a tragedy hit Philadelphia. A local bridge was about to collapse with thirty people on it. Most of the staff was sent out to cover this story, but the editor asked Gibson to stay behind. In order to comfort Gibson the editor promised him that if any big stories came through that day, he would get the first chance to cover them. A few minutes after announcing this, the telephone rang. It turned out that President Warren G. Harding was in Philadelphia and was willing to speak with reporters. This was Gibson's chance. He rushed out and exclusively interviewed the President. Gibson found that "'he just happened to be passing on his way to Atlantic City.'"[9] The interview went very well. Gibson said that he had "'...a good feeling about President Harding. He was a newspaperman himself and owned a paper, so he understood reporters.'"[10]

In 1921, Gibson moved across town to join the staff of the Philadelphia *Evening Public Ledger.* With the job move Gibson received a pay increase to around $25 a week. It was here that he got to draw on his many talents and interests to make his writings more entertaining. In an era before television and before the mass spread of radio, people looked to the daily newspapers to provide a means of entertainment. As a result of such a cry, Gibson was one of the first to offer his readers the entertainment of crossword puzzles which he created himself. "One day a week he'd go into a trance and write fourteen crossword puzzles," recalls his son, Dr. Robert Gibson.[11] Walter Gibson would sit with a pen behind each ear, one for blocking, the other for writing; the young Robert would often crawl around with pens over his ears. In later years, Gibson could quickly go through any *New York Times* puzzle. His crossword puzzles were a hit in his day, and they were syndicated to other papers. Of course, today the crossword puzzle is an ever-present feature in most newspapers, but during the early 1920s this was a novel idea.

Gibson's syndicated work spread from crossword puzzles to tricks. It was here that Gibson created his first feature for the *Ledger* syndicate, "After Dinner Tricks." Gibson wrote a daily feature that described the working of a single magic trick. Only expected to run a few weeks, the series ran for nearly five years until March 7, 1925. Selected tricks from this series were compiled to produce Gibson's first book, *After Dinner Tricks,* published by Magic Publishing Company in 1921.[12]

Gibson's second book was published this same year as well. It was patterned after his series in *The Magic World,* "Practical Card Tricks." The book, *Practical Card Tricks,* was filled with new tricks that were not part of the series in the magic magazine. The book was number one in a series of four that were intended to be bound together by the reader (for they were paginated consecutively, except for the last volume *Sixteen Master Card Mysteries,* which was intended to stand alone).

Other syndicated features arose from Gibson in the years to follow. In 1922, he contributed two separate articles to the *Ledger* syndicate: "Easy Magic You Can Do" and "Miracles—Ancient and Modern." In the former articles (twenty in all), Gibson demonstrates to his readers his ability to describe more complex tricks in a simple manner. The latter articles, running in fifty parts, give the reader ideas of how the most talked about illusions of all time were performed. From "Sawing a Woman in Half" to "The Hindu Rope Trick," explanations are offered in the brief, illustrated articles (a series of exposures to which Houdini did not take too kindly.

See Chapter 5). The articles from both of these features were revised and put together in *The Book of Secrets* published in what would become Gibson's seventh book in 1927.[13]

Gibson's involvement with magic and magicians was fruitful. He had a friend who owned Greenwood's Magic Shop. Gibson would write the instruction sheets for the various tricks produced here. Mr. Greenwood was one of the early manufacturers of metal magic products. His son, Bill, also worked with metal lathes. Gibson recalled that "'He had a metal shop, and he thought up tricks, which I would write out for him. One trick he made a fortune on was the nickels and dimes trick, though he was afraid to advertise it because in those days there was a law against mutilating coins. I asked him, why did he have to use coins— he could use brass things instead, and put a real nickel on top to make it look higher. He didn't go for that though, he wanted to do it the same way.'"[14]

Gibson soon became involved with his own magic shop in Philadelphia.[15] He had a friend, Bill Kofoes, who was interested in magic. Kofoes published a few magazines such as *Brief Magazine, Laughter*, a humorist magazine, and *Paris Nights*, a risqué magazine (at least as risqué as you could get in those days). It was he who encouraged Gibson to gather together his *Bunco* syndicated features into a book. He also encouraged Gibson to start up a magic shop. The shop opened in 1925 with Kofoes as the silent partner. Kofoes had an office in the back for his magazines and he advertised the shop in them. He was interested in magic but he did not want it to look like he was going into the magic business. He used the shop as a "backer" for his magazines.[16]

In addition to his writing, Gibson also appeared on the radio. He had a job with station WIP in Philadelphia. Gibson would create, announce and solve puzzles and tricks on the air twice each week. One of Gibson's brothers wired a crystal set in the attic of the family home in Germantown so the family could hear Gibson's voice on the airwaves, taking turns with the earphones.

Then, after the summer of 1922, the Cleveland *NEA* discovered the fertile mind of Walter Gibson. His syndicated feature "A Puzzle a Day" was picked up by this publication. They considered him part of the staff. Ever since Gibson was young he adored puzzles, and now he had a chance to show the world his love. The *NEA* wrote about Gibson on July 24, 1923. "'A Puzzle a Day' doesn't just simply happen, or grow. No puzzle does. In the first place puzzles have to be thought up. It's a very highly specialized class of work. To do it, and to do it right, takes an expert. Likewise it's a gift. Clever puzzle-makers must be born. They can't be made." They prided themselves on having one of the most tricky minds in the magic world and his magic words appeared on their pages each day. Gibson wrote this feature through 1923 and included the answer to the puzzles, which required observation and logic to derive, on the following day. This format was relatively the same with another two syndicated feature columns called "Intelligence Tests" and "Brain Tests" (also called "Your Brains If Any"). The latter feature of 1928 became a book by the same title in 1930.

Walter Gibson was truly making a name for himself in the magic world. But just when one would think he would take off to become a star, Gibson slumped back into the shadows, at least as far as the public was concerned. In reality, Gibson started working harder than ever. Yet he did not take the name credit for any of these writings, a trend that would continue into his later life. The man working from the shadows with seventy-nine different disguises was Walter B. Gibson!

4

Howard Thurston

*So, in the years that have passed, and in the years that are to come,
Howard Thurston will be recognized and remembered by the title which he
has richly deserved — 'The World's Master Magician.'*
— *Walter B. Gibson,* Thurston's Book of Magic,
Edward J. Murray, 1927.

Gibson made many connections in 1919 in the magic world, and performed
many shows. His repertoire expanded. His family even helped him out a bit in creating some magical props. His Aunt Sarah had designed an "egg bag" for Gibson, in
which an egg magically appeared and disappeared. "I will probably keep [it] for an
encore," wrote Gibson on April 5, 1919. On Saturday, May 24 of the same year, Gibson was fortunate enough to see another one of the great magicians of the century
perform: Howard Thurston. On that day Gibson reflected that he "saw Thurston,
with father. I had on my S.A.M. pin, so when I went up on the stage, Thurston gave
me a wink, so to speak. His show was great." Soon Gibson would meet this
magnificent magician through a good friend, James Wobensmith.

James Wobensmith, the president of the Philadelphia assembly of the S.A.M.,
was a neighbor of Gibson's in Germantown. He was closer to Gibson's father's age
than Gibson's own, but nonetheless the two became good friends. It turns out that
Mr. Wobensmith was the patent attorney for Howard Thurston, the popular stage
magician of the time. Mr. Wobensmith would look into patents for illusions and
tricks that the Great Thurston created. It was through Mr. Wobensmith that Gibson
eventually became acquainted with this star of magic for whom he would ghost-
write numerous books. Magic became an ever-growing part of Gibson's life. Every
day Gibson mentioned something about magic in his diary. The magical cherub sat
on Gibson's shoulder. A sly smile crossed its lips as it watched Gibson pen these words
on Tuesday, May 4, 1920: "...dropped in on Thurston at the Walton and had a chat
with him and Mrs. T."

Howard Thurston (1869–1936) toured the world with his stage show during the first quarter of the 20th century. He would gain fame with his adaptation of the "Rising Card Trick" in which cards rise up out of the pack and into his waiting hand. Thurston adapted this trick during an engagement with a variety troupe in Boulder, Montana, where the theatre was a billiard parlor and gambling hall by day. Thurston was setting up the show and a fight broke out and a shot flew through the curtain and shattered the glass for the "Rising Card Trick." Having no other suitable glass, Thurston improvised his own version.

The "Rising Card Trick" carried Thurston to fame. It was in October 1898, that a request to see this trick brought Thurston closer to the spotlight. He was playing at the Alcazar Theatre in Denver, Colorado, where Leon Herrmann, nephew and successor of Alexander Herrmann, whose grand stage production Thurston had always admired, was also playing at the Tabor Grand. Though in competition with each other, the two magicians desired to see the other's show. Thurston was able to catch Herrmann's, yet Herrmann was unable to see Thurston's; and he desperately wanted to see Thurston's "Rising Card Trick." Thurston agreed to perform the trick backstage before one of Herrmann's evening shows.

Herrmann's excitement to see the trick delayed the opening of his show. He watched Thurston in amazement. He was baffled. That was just the response Thurston was hoping for when he invited a reporter from the *Denver Post* along to witness the miracle. The next day the story hit the papers: "The Man Who Mystified Herrmann."[1]

Once Thurston arrived in New York City he added card manipulations to his act which increased his bookings. Thurston was soon booked at Tony Pastor's famous vaudeville house with one assistant, an African-American boy named George White. Thurston never again did a performance without him. Gibson often heard Thurston say, "'I've never given a show without George White, and I never will. Without George, my show just can't go on.'"[2] Added to his rising repertoire and increasing fame, was Thurston's improvement on the "Rising Card Trick" in which now he could levitate any card called for by the audience.[3] Thurston's fame grew and he was booked in England to play a four-week engagement at the Palace Theatre in London beginning November 12, 1900; yet his stay stretched to a twenty-six-week engagement. Then Thurston performed in vaudeville houses throughout England before touring Europe.[4] Thurston brought magic to the eyes of such royal rulers as King Edward VII, President Loubet of France, The Emperor of Germany, and the Czar of Russia.[5]

By May 1902, Thurston had returned to America to put all his money into staging an even larger show with a dozen assistants. Thurston worked hard for a show as great as Herrmann's; yet unwilling to compete with Kellar's fame in America, Thurston took his show on a world tour, starting in Australia. He spent much more money on this production as he toured Australia and moved on to China, Japan, Indo-China, Sumatra, Java, the Philippine Islands, Burma and India. Thurston played to packed houses and performed for numerous rulers. In America Kellar's popularity had grown enormously,[6] but by 1907 Kellar was looking for a successor. He chose

Thurston and combined their shows for a full season after which Thurston took over.[7] In May 1908 at Ford's Opera House in Baltimore Kellar announced Thurston as his successor.[8]

Thurston's show continued to grow each season. By the late 1920s the show was twice as large as it was in 1909. The show consisted of 30 assistants, 3 cars of magic and a number of animals.[9] He was very smart financially by hiring married couples as his assistants. In this way he could pay the male assistants a lot and pay the female assistants a much-reduced rate.[10] He played only the largest of theatres due to his enormous production. This gave him some difficulties for he could not play in many towns that desired to see his mysteries. Thurston solved this problem by dispatching another magic company headed by a magician named Jansen who performed as Dante. Dante kept in constant contact with Thurston to update the show with Thurston's latest illusions. The show soon grew so big, consisting of 17 tons of baggage, that Thurston sent the show on a tour of South America in the late 1920s. Dante continued the tour on his own in Europe. Thurston introduced another company headed by Sugden under the name of Tampa. On February 15, 1926, Thurston issued a release: "Dear Reader: In as much as I am unable to fill all of the engagements requested of me, I have pleasure in offering to the public the famous Mystifier, 'Tampa,' England's Court Magician, who will present the best of my illusions as well as many of his own masterpieces. Sincerely, Howard Thurston."[11] With 15 assistants and 6 tons of baggage, Tampa toured the cities that Thurston was unable to visit, performing a 45-minute show. Thurston's brother, Harry, later presented a show in smaller cities called Thurston's "Mysteries of India." [12, 13] So by the time he found Gibson, he had quite a story to tell. Gibson would later ghost-write six books for Thurston in the mid to late twenties.

Howard Thurston (1869–1936). This image is housed in Ray Goulet's Mini Museum of Magic in Watertown, Massachusetts. Photograph by Thomas J. Shimeld.

At around the same time the *NEA* publication discovered Gibson's feature articles, he had been meeting with Howard Thurston. The two worked together on many projects. It all began with Gibson researching material for a new edition of a pocket book of tricks which Thurston sold at theatres after his performances. John Mulholland, a writer of Thurston's, had been working on a show book when the Sykes & Thompson Candy Company of Cleveland offered to produce a million boxes of candy that had instructions for fifty different tricks, selling for ten cents each. Mulholland, busy with other projects, called on Gibson to work on the "Thurston Magic Box of Candy." Enticed by the money the company offered (much better than a reporter's salary), Gibson accepted. As Gibson recalled in a letter dated April Fool's Eve, 1982 to Jane Thurston, the daughter of the great magician: "So I came to New York and John & I went out to Beechhurst, where we met Jane's dad and Jane as well, as John had everything all set to take photos for the show book that evening. Also present was Stouder Thompson of the candy company, so we all went into New York, as I recall it, in the Thurston limousine." Gibson later prepared a list of materials for the series and visited the factory in Cleveland. He spent three months there preparing the instruction sheets and working on the advertising campaign. It was during his stay in Cleveland that the *NEA*, based in this city, took an interest in Gibson.

Thurston was very impressed with Gibson as a friend. The two often connected at Thurston's various show engagements. In fact, Thurston wanted Gibson to travel with him for some time, but at this stage in life, Gibson was not ready. He had a steady job doing his syndicated work, and he had just married Charlotte on November 5, 1923, in Philadelphia, Pennsylvania. Charlotte was Gibson's first wife and mother of their son, Robert. They lived together at 5400 Walnut Street and then later resided at 4029 Walnut Street and Concord Hall, 45th and Spruce Street in Philadelphia. But Thurston wouldn't let Gibson get away that easily. Thurston was so impressed with Gibson's skill as a writer that he enlisted him as the author of his books. Gibson ghosted six books under Thurston's name. Howard Thurston's *200 Tricks You Can Do,* was the first of the books, published in Philadelphia by George Sully and Company in 1926. This was Gibson's first substantial book of over 100 pages. The following year *200 More Tricks You Can Do* made its magical appearance. The two books have been republished at various times and in various places after their original publishing dates. Gibson also wrote Thurston's program, *Book of Magic,* published in Philadelphia by Edward J. Murray in 1927; and *Fooling the World* and *The Thurston Magic Lessons,* both published in New York by Howard Thurston in 1928. Furthermore, Gibson contributed articles to various periodicals under Thurston's name. Such magazines include *Popular Mechanics,* the *Saturday Evening Post, Collier's Weekly,* and *Tales of Magic and Mystery.* Gibson's last book for Thurston was his autobiography. Howard Thurston's *My Life of Magic* (as told to Walter B. Gibson) is said to be Gibson's "first substantial contribution to the history of magic."[14] Published in 1929 in Philadelphia by Dorrance and Company, it is the story of Thurston's life as dictated to Gibson at Thurston's Long Island home.

Thurston asked Gibson to help him develop his autobiography. Thurston had already written most of it, but he had gone into his distant past. He had written about his youth in Columbus, Ohio, and how he was somewhat of a "'roustabout'"[15, 16] as a newsboy "'on fast trains running from Columbus to Akron and Pittsburgh,'"[17] selling programs with a racing circuit. In the spring of 1886, Thurston left home. He had stayed away from home previous years because of his job as a traveling newsboy. Thurston sent money home to his mother, who was unhappy with his leaving and with his being involved with the races. Thurston's life began to turn around in New York where he became ill and had to stay while the races moved on. He was poor, had no friends, and no job. At this low point in his life, he attended a revival meeting given by Dwight Lyman Moody (1837–1899), the famous American evangelist; it was after this that Thurston became heavily involved in religion. He loved it and decided to be a medical missionary. Thurston became a student at Mount Hermon School in Massachusetts[18] in order to study for the ministry. Thurston attributed his later success to the physical and mental pursuits of this time.[19]

Thurston further dove into the struggles of his life with two divorces before finding a happy marriage. Gibson immediately told Thurston that he must take all of this out. As interesting as it may be to historians, Gibson had his eye on the public's taste and he understood that they demanded to know about Thurston's magic; he should not talk about the valleys of his life, but rather focus on the peaks. The public wanted to know about his inspiration in magic: Alexander Herrmann, known as the Great Herrmann, whom Thurston saw perform for the first time during the summer of 1876, in Columbus, Ohio.

The public may like to know about Thurston's first performance at Mt. Hermon, thought Gibson, where he performed a rising card trick he learned from Professor Hoffmann's book, *Modern Magic*. Thurston had also performed an improvised decapitation illusion similar to that which he had seen in Herrmann's show. After seeing Herrmann again in Syracuse, New York, Thurston decided he'd become a magician. After a small and slow progression in magic,[20] his life took an unexpected turn when he was traveling to Philadelphia and ran into a man named Herman Schnell who subsequently got Thurston more interested in magic. Thurston became a magician and began traveling around the country with carnivals. This history of Thurston's magical progression through the years is more of what Gibson had in mind for the biography. So they started over from square one.

Gibson recalls vivid images of this summer of 1928 spent with Thurston: "'I would sit out every day with Thurston on a screened porch. He'd like to sit out in bathing trunks and a straw hat and get sunburn [*sic*], while dictating the stuff. We rigged up a canvas thing so I could sit in the shade.'"[21] They sat here by the garage throughout the hot days. Gibson recalled in a letter to Jane Thurston, "I would poke my head up toward the kitchen and ca;; [*sic:* call]: 'Hitherao, Mohammed!' and he would show up brin[g]ing a pitcher of ice-cold lemonade and two glasses on a tray, which he would [?] with us. Always he would have two glasses already poured and would personally serve one to each of us.

"The reason was that your Dad had decided that lemonade, to be healthy, should *not* contain sugar, so there was none in his glass or the pitcher. But Mohammed had overloaded my glass with so much sugar that I could fill it each time I'd finished about a third, thus keeping it pretty well sweetened all along."[22] In the evenings when they finished up their day's work, around 1:00, Thurston would often go in and get a scotch and soda. Gibson was the only other person that Thurston trusted with the keys to the liquor cabinet, for it contained three very valuable things: the liquor, the original autobiography that Thurston wrote himself, and a "workbook," which was a book of pictures of all of Thurston's magic tricks. Throughout the summer, Gibson would come and go from Thurston's home on Long Island. On the way through New York, Gibson would always stop at all the magic shops, but he was careful never to reveal where he was going and what he was doing; the autobiography was to remain between them for now. Their long days paid off when they completed the first draft of Thurston's autobiography. Like any writing, there were many corrections and pages to be retyped. Thurston urged Gibson to finish through to the last chapter and they would overhaul and rewrite the entire piece before the performance season began. Yet Gibson did not want to change anything in the writing, he was satisfied with its overall composition. He begged Thurston for a three-day extension. Gibson took advantage of this extension and immediately brought the manuscript to an editor. Gibson had written many articles under Thurston's name for the *Saturday Evening Post,* but Gibson decided to take his work to another magazine, *Colliers.* At *Colliers* he asked to see the editor, Hugh Leamy, and spoke to him about other articles that were in the *Evening Post* that "Thurston" (Gibson) had written. He requested that the editor give it a brief reading over the weekend. The manuscript was out of his hands now. He knew it was salable, and he hoped the editor thought so too for Gibson would have to answer to Thurston at the end of the weekend about rewriting the entire work. Gibson rushed back to the magazine company that Monday and he was immediately taken to see the editor-in-chief, William Chenery, and the managing editor. The two had read the manuscript and truly enjoyed it: "they liked it, wanted it and would run it as it was, with no re-write."[23] They questioned Gibson about how much Thurston wanted for it. Gibson was a bit taken aback. He knew that it was a salable autobiography, but he never thought about haggling over prices. He knew that Thurston would want a good price for they had spent so much time transcribing it over the summer. Gibson explained to them that Thurston had taken the summer off in order to write his autobiography. He mentioned that Thurston usually took home about $75,000 a year and had many expenditures. *Colliers* offered $8,000 and would divide the work up into five articles up to the part of the book where Thurston came back from India. They figured that the public at the time would know the rest of the story. They gave Gibson a letter to deliver to Thurston asking for his confirmation on the deal. Gibson was a bit nervous to take the letter for he knew that "'when Thurston saw something big, boy his ideas would get bigger. It was like where he went with the gold mine. The people would tell him, look, the reason the gold mine isn't paying off is because we need new machinery. They would get him as a sucker."[24] *Colliers* further promised that they'd also sell the articles to a publisher. Yet the book itself would not be printed until five months after the articles appeared in the magazine. The articles appeared in the fall of 1929. (Because of this Milbourne Christopher, a prolific writer and historian on magic, assumed that they were written during the summer of 1929. This just proves how secretive Thurston and Gibson were during the summer of 1928 when the articles were actually written.) Gibson immediately took the book to a publisher he knew in Philadelphia called

Dorrance. They knew that Gibson actually wrote it, but Gibson directed them to Thurston to finalize the deal. After that, Thurston never saw the manuscript again. The manuscript never got the overhaul Thurston intended. This just shows how good Gibson's writing had become, for it only took a minimal amount of rewriting. His system of clean first drafts would aid him greatly in the near future when he would undertake *The Shadow Magazine.*

Thurston acquired an agent who wanted 25% of the profits from the book sales. This deal did not work out, so Gibson stepped in briefly and worked out a deal. He expected to receive about a third of the profits, but he wound up getting around 15%. Thanks to the work of Gibson, Thurston's name has remained in the public eye.

Thurston's shows grew through his wonderful abilities to adapt new magical inventions to his own needs.[25] Thurston spent the summer in researching and developing new illusions. He kept up with the scientific breakthroughs and the newest vogue in art. He used his workshops in Whitestone, Long Island, for this. Gibson recalls that "The shops occupied the grounds of a small amusement park, which was surrounded by a high board fence, keeping it immune from the public eye. One of the buildings had a fully equipped stage on which new illusions could be tested and rehearsed after they were completed. The security measures around the workshop resembled those of a modern A-bomb project, as Thurston did not want his next year's novelties to be copied before he could present them."[26]

Gibson described an illusion Thurston developed for a climax to his show, called the "Vanishing Automobile":

> The curtain rose to reveal a triangular framework with upright slats or pickets. Above it was a sign that read: GARAGE. The back and sides of the stage had curtains with horizontal red and white stripes. The curtain on the right was lifted and a sports car rolled in view, carrying half a dozen passengers along with the driver. It stopped behind the slatted frame, with its occupants waving and shouting to the audience.
>
> Then, Thurston took control. He fired a pistol, there was a great puff of light, and the sports car vanished. The audience could look right through the slats of the garage to view an absolute void! [27]

A number of years after Gibson completed his writing for Thurston the two remained good friends. Gibson recalls seeing a performance of this illusion and told Thurston about its problem: it left people blind; the flash was just too bright. Gibson suggested using a strobe light instead, like the one Thurston's daughter, Jane, used on-stage during a dance number in the show. With the light blinking it would give the impression that the car just dissolved into nothingness. Thurston liked the idea and was eager to try it out immediately at the theatre. Unfortunately the theatre was locked up and the two could not get in. Thurston did adapt this version but also experimented more with the flash, until he got it just right.

Thurston wanted to purchase the Herrmann mansion only a mile away from the workshops in Beechhurst, but unfortunately the mansion was already slated to be replaced with an apartment house. Thurston, unable to give up on his inspiration's home, instead purchased a stable that was on the property. Gibson recalled that Thurston "expanded it to an impressive home, with broad verandas opening onto shaded lawns and well-kept tennis courts."[28] Thurston lived a wealthy lifestyle. He invested in a gold mine and other such extravagances. He had a Cadillac and a chauffeur. Many of the people who worked in the show found a permanent job in Thurston's home as gardeners, maids and the like. He had two Hindu servants to serve dinner. He also had a tennis court, which he didn't play on much for over five years.[29] It was here that Thurston spent his summers from 1915 to 1935.

Gibson stated, "I was sort of without portfolio after Thurston went out that season"[30] after the book was completed. This was the last book Gibson did for Thurston. In 1966 Gibson completed the life story of Thurston in a chapter in his book about the anecdotal history of magic entitled *The Master Magicians*, published by Doubleday. In it Gibson updated Thurston's story through his death. The rise of movies caused Thurston's engagements to decline. The larger movie houses showed live stage shows in conjunction with the movies. Thurston reduced his act to one hour so he could play in this venue, performing five shows a day. He was sixty-two. Gibson explains, "The going proved more arduous than he anticipated. Already, he had lessened the strain of his full-evening show by introducing his daughter Jane to the stage as a *magicienne*, and the clever novelty acts that she presented gave Thurston longer rest periods during his regular performances. He thought that the one-hour presentations, in which Jane also appeared, would not be overtaxing. But he was wrong."[31] After a season of these performances, Thurston switched to presenting a dramatic radio show for a few months with a magical theme.

In a 1980 interview, Gibson recalled working with Thurston in 1930 in developing this radio show. It happens that they were at Thurston's home on Long Island. Thurston was enthusiastic about this idea. Gibson: "we were discussing radio, so naturally we turned the radio on to hear what was on it." As the radio tuned in a sinister laugh filled the room. A foretelling laugh that instructed Gibson toward his future calling. Gibson was oblivious to the significance of this sinister character narrating the radio show with his cryptic laugh; but the Shadow knew!

The Thurston radio program developed into a short-lived series. Thurston would tell strange tales, or he would conduct a game over the air in which the listeners would answer personal questions about themselves and gain a number of points depending on their answers. Thurston would then reveal the listeners' character traits in accordance with their total number of points.[32]

Thurston soon returned to the five-a-day shows, yet, Gibson explains, Thurston was "weakening more and more, though he masked that fact from his audiences, from his company, and even from himself."[33] Thurston suffered a stroke in October 1935. He recuperated well, but died from a second stroke on April 13, 1936. He was sixty-six years old. Gibson presented a wonderful description of Thurston in *The Master Magicians*: "Where other magicians injected dash and vigor into their presentations, Thurston depended on poise and deliberation.... Though his manner was restrained [when inviting members of the audience onto the stage], he projected a sincere warmth and impressed onlookers with his somewhat ministerial air."[34]

Yet Howard Thurston was not the only magician that enlisted Gibson for his writing services. Gibson stated that after writing articles and books for Thurston he "became a kind of clearing house."[35] Originally the writing and promotional work that Gibson had done for Thurston was supposed to have been for the great escape artist Harry Houdini.

By 1930 Gibson had proven himself to be a prolific writer. From 1920 to 1930 he wrote no less than twenty-seven books, 212 individual articles contributed to magazines, and at least 44 separate syndicated feature titles comprising over 9,000 articles. Many of Gibson's early books were simple collections of material from his articles in magazines and syndicated features. Yet with each collection sections were revised and essays accompanied the tricks. Such essays truly revealed Gibson's love for magic and proved to the reader that magic was an art form that should be taken seriously. Gibson's writing had a flair. His writings on performing magic demonstrated his no-nonsense, simple to follow style. Each trick provided the reader with a miracle that required no elaborate equipment and minimal set-up. Gibson would include only a minimal amount of patter to say to accompany the trick. He was a firm believer that what one said when performing was such an individual thing he did not want to influence another's creativity with suggesting patter.

Gibson's writings during this decade would seem to many to be an author's whole lifetime achievement, but for Gibson this was just the beginning of an amazing writing career. He had gained the attention of Howard Thurston, and now he would work with Harry Houdini.

5

Harry Houdini's Final Escape

*By the way, in the Newark Sunday Call, Mr. W. B. Gibson is exposing
an illusion, "Sawing a Woman in Half", (although he is doing it incorrectly).*
— Harry Houdini, April 25, 1922,
letter to Richard Van Dien.

One famous name Gibson wrote under was Harry Houdini. Harry Houdini. The name itself conjures images of a magical enigma who could free himself at will from any such bond that vowed to steal his freedom. A man of mystery, fascinated with death and the beyond, he could escape from every constraint, no matter how many handcuffs, chains and ropes that bound him; Houdini could almost melt through such toys. But there was one escape he never pulled off. If anyone could, it would be Houdini. He vowed that if it were at all possible, he would accomplish it: to escape from the bonds that tie us all together in the same fate, the bonds of death.

Houdini was an idol, a symbolic representation of everyone's desire to escape his troubles. Articles, books and movies have all attempted to answer the questions surrounding Houdini's escapes. A single gentleman, outside of Houdini's close relatives, was allowed to see into his private world of mystery, a gentleman whose future writings would be as mysterious as the enigmatic escape artist himself: Walter B. Gibson.

Thanks to Walter B. Gibson's dedication to magic and writing the world was able to get to know the man who was born Ehrich Weiss in 1874 and would gain fortune and fame as the master escape artist Harry Houdini. Gibson exposed the escape artist's life to the public through books, articles, and radio programs. Gibson's personal friendship with Houdini prompted him to keep Houdini's name in the minds of the public well after the death of the escape artist. So it is Gibson who helped Houdini break the bonds of death, giving him eternal life in the minds of the public.

Gibson recalls that Houdini jumped into the spotlight during the rise of vaudeville around the turn of the 20th century. During his early struggle toward fame, Houdini performed an act that was similar to a typical séance of a spirit medium. One of his specialties was slate writing in which a "ghost" seems to respond to questions by writing on two slates that are sandwiched together around a piece of chalk. Furthermore, in his practice to become "a medium," Houdini became adept at escaping from bonds. A typical medium would be placed in a "spirit cabinet," bound to a chair and then left alone. Ghostly noises and objects emerged from the cabinet. When the guests inspected the cabinet, they found the medium still bound to the chair. Yet Houdini found he gained much more attention and notoriety if he stopped halfway and stepped out of the cabinet, showing that he had escaped. Gibson states, "So Houdini, who was very smart, cut the act at the turning point. Once out of the bonds, he came from the cabinet and took a bow, claiming credit for the whole thing."[1] Houdini then presented more escapes than he did medium work. He set records with his handcuff escapes. He performed two shows a day on the Keith and Orpheum Vaudeville Circuits,[2] performing jail breaks for publicity. He eventually began performing specialty acts which centered more around magic than the escapes.[3]

As vaudeville began to decline and the trend moved more towards feature films, Houdini took the role of a hero in a series of movies, which include *The Master Mystery*, *The Grim Game* and *Terror Island*. The films did well. Their popularity encouraged Houdini to look into a filmmaking venture. The Houdini Picture Company made its magical appearance in 1921. The company made only two serials, *The Man From Beyond* and *Haldane of the Secret Service*. His company never did well. Losing money, it eventually folded.[4]

Walter Gibson, being a fan of magic, of course was greatly interested in Harry Houdini. Gibson read of the marvelous escape artist's impossible liberations from every sort of contraption that bound him. Yet it was not until July 1915 that Gibson first met this world sensation.

At age seventeen, Walter Gibson was visiting Atlantic City where Houdini was performing at the Keith's Theatre on the Garden Pier. Gibson arrived at the theatre wearing a sports coat with a lightweight, blue handkerchief adorning his breast pocket. This handkerchief was of the purest silk, the type magicians use in their performances. Gibson always carried such an object so he would be ready at a moment's notice to give a brief magical performance.

Gibson watched the marvelous show unfold before his eyes. As if witnessing Houdini's live performance wasn't amazing enough, Gibson was selected to join the master escape artist on-stage as a member of the committee who would examine the Chinese Water Torture Cell. The cell was a tall box filled with water. Assistants would strap Houdini's ankles into a stock, which would act as the lid to the cell. Assistants hoisted Houdini into the air and then plunged him, head first, into the water cell. The lid was locked in place. The audience could see the master escape artist in what could be a watery grave through the glass panels on each side of the cell. A curtain dropped around the box, and within a long three minutes, with gasps of anticipation hissing from the audience, Houdini would emerge from the curtains, dripping wet in his bathing suit. Assistants removed the curtains to allow the thrilled audience to view the Water Torture Cell, completely sealed and intact. As the committee arrived on-stage to aid him, Houdini spotted the blue handkerchief in Gibson's pocket. Houdini strolled over to Gibson and removed the handkerchief. With the words "Watch this," Houdini rolled the handkerchief into his right hand. With a bit of magic the handkerchief disappeared. Houdini, showing his left hand empty, reached up beneath Gibson's coat and produced the blue handkerchief at his fingertips. "This brought smiles from the committee and an appreciative ripple of applause from the audience," explained Gibson.[5] Houdini stuffed the blue silk handkerchief back into Gibson's breast pocket and proceeded with the show.

After Gibson saw this performance of Houdini's, he became even more interested in the man. When Gibson's father traveled on business trips, he would often send home newspaper accounts of Houdini's performances. Gibson saw Houdini a few other times with his father: once in January 1917 and a second time in September 1918 at the Hippodrome in New York.

When Gibson joined the Society of American Magicians he got one step closer to meeting Houdini personally. At the time, Houdini was president of this growing fraternity. He held this office from June 1917 until his death in October 1926. Gibson was sure that he would be able to meet Houdini at the S.A.M. banquet in June 1920. Unfortunately, Houdini was in England at the time and did not make the banquet. Yet Gibson's disappointment would not last too long.

Gibson took a return trip to New York shortly after the banquet. It was here at a magic shop that Gibson met Arthur Felsman, a Chicago magic dealer. Felsman told Gibson that he had a business appointment with Houdini the following day, and invited Gibson to join him. Gibson was thrilled.

The next morning the two traveled to Houdini's brownstone on West 113th Street in New York City. The two magicians were greeted and shown into the first-floor reception room to wait for Houdini. While seated in the room, Gibson began making small talk with Felsman until he interrupted Gibson's talk with a single finger pressed to his lips. Felsman quietly removed a pencil and envelope from his pocket and wrote on it, "Things said here may be heard." Gibson would later confirm this statement. Houdini had the room wired and would listen in on the conversations of guests. He would later use this information to perform mind-reading acts to the amazement of his guests. So Gibson and Felsman, assuming their conversation would be heard, began speaking about how wonderful the membership growth had been in the S.A.M. since Houdini became president. Gibson pointed out the growth of his newly formed Philadelphia Assembly as an example of the great improvement. Felsman made similar remarks regarding his assembly.

The two were deep in conversation when Houdini strode into the room carrying a deck of playing cards. He greeted his guests and then proceeded to show them the latest craze in card magic in England. It was a trick entitled "Instanto." Houdini began quickly cutting the cards and naming the cut-to card before turning it over. He kept repeating this and announced his thoughts about the trick's originator. Houdini thought that Billy O'Connor, the magician responsible for this close-up miracle, had not invented the trick. He guessed that O'Connor got the idea from someone

Harry Houdini sits among his vast collection of magic books. It was in Houdini's library that Gibson had his first personal conversation with the world's greatest escape artist. Photograph courtesy of the Sidney H. Radner Collection, Houdini Historical Center, Appelton, Wisconsin.

else, but he did not know who. Gibson thought the trick was similar to a trick deck put out by Theo Deland, which used marked edges. But none of them could think of the trick's name. Houdini, still searching for the specific name of the trick, was partly satisfied with the answer to his thoughts. He ushered his guests to the library.

The room was filled with bookshelves stuffed with magic books. Books were everywhere. Houdini explained the room's mass disarray. Alfred Becks, a professional librarian from England, was categorizing the books in Houdini's library. Among the books sat two of Houdini's assistants. They were studying the origins of various tricks by perusing magic publications. Houdini added a new task to their list: compare the ad descriptions for "Instanto" and Theo Deland's "Wonder Pack." Miraculously Houdini recalled the name of the trick that Gibson and Felsman had forgotten. Such was the memory of Houdini.

The three magicians settled down to talk in Houdini's third-floor study. Houdini produced a list of gadgets that he wanted Felsman to make. The gadgets were those used by mediums. Houdini intended to produce a show that exposed the methods of fake mediums. The conversation soon turned to the topic of the supernatural, a topic that Gibson thoroughly enjoyed. The three spoke at length on this topic until Felsman and Gibson departed prior to lunch. This initial meeting with Houdini would eventually lead to a great friendship between the escape artist and Gibson, though some of Houdini's first impressions of Gibson were not in the brightest of light.

In 1922 Houdini discovered an article in a paper exposing the secrets of magic to the public. Houdini did not like this at all. Being national president of the Society of American Magicians Houdini decided some action should be taken against this author. In a letter on official stationery of the S.A.M. dated April 25, 1922, Houdini wrote to National Secretary Richard Van Dien of Jersey City, New Jersey:

My dear Van Dien:

Am mailing you a parcel of two color letterheads.
By the way, in the Newark Sunday Call, Mr. W. B. Gibson is exposing an illusion, "Sawing a Woman in Half", (although he is doing it incorrectly). If I am not

mistaken he is a member of the Philadelphia Assembly. Will you please write to the secretary asking about this? Enclosed you will find a clipping from the Newark Sunday Call, which please return after perusal.

With kindest regards and best wishes, I remain

Fraternally yours,
Houdini

When Gibson got a hold of a copy of this letter, he made copies of it and distributed them among all of his friends. Oddly enough, a short time later Houdini would be calling on Gibson to ghost-write books for him, exposing the secrets of magic to the public.

Gibson and Houdini met at intervals throughout the following years, at S.A.M. banquets and after performances. On one occasion Gibson's S.A.M. assembly hosted a dinner at the Hotel Hanover, to which Houdini was invited as the guest of honor. The assembly performed a magic show for their guest, and Gibson was on the bill. He performed one of his favorite routines, the "Hindu Wand Trick." The audience loved the trick and were thoroughly entertained. Houdini was so impressed by the audience's reaction that he became very interested in this particular apparatus and wanted to know more about who made it. Houdini approached Gibson after the show. Gibson was very proud to direct Houdini to the builder, Carl Brema. The next day the two magicians arrived at Brema's magic shop on the third floor at 524 Market Street in Philadelphia.

Brema was a manufacturer of metal conjuring apparatus. He specialized in coin tricks and turned out various brass gadgets for the magic world. Many of these tricks Gibson invented himself, or he helped Brema improve on old concepts. In his shop was a special back room in which no one was allowed. Many noted magicians would be standing in the shop when a quick-moving young man would rush in and head for that back room. Later the youth would rush out past the other magicians. Of course all these top magicians became very interested to find out who this young magician was who was allowed in the back when they were not. It was none other than Walter B. Gibson.

Gibson had something these other magicians did not: an endless supply of good ideas and the means to make them come true. Gibson's father had many top engineers and metal turners working for the Gibson Gas Fixture Works. Thus Gibson would often take brass gadgets from Brema and bring them to his friends in the company. He would then question them about improving the apparatus. The engineers would immediately take the pieces and figure out a better way of accomplishing the same effect. Gibson would rush back to Brema's shop and pass this information on to him. Gibson and his father's workers were heroes in Carl Brema's mind. Thus Gibson was one of the few allowed in the back room.

Houdini eventually became good friends with Brema and had him produce some apparatus for his séance exposés. Whenever Houdini was in the Philadelphia area he would meet with Gibson and Brema to discuss magic and the latest gadgets on the market. Gibson recalls one of these engagements. "...When Houdini was again playing

Keith's [Theatre] in Philadelphia, he would finish his act in the afternoon and call a cab to take him down to Brema's. There, he would tell the cabby to wait for 10 or 15 minutes. Hours later, Houdini would come down from Brema's shop to find the taxi driver asleep and the meter running, piling up the dollars. That didn't bother Houdini."[6] When magicians get together to talk about magic, they will talk until all hours of the night, regardless of other obligations, and obviously Houdini was no exception.

Gibson and Houdini became great friends through the years. When Houdini was playing to packed audiences at Keith's Theatre he would often invite Gibson backstage. Gibson recalls that the act Houdini performed still included the Needle Trick and the Substitution Trunk that Gibson had witnessed during Houdini's first run at the theatre. In fact, one evening Houdini confided in Gibson, "'This act that Bessie [his wife] and I are doing here is the same act we worked in dime museums, nine times a day for eighteen dollars a week. Now we're doing two a day and getting eighteen hundred.'"[7] Houdini's fame had obviously won out.

Houdini was known to be the one man who could not be contained. Yet there was one situation that he was helpless and unable to escape, all as a result of Gibson's baby, the yet-to-be-born Robert. The very pregnant Charlotte, Gibson's first wife, squeezed against Gibson in the front seat of his brand new Model T Ford coupe to make room for Houdini. The three, or rather four, passengers were driving to a magic meeting on Girard Avenue in Philadelphia. Soon they arrived at the meeting and Gibson noticed Houdini groping for the door handle. He was accustomed to the old model cars in which the handle was at the front and the door would swing backwards. The new Model T was equipped with the handle toward one's elbow, and the door swung forward. Houdini's hand fished backward along the door when it didn't find the handle in the front. He finally found it but couldn't get enough leverage to push the door open because the handle stuck due to its newness, as well as the lack of personal space in the seat due to Robert's expected arrival. With great annoyance Houdini proclaimed:

> I've escaped from practically every type of a container and every size, shape, and weight of boxes, trunks, and other such things, but I wish someone would tell me how I can get out of this darned automobile![8]

Gibson reached across and with a push released the latch to free the great escape artist from the automobile. Gibson recalled that this was one of the few times he ever heard Houdini laugh. The world's greatest escape artist contained by an unborn baby!

Houdini was looked upon by others as a serious individual. He could be rather friendly to those in the magic world, just as long as those fellow magicians did not present any escapes in their acts. Houdini saw all escape artists as imitators, and he would go to great lengths to see that they never made a name for themselves. One such case involved a young woman by the name of Miss Undina. In Germany she had built and advertised an escape that duplicated Houdini's Chinese Water Torture Cell which he constructed around 1913. Miss Undina had constructed a similar apparatus.

A poster depicts the woman escape artist being plunged into the cell upside down. Houdini sued the woman for using his escape. He won the suit, and the woman had to destroy all of her posters. One of them was saved by Houdini and his attorney and eventually ended up in the hands of Walter Gibson. This poster has been restored to its former glory and now hangs in the living room of Sidney Radner. Another such poster revealed itself in a collection bought by David Copperfield, yet the poster disappeared from the collection after Copperfield acquired it.

Houdini's vengeance on others who attempted escape acts or to imitate him in any manner was intimidating. Gibson witnessed many incidents of the master escape artist losing his temper over supposed imitators. One such example, and one of Gibson's favorite stories, revolves around a series of articles Houdini was to write every Sunday for the *New York World*. The section of articles would be called "Red Magic" and would feature various puzzles and simple tricks with which the reader could amuse himself. Houdini wanted Gibson to write these for him, but Gibson was already under contract with Howard Thurston to provide a similar series, "Lessons in Magic," as an expansion from the candy box tricks Gibson had done. Thurston's articles were syndicated on a yearly basis, and were picked up by a variety of papers including the *Brooklyn Daily Eagle*. (One paper eventually picked up Houdini's "Red Magic" as well as Thurston's lessons, printing them under the heading of "Green Magic". Houdini was not amused.) Houdini worked it out with the *World* writers to provide them with the articles and they would edit them so he would not need a professional writer to write them. Each article would be accompanied by an artist's rendition of the featured trick or puzzle. The writing of the articles had been figured out, but the *World* and Houdini were just waiting for the right artist for the job.

One day as the editor of the *World* was sitting behind his desk a gentleman walked into the office. He carried some artwork under his arm and presented it to the editor, along with his card. The editor glanced at the business card to find that the young man's name was Hugh Deeny. With a chuckle the editor questioned the artist about the origins of his name. Deeny said it was his birth name. The editor replied that he had a wonderful job for him.

The editor discussed the type of artwork they needed to accompany the "Red Magic" series. He wanted Deeny to show Houdini his artwork. The editor made it a point to tell the young artist to give Houdini's secretary his card. Houdini would be quite amused; at least that's what the editor thought.

Hugh Deeny arrived at Houdini's brownstone and entered with his artwork under his arm. He proudly presented Houdini's secretary with his card. Deeny was asked to wait there. Soon a man burst into the foyer. The man screamed about impostors and imitators. He demanded to know who had put Deeny up to this horrible joke. Deeny attempted to explain about the artwork for "Red Magic," but the man ignored him. Deeny held onto his artwork as tightly as he could out of fear that this madman would rip it up. The man descended upon Deeny, pressuring him toward the door. Deeny meekly explained the situation. With a tight grip, the man ushered Deeny into the library. He snatched the artwork out of Deeny's arms and pushed it towards a couple of secretaries, demanding that they look at it while he got to the bottom of this horrid imitation. It wasn't until this moment that Deeny realized that this crazy man was Houdini himself.

Houdini rushed to the phone and dialed the "Red Magic" editor. Houdini's voice thundered through the phone, demanding an explanation. He threatened the editor that he would speak to the chief editor and others about this cruel joke.

The phone lightly clicked back into its resting spot and Houdini slowly turned to face Deeny. Houdini's somber eyes looked into Deeny's. His hands touched the artwork. His eyes glanced at each piece, studying the skill of the artist. Silence filled the air. Houdini slowly looked up at Deeny and calmly remarked about the artwork, "They're all right, the kind we want. Sit down, *Murphy*, and we'll go over the work we want you to do. Murphy, that's to be your name whenever you come here. Remember it." Deeny complied, and he received the job. The two became good friends after this initial incident. Maybe that was due to the fact that Hugh Deeny decided to change his birth name to Joe Bowers when he was doing other professional work so he would not offend Ehrich Weiss, or, rather Houdini. It was years later, as Joe Bowers, that he related this story to Gibson when the two worked together at the *Ledger* syndicate in Philadelphia.[9]

Gibson often noted that Houdini was a master of publicity stunts. Gibson recalls that there was a company which supplied radio equipment, called the Houdina Company. This company was staging a huge publicity stunt at around the same time as the Deeny incident mentioned above. The Houdina Company planned on driving a radio-controlled automobile down Broadway. This attention-getting stunt would truly get the company's name to stay in the public's mind, and when Houdini heard of their idea, he couldn't get it out of his mind.

Houdini couldn't stand the fact that this company's name was so close to his stage name. Wouldn't it be horrible if the public remembered the name *Houdina* instead of *Houdini*? To terminate this threat, Houdini and his secretary, Oscar Teale, paid the Houdina Company a visit. They entered the offices and abruptly destroyed almost all of the office furniture by smashing it against walls and floors. One must learn not to mess with Houdini![10]

Gibson recalled seeing Houdini's fury firsthand when he was backstage with Houdini and Hardeen, Houdini's brother, at the Chestnut Street Opera House in 1926 in Philadelphia. Gibson was backstage arranging with Houdini a special evening called "Magicians' Night." As the two were discussing this night of magic a messenger from the *Evening Bulletin* arrived holding a want ad that someone had placed in the paper as a publicity stunt for a show. The young man was attempting to find someone backstage who could confirm the advertisement. The message had nothing to do with Houdini, but when he found out about the publicity stunt he simply lost his senses. He viciously grabbed the piece of paper from the young man and exclaimed: "'Who is responsible for this hoax? Who thinks that I would stoop to a cheap publicity stunt like this? Go back and tell your editor that when he puts anything in his paper about Houdini, it will be front-page news!'"[11] Gibson attempted to calm Houdini down and to explain the situation, but Houdini wouldn't listen. The words exploded from Houdini as he attacked the poor messenger. In desperation, Gibson turned to Houdini's brother, Hardeen, figuring a family member could calm Houdini's rage. Gibson recalled that "...Hardeen simply spread his hands and gave me a broad, knowing smile. 'When he starts a streak like that,' confided Hardeen, 'don't try to stop him. You can't. Nobody can stop him — except Houdini.'"[12] Eventually the master escape artist quieted himself. With a grin of satisfaction he turned toward Gibson and Hardeen, as if they should congratulate him on his outburst.

After this hectic evening, "Magician's Night" was finalized and was a great success. The evening of entertainment was a sell-out, and Houdini was in attendance as a guest. Gibson was performing in the show along with about five other magicians. Gibson again entertained the audience with his Hindu Wands routine. He showed two wands with a short tassel dangling from one wand and a second tassel dangling from a long string attached to the second wand. If one were in India, he said, one could easily discover the Hindu fakir, for he would be pulling the tassels back and forth, making one short, the other long, and then vice versa. This would inevitably draw a crowd, explained Gibson. He went on to explain that the Hindu fakir would sever the string that attached the two wands and then proceed to show that the two tassels were still magically attached, and when one pulled down on the short tassel the long tassel would still go up. Gibson exposed the secret of the Hindu fakir: he actually destroyed a fake string and another string which connected the wands protruded out the back of the wands. Thus, Gibson explained, if one was ever in India one should cut this real string, making it impossible to perform the trick. Gibson proceeded to do just this. He showed two unattached wands, yet as soon as he pulled on the short tassel, it magically pulled the long tassel up, to the great amusement of the audience. This was the same routine that Gibson had impressed

Walter Gibson performs his Hindu Wand routine — the routine Houdini was so interested in performing himself. From the collection of William V. Rauscher.

Houdini with four years earlier. This evening the wands got such a great response (even Houdini was wildly applauding) that Houdini approached Gibson after the show, wanting to learn the routine.

The next day, Gibson and Houdini went to Brema's shop, and Houdini ordered a set of oversized Hindu Wands made of imitation bamboo. Gibson joyfully went over the routine with Houdini, and soon they returned to the theatre to practice some more. Houdini asked Gibson to dictate the routine word for word to his secretary. Gibson went through the routine in great detail with Houdini's secretary to make sure that he wouldn't miss a move (Houdini died before ever performing the wands).

It was at this moment that Houdini asked Gibson for another favor. He wanted Gibson to ghost-write books for him. Houdini had already published some books himself, but he was interested in publishing more. Houdini wanted to publish a whole series of books from beginning to advanced magic. He also wanted to include some of his closely guarded secrets of escape and illusion. He wanted to start with a few books for the beginning magician. Each book would be dedicated to clearly demonstrating simple magic tricks that the reader could do. Gibson had just done

These are the Hindu Wands Houdini had Carl Brema make in order that Houdini could reproduce Walter's routine. Houdini died before he could perform the routine. The wands are part of the annex collection of Ray Goulet's Mini Museum of Magic in Watertown, Massachusetts. Photograph by Thomas J. Shimeld.

research on such tricks for Howard Thurston for the ghost-written book *200 Tricks You Can Do* and had literally hundreds of extra tricks as a result of his research: thus there would be no duplication in Houdini's books. Gibson quickly agreed. Houdini collected notes on tricks and performing for the purpose of writing after he had retired. Houdini dictated many of his notes to Sagent, his secretary, in order to be later published. Sagent had written such books as *Miracle Mongers and Their Methods* and *Magician Among the Spirits* under Houdini's name. Gibson took over Sagent's work in writing for Houdini after Sagent died.[13]

The two magicians stayed in contact through the next few weeks. Gibson would meet with Houdini every now and then at various public shows in which Houdini dedicated a portion of his show to exposing the secrets of mediums. At the close of Houdini's touring season, Gibson frequently visited the escape artist at his brownstone in New York City. The two would discuss materials that should be presented in the books. Houdini wanted to approve each trick and modify, add or subtract tricks as he saw fit. The discussions took place often in Houdini's study, sometimes in various local magic shops, and even walking down Sixth Avenue to the New York Hippodrome where Houdini was performing. As the book was taking form, Houdini would dictate various notes to his secretary that would be given to Gibson to use in newspaper articles under Houdini's name.

By early October, Gibson had the first book complete. Yet, always one to go above and beyond people's expectations, he withheld sending the book so that he might finish the second book and send them both to Houdini. He anticipated that the second book would be complete by the end of October and he would send off the set during the first week of November. Unfortunately, Houdini would never see either completed volume, for he died on October 31, 1926.

The first in the series of Houdini books was complete, and Gibson did not know what he should do with it. He approached Mrs. Houdini after her husband's death to see what should become of the book. She thought that the book should definitely be published, but she was too busy with finalizing her husband's affairs. Gibson's nephew Wendel recalled that "Houdini had a fantastic warehouse full of magic. Talk about a collector! He had everything…. She [Houdini's wife] had to liquidate all this and the estate had to be settled and it was not the propitious moment to do what he [Walter Gibson] wanted to do…." Because Bess Houdini was so busy taking care of the estate, Gibson was given permission to publish the book under his own name. *Popular Card Tricks* was published in 1926 by the E.I. Company. This forty-eight-page book included 91 various card tricks with suggestions on presentation. The book, originally intended to be the first in the series of Houdini books, was the only one published.[14]

After Houdini's death, Gibson continued his commitment by writing books on Houdini's life. From 1927 through 1976, Gibson published six books dedicated to Houdini's life, magic, and escapes. Gibson worked with Bess Houdini and Bernard M. L. Ernst to have the memory of Houdini live on. Each book contains some previously unpublished material from Houdini's private notebooks. The popularity of

Houdini resulted in many of Gibson's books on him being republished and reissued a number of times. *Houdini's Escapes* became one of Gibson's greatest contributions to magic history. This book was prepared from Houdini's private notebooks and demonstrates the methods Houdini used in rope, box, and underwater escapes. It also explains how to walk through a brick wall. This book has been reissued and is still among libraries' collections today. It is possible that this is the only copy surviving of Houdini's notebooks, for the originals are said to no longer exist. The originals were part of a collection stored in two trunks, which Gibson was given sole access to. As a result of Houdini's continued popularity, Gibson put together *The Original Houdini Scrapbook* in 1976. It includes numerous photographs, newspaper clippings, magazine articles and posters from various collections, including Gibson's own. The book, written by someone who actually knew Houdini on a personal level, was the great work to satisfy people's appetite for Houdini and their "Houdinimania."[15]

Houdini's fame has sparked many books, documentaries and even movies and plays in which he is the center of attention. In one famous movie, Tony Curtis played Houdini. But Gibson disagreed with Curtis' interpretation of Houdini: "'Tony Curtis wasn't a very good Houdini.... He made him suave. Houdini was very rough and ready.'"[16] Houdini's fame has reached such immense proportions that many museums have been dedicated to this escape artist. In Niagara Falls, Ontario, Canada, the Houdini Magical Hall of Fame had collected a vast amount of paraphernalia and memorabilia relating to Houdini, before much was lost in a fire (see Afterword).

Thanks to Gibson's unique gift of storytelling on radio and various television talk shows, as well as on paper, Houdini's mysterious life has been opened for the world to view. The enigma of an escape artist was solved first by a man with an incredible propensity for mystery and magic. Gibson knew the real Houdini and not just the myth. Gibson wanted the fame of his friend to live on, untarnished, yet in each book, article or interview Gibson would always slip in a glimpse of the true persona of Houdini.

6

Casting the Shadow

Why? Why in all the modern movies, stories, [and] novels, does the villain get away with all sorts of wild stuff, and the hero act like a hick, until just at the close, when the villain has but to pull some easy stunt, he makes a mess of it, and the insipid hero, has, simultaneously, an inspiration and an acquisition of superhuman skill, so that he thwarts the villain's vile purposes and brings everything to a lovely conclusion? I must confess a weakness for the villain, but my hopes are never realized.

— Walter B. Gibson, 1918 diary,
February 14th entry.

That little cherub that played such a vital part in guiding Walter Gibson's life would soon reveal the reason for its guiding hand toward a particular goal: the creation of the Shadow.

Street & Smith, the leading publisher of pulp-fiction magazines of the early 1920s and 1930s, of 79 Seventh Avenue in New York City, hired advertising executive Dave Christman of the Ruthrauff & Ryan Advertising Agency and writer-director Bill Sweets to produce a radio program to aid in the promotion of its *Detective Story Magazine*, the world's first detective fiction magazine. In 1929, Street & Smith had purchased two years of radio time for *The Detective Story Hour*.[1] Christman and Sweets decided the program would be introduced by a sinister, all-knowing voice; a voice that had no name at first; but the scriptwriter assisting Sweets, Harry Charlot, would soon dub the famous voice the Shadow. The Shadow was the first mysterious storyteller on the radio that introduced and narrated the dramatized radio stories from the first ever detective fiction magazine, the *Detective Story Magazine*. The Shadow began as a narrator, not a character, to promote the magazine on the *Detective Story* program on the radio. The radio show premiered on Thursday night, July 31, 1930, featuring James LaCurto as the sinister host. After a few weeks, Frank Readick, Jr. soon acquired the role of the host as LaCurto's successor. Readick began his radio career in 1928 as the producer and director of the Hank Simmon's *Show Boat* program. He was also featured in *The March of Time, Joe Polooka, Smilin' Jack,* and

Meet Mr. Meek radio shows. The half-hour *Detective Story* show would continue on CBS each Thursday night thereafter. People could then purchase the new issue of the *Detective Story Magazine* the following day. After the knowing, mysterious laugh, a voice would announce: "I ... am the Shadow! Conscience is a taskmaster no crook can escape. It is a jeering shadow even in the blackest lives. [Sinister laugh] The Shadow knows ... and you too shall know if you listen as Street & Smith's *Detective Story Magazine* relates for you the story of ... [for example] The House of Death." It was this same sinister laugh that Gibson had heard when tuning in the radio with Howard Thurston in 1930.

Listeners were so enthralled with the narrator of these programs that they would go to their newsdealers requesting "that shadow detective magazine."[2] (This was not good for the sales of the *Detective Story Magazine,* so Street & Smith soon decided it was necessary to reenter the "character magazine" field to feature the Shadow in his own magazine. The publisher had dominated the field at one time featuring the exploits of Nick Carter, and it was willing to attempt another magazine based on the Shadow, although it was hesitant. Meanwhile, Street & Smith removed *The Detective Story Hour* during its second season and replaced it with *Love Story,* retaining, oddly enough, the popular sinister Shadow as the narrator.

Around the time of the development of the radio narrator now known as the Shadow, Gibson was writing stories for a magazine called *Tales of Magic and Mystery.* The series ran for five issues appearing once a month from January through May 1928. Gibson wrote a number of articles for each issue under various names including Thurston's. He included a series of articles on Houdini and a section devoted to simple tricks.[3, 4]

After this magazine folded, Gibson went to the editor of the *Liberty* to talk to him about taking over the magazine. Gibson suggested titling the new magazine *Strange Stories.* The editor had been considering such a venture under the name *True Strange Stories,* and already had someone working on it. Gibson became the editor of this magazine around 1928. He took the job with the understanding that he would step down after the first issues were published, since he really wanted to write for the magazine. Gibson commuted from Philadelphia to New York in order to work on this magazine. After several months of work on it, Gibson turned the magazine over to Ray Wilson, a veteran editor of the company. This eased Gibson's commuting lifestyle for he would not have to be at the office so often if he were to just write for the magazine. He further

Walter Gibson at the time he began writing the Shadow stories. From the collection of William V. Rauscher.

kept up his work with the *Ledger* syndicate which gave him access to files for story ideas.[5]

It was his factual writing that added greatly to Gibson's fantasy creations. One such creation appeared as the lead story of *True Strange Stories*. He explained his work for this magazine in a 1980 interview: "Now this was somewhat pathetic, a lot of people don't know about this story.... *True Stories*, although those magazines were supposedly true, you could develop them as you saw fit. And many of them were true in the sense that they could have happened and probably had happened." At the time in Pennsylvania there was an outcry over witches. Gibson was excited about the idea of an article on witchcraft and produced a story as told to him by the fictitious character Madeleine Grover. The story was titled "Why I Am Called a Witch" and ran 13,500 words and was written in the first person. The story was told by a girl who had been mistaken for a witch during a visit to the county in Pennsylvania where there was a concern about witchcraft. He gave it to *True Strange Stories* for a reading in the morning. When Gibson returned to the office to see how they liked it, he discovered that they were already in the process of typesetting it as the cover story. This story is held to be Walter Gibson's first fictional story for a large-scale audience.

Gibson continued to write for *True Strange Stories* until 1929 when the magazine folded due to the stock market crash. Gibson continued writing syndicate features, yet he yearned to write more fiction. He submitted stories to various magazines. He even completed a full-length mystery novel. The intent was not really to get it published, but just as an exercise to see if he could actually do it, and he certainly could. Instead of editing this novel to his satisfaction, Gibson began pursuing other projects. This was a time of constant writing for Gibson on various projects just to make a steady income.[6] He was interested in the pulp magazines and submitted some short crime stories to Street & Smith publications to be published in the *Detective Story Magazine*. Gibson had established himself over the previous ten years as an efficient writer, and his bid to be published at Street & Smith was encouraged by the fact that an editor friend, Lon Murray, had recently acquired a job with the company. One of Gibson's short stories, "The Green Light," seemed to get some attention from the editor-in-chief, Frank Blackwell. Henry W. Ralston, the business manager at Street & Smith, who would later become vice-president of the company, designated Blackwell to begin work on a new pulp magazine featuring the Shadow. Ralston had thought that the quickest way to get this new *Shadow Magazine* out to the public was to rewrite an old Nick Carter novel.[7] Blackwell noticed Gibson's flare for fiction and he had heard about his other writings; he figured Gibson "was worth a try with this new character, the Shadow, because they wanted something fictional that sounded like fact,"[8] a genre of writing with which Gibson was most familiar.

Through Gibson's connection with Murray he met Blackwell. When Blackwell told Gibson about Ralston's ideas of rewriting the Nick Carter series, Gibson thought it would not work. Gibson saw Nick Carter as a "'stylized detective'"—to turn him into a mysterious figure "'would be somewhat incongruous.'"[9] Furthermore, for an author to rewrite another author's story, he would be compensated half the usual rate, or less, for an original story. Gibson would create a whole new character for the series.

The editors had only a few simple suggestions for Gibson to begin his writing: to make the character mysterious, to create agents to aid him, and to utilize modern technology in the stories. These acted as general guidelines beyond which Gibson was left entirely free to develop characters and plots as he saw fit. Gibson remembered, "'...I always thought it would be good to have a fictional character — a strange weird person. I took the story with the understanding that if they liked it they'd give me three more. At least I'd get paid for the one story. If they didn't like it they'd junk it and give the concept to somebody else.'"[10] Thus Gibson accepted the job with the understanding that he would provide the complete year (four stories in all) if they approved of the first story; that Gibson would remain as the author, developing his own stories, thereafter if the magazine proved successful in its first year; and that Gibson would be compensated accordingly on future stories if the magazine became popular. Conditions seemed right and Street & Smith agreed. Gibson explained his idea for the characterization of the Shadow:

> For that, I needed an outstanding character and I had been thinking of one who would be a mystery in himself, moving into the affairs of lesser folk much to their amazement. By combining Houdini's penchant for escapes with the hypnotic power of Tibetan mystics plus the knowledge shared by Thurston and Blackstone in the creation of illusions, such a character would have unlimited scope when confronted by surprise situations, yet all could be brought within the range of credibility.[11]

The Shadow knows, and so too did Gibson.

Street & Smith wanted a novel-length story around 75,000 words immediately. They wanted to see a few opening chapters and a general chapter outline within a week. On the train back to Philadelphia, Gibson began working out ideas for the chapters. He began writing the very next morning.[12]

Gibson returned to Philadelphia to write the first few chapters. He luckily showed Blackwell his progression for he would have to add a Chinatown slant to the story because the cover art was already chosen. The cover was recycled from a 1919 magazine. Gibson explained: "'It seems the publisher, for purposes of economy, had decided to use an old cover painting for the new magazine, and the only one that tied in with the Shadow was a man in Chinese costume, clutching an upraised hand that cast a huge shadow on the wall behind him.... I simply changed one of my scenes to Manhattan's Chinatown!'"[13] He titled chapter eight "The Tea Shop of Wang Foo."[14] During various conferences, the editors at Street & Smith publications had agreed (although Gibson later found that his friend Murray was not in accord with much of this) that the stories should be written under a "house name" owned by Street & Smith. When Murray informed Gibson of this news, Gibson objected, figuring his creation of plots and characters and the development of the Shadow as a character should be credited to himself. The two came to a compromise resulting in Gibson using a pen name. Gibson went to work on this. Reverting back to the area he knew best, Gibson compiled a list of magic dealers with whom he was acquainted. He listed the names in two columns, one for the first name and one for the last. Using his gifted genius for solving puzzles, Gibson arranged the names into combinations that sounded good and that would attract a reader's attention. He struck upon one combination that rang in his ears: Maxwell Grant.[15] Gibson acquired this famous name through the combination of the names of two magic dealers: Maxwell Holden and U.F. Grant. Holden was a famous New York magic dealer at the time, and Grant sold his tricks of the trade from his store in Pittsfield, Massachusetts.[16] The two names were perfect, for Holden performed a specialty branch of entertaining with hand shadows, and Grant had developed a "Shadow Illusion" in which he could walk away from his own shadow.[17, 18] The public would then see Maxwell Grant as the biographer of the Shadow. The pen name also allowed Street & Smith some leeway in dealing with Gibson for they could always substitute another author's writing for Gibson's.

The editors approved of Gibson's pen name and Gibson thought that it would be nice to have such a name that he could use in certain writings, especially novel-length ones. Furthermore, Gibson readily accepted this name change, for a short story under his own name would also be appearing in the first issue of the magazine. Gibson was certainly familiar with using pen names in magazines when more than one article by the same author was published in the same issue; besides, Gibson wanted to become better established in the short story market. Street & Smith used the name Maxwell Grant for some time on other publications, such as *Sports Story*, in order to further publicize it as that of an actual and credible author.[19]

Gibson finished the first story ahead of schedule[20] and it appeared in the spring of 1931 in the April–June issue of *The Shadow Magazine*. The first book-length novel, entitled *The Living Shadow*, was inspired by elements of Robert Louis Stevenson's "The Suicide Club." The Shadow's adventures begin on page two and run through page 113 of *The Shadow Magazine*. From page 117 through 125 one finds "The Green Light" story that Gibson had submitted to Street & Smith, published under his own name. There are two other stories that accompany the main Shadow story: "Crime Detection in the Philippines," by Charles A. Freeman; and "The Bounty Racket," by Captain Bruce. The first issue of *The Shadow Magazine* introduces readers to this dark character through the eyes of Harry Vincent, who, in the opening scene, intends to take his own life. A mysterious figure appears out of the mist to rescue him. The saved man "faced a tall, black-cloaked figure that might have represented death itself. For he could not have sworn that he was looking at a human being. The stranger's face was entirely obscured by a broad-brimmed felt hat bent downward over his features; and the long, black coat looked almost like part of the thickening fog" (pages 4–5 of *The Shadow Magazine*, volume 1, number 1). Vincent is now the Shadow's agent, in a life that is mysterious and full of adventure. The Shadow was treated as "a discovery" that readers, along with Gibson, would learn more about in each successive novel.

Anthony Tollin thought Street & Smith smart for choosing Gibson to write the Shadow: "Walter Brown Gibson was the perfect choice to chronicle The Shadow's mysterious adventures. His writing combined a journalist's crisp, no-nonsense prose with a magician's talent for misdirection."[21] Gibson figured he would be done with this project and move on to another in a couple of months after the first four issues were written. Gibson stated that after the first issue was completed, "'I wrote the next three in a hurry in order to get 'em out of my hair and get back to work. But the editor contacted me and said, "'Hurry up, we're selling 'em out!'"[22] The Shadow had taken off in popularity. Gibson explained "'that was a bad year. The only two pulp magazines that sold out in 1931 were the Shadow and Ballyhoo. The second issue also sold out, so I was told to keep writing.'"[23] The magazine had a run of approximately 300,000 copies per novel and they sold almost as fast as they could print them. The demand for these first issues of *The Shadow* became so great that Street & Smith published the first three issues in three separate books from 1934 to 1935[24] (Gibson received no compensation for these reprints, for in 1932, when Gibson signed a contract with Street & Smith in which all rights were reserved by the publisher, "all rights" meant only magazine rights, for this was all Street & Smith wanted at the time and all the company would ever be concerned with). Gibson was paid $400 for his first novel.[25] This was less than 1 cent a word. The best rate at the time for these magazines was 2 cents a word, but these were magazines that sold for 20¢. *The Shadow Magazine* cover price was 10¢.[26] But $400 a novel was a good income for this young newspaper writer. Gibson made approximately $80 for features at the *Ledger* syndicate and around $40 for crossword puzzles. Gibson reported that Street & Smith "'were good pay in those days when some magazines paid only on publication, and some of them never.'"[27] By the third issue the magazine was so popular it went monthly. Gibson was thrilled, "'A novel a month was a nice prospect, and I hoped the demand would last for two, three, or four years. It didn't.'"[28] By March 1932, the magazine was published on a never-before-seen twice-a-month basis, and would continue at this rate for the next decade, and Gibson began making $500 a story, and towards the end of his fifteen years writing *The Shadow* he made $750. Gibson reminisced about this time:

> If I wanted to buy a car I could do it with two books. But I never really did make any money. If I had invested in things like real estate, I would have come out very well. But I was so busy, so wrapped up in things.... I didn't get as much as a typist would today for typing them. And copies of the originals are worth more ... now than I got for writing them.[29]

The Depression brought the Shadow to life. One needed a diversion at this time, an escape from one's troubles. Sampson speculated on the popularity of the Shadow: "The Depression was just getting into full collapse. What was needed was some sort of a figure acting within the popular mythology to strike out against all the menaces, from gangster domination to government corruption, that everybody perceived were floating around, destroying the society, ruining the economy and otherwise causing havoc."[30]

"The Shadow did not die in 1952: Today, as part of the interest in nostalgia, there are Shadow clubs, Shadow collectors, and correspondents who write Gibson letters addressed simply, 'The Shadow, 12426' his ZIP."[31] The Shadow continues to have a following of dedicated fans.

The Shadow stories are not only significant to nostalgia-loving collectors, but also to literary professors. The Shadow offers a unique insight into the mentality of people living during the years of the Depression and World War II.[32] Displaying the deep undercurrents of the American psyche to future readers and researchers was not Gibson's intent. "I saw it as a job," stated Gibson plainly. [33] The Shadow stories contained much violence. They were "long on violence and short on sex." Gibson explained that "'World War I had had a violent impact on audiences, and we were starting to get a foretaste of the world we have now, with crime and violence everywhere. I wish I could have left out some of it, but that's what the public liked.'"[34]

Through the first year, after beginning writing, Gibson's *only* contact with Street & Smith was through Lon Murray. This left Gibson on his own, free to develop stories himself without editorial guidance. Finally, in March 1932, Gibson met, for the first time, with Ralston. Ralston offered Gibson a contract, based on the increased demand for the magazine. The contract ensured the exclusive use of the name Maxwell Grant for the sole purpose of writing the Shadow novels.[35] Gibson had first objected about Street & Smith obtaining exclusive rights to the Maxwell Grant name, but he understood that under this name Gibson had established something no other writer had ever done: writing 1.5 million words of mystery about a single character in a single year. He thought after producing such an output that he would have "exclusive privilege to the further exploits" of his character.*

Gibson insisted that one clause be added to the contract — that he would be informed prior to Street & Smith assigning a Shadow story to another writer. Prior to this Gibson had produced the beginnings of a legend, all on his own. As Gibson writes in his personal papers:

> I had put honest effort into developing a most profitable product. I had done this despite editorial contacts instead of through their help.... Simply put, however, the whole subsequent history of "The Shadow" as a commodity can be attributed largely to my fortitude during that period prior to March 1932. I delivered and asked questions afterward. My policy brought results— at the time — so I stayed with it later, which proved in some ways to be a mistake.

The popularity of *The Shadow Magazine* encouraged Street & Smith to offer Gibson a contract to produce twenty-four Shadow novels in twelve months, a task no other writer had ever accomplished. "It was obvious that if I could not meet the strain," Gibson writes in his personal papers, "I would suffer along with Street and

---

Opposite the table of contents page of the first isssue, the reader may note the following:

> *This is to certify that I have made careful examination of the manuscript known as "The Living Shadow," as set down by Mr. Maxwell Grant, my raconteur, and do find it a true account of my activities upon that occasion. I have therefore arranged that Mr. Grant shall have exclusive privilege to such further of my exploits as may be considered of interest to the American public.*
>
> — The Shadow

Smith." Gibson felt that if he could prove he could meet this demand, that Street & Smith would have no other choice but to allow Gibson to be the exclusive author of the Shadow. There was another clause in the contract stating that if Gibson completed more than 24 novel-length stories in a year that Street & Smith would give him other assignments to "fill my 'slack time' ... I liked the humor of that," so in just ten months, from March 1 through December 31, 1932, Gibson wrote the twenty-four Shadow novels averaging 60,000 words each. In the remaining two months of the contract, until February 1933, Gibson completed four additional novels bringing his total word output for this twelve-month contract period to in excess of 1,680,000 words.[36] This got Gibson ahead of schedule. This was all part of Gibson's "plan" to demonstrate to Street & Smith his ability to deliver quality writing. Gibson now thought he had proven his exclusive use of the Maxwell Grant name as a result of this spectacular output. It seemed that Street & Smith agreed, for they used Gibson's picture as Maxwell Grant in promotion pieces. The Corona Typewriter Company recognized Gibson's, or rather Maxwell Grant's prolific writing, in an ad campaign in New York City in 1933. A picture of Gibson was blown up to a life-size display featured in shop windows throughout the city. The display announces at the top, "A NEW WORLD'S RECORD" and depicts a young "Maxwell Grant" standing above a Corona typewriter with a long curled sheet of paper protruding from the typewriter and being displayed in Grant's hands. A dark shadow wearing a slouch hat shades the writing on the paper which states:

> **1,440,000 words** were written by **Maxwell Grant** in less than **10 months** on a **Corona** typewriter in the creation of the sensational character *The Shadow* featured in *The Shadow* magazine a Street & Smith Publication

Under the picture the display continues:

Making a Record with a Record-Maker

> Two champions— THE CORONA and THE SHADOW. Corona is a good typewriter but Maxwell Grant is a great typewriter — and THE SHADOW is one of the most amazing types in all fiction.
>   Making records is nothing new for THE SHADOW MAGAZINE. Right from the start THE SHADOW has been a record-maker and a record breaker.

In the following twelve-month period, from March 1, 1933, until February 28, 1934, Gibson rapidly produced another twenty-four novels totaling greater than 1,440,000 words. Gibson was so far ahead that he could relax into producing 1,000,000 to 1,200,000 words annually, a rate which he would continue at for the next twelve years. It would not be until Gibson's fifteenth year writing the Shadow novels that his prolificacy would drop beneath a million words a year. All these words were nimbly typed out on an eighteen pound, semi-portable, noiseless, Corona typewriter.

Each successive year after the beginning of the second year Gibson and Street & Smith established a verbal agreement in the extension of the contract. Five years into the Shadow writing, with no sign of declining demands (even though five years was the absolute limit that Street & Smith had anticipated producing this magazine), a *Shadow Magazine* appeared by another author.

As the Shadow became more and more popular, other magazines began imitating him with other mysterious characters. This really scared Street & Smith. To keep ahead, Ralston thought the magazine should change its angle and have the stories split up more so they could be read as individual works rather than the building upon one story. Since Gibson was six months ahead in his writing, Ralston decided to contract out for another writer instead of disturbing Gibson's output. So they asked Ted Tinsley to write four stories under a year's contract. Tinsley wrote slower than Gibson, completing a Shadow story in about two months, but his stories were good and meticulous. Tinsley was a modern writer who depicted the Shadow as "less awesome and more human."[37] Gibson was surprised at the appearance of this other author's story, since

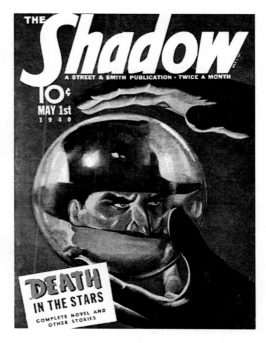

Gibson's love of psychic phenomena and astrology often shone through in his stories, such as this one, *Death in the Stars* (May 1, 1940). From the collection of Marc Sky, retouched by Jennifer Ann Shimeld, reproduced with permission from Condé Nast.

Street & Smith gave no warning of such an intention (thus violating the contract Gibson had signed four years prior). Gibson's quick yet succinct writing had elevated the character magazine into popular demand; just imagine if he had been given a couple of months to write *one* issue.

Years later in reflecting on this period in his life, Gibson was grateful for this work for "'this was the Depression, and it was a good thing to be doing. I just dropped everything else and did the Shadow for fifteen years. I was sort of depression proof.'"[38] Gibson stated in an interview, "'The 10 years I worked as a reporter provided me with valuable experience and ideas,' he recalled. 'For one thing I learned to write and think fast. Many authors including Charles Dickens got their start as newspapermen and it is a misconception that good writing has got to be done slowly. The faster you can write the faster the ideas come to you.'"[39]

The public demanded more and Gibson responded. Being a man of deadlines, Gibson encouraged himself to write furiously to finish the novels. What was created in Gibson's mind and interpreted onto the page by his fingertips was final: there was never any rewriting. "'I didn't have any time,'" admitted Gibson.[40] "'I did all the typing myself, and everything on first draft. Occasionally if I noticed a weakness I might redo a couple pages.'"[41] Street & Smith had a staff of editors who would make sure that character and scene details remained the same throughout the novel, but they never requested a rewrite. This speed of production was the only way Gibson could write. "'Speed writing is really the only way to get good writing,'" thought Gibson. "'The characters begin to talk for themselves.'"[42] For each Shadow novel Gibson would submit a 2,500–5,000 word synopsis, which the editors at Street & Smith would approve. The synopsis included background and an outline of the story. Gibson explained his formula in working out the synopsis:

> First: I find a crime and a man to do it. I figure possible complications for him, and how he might handle them. To a degree, I'm using the "plot from character" process with him. At any rate, this goes into a couple of pages called a "Background."
> Next comes the "outline," three to four pages. It brings the background people into conflict with The Shadow, and introduces the "proxy hero" or his equivalents.
> Then I write a synopsis. It runs twelve pages, sometimes more, and brings in the features of each chapter, even to snatches of dialogue. [43]

The editor, John Nanovic, would often read the background of where the story took place. Ralston read what went on in the story. Each chapter would be broken down into precise characters and plots, so it would be very easy for Gibson to write from these. "The headaches that accompany a synopsis eliminate those that would otherwise occur when writing the story."[44] Gibson remembered:

> Sometimes, I would call John and say I was going to get rid of such-and-such a character and switch this thing that way. And he'd okay it while the story was in progress. But originally I had trouble with that and I had to do lots of changes, and I cluttered up with too many characters. Well, I would have these synopses absolutely licked and that formula would take me three or four days. That was why sometimes I sped up on the writing of the stories. But the stories from then were duck soup.[45]

The detail of the synopses provided Gibson with a foolproof plan for his writings. "'I think that's one reason I was very happy at doing the work; I never had anything in the way of a hitch.'"[46] Gibson would then write 10,000–15,000 words daily, finishing a novel in four to five days. This translates into approximately sixty typewritten pages a day, around four to five pages an hour for twelve to fifteen hours. This was at his best and most productive. Many of the novels averaged closer to eight to ten days to complete, setting a minimum of twenty pages to write a day, but he usually accomplished an average output of thirty pages daily.[47] He would then take a brief rest to allow his fingertips to heal before pounding out the next novel.[48] Gibson recalled that "By living, thinking, even dreaming the story in one continuous process, ideas came faster and faster. Sometimes the typewriter keys would fly so fast that I wondered if my fingers could keep up with them. And at the finish of the story I often had to take a few days off as my fingertips were too sore to begin work on the next book."[49] "'I'd used to knock 'em out one a week,' Gibson said. 'In between, I'd take two or three days for plots and outlines. I was living the thing all the time, and one story just merged in with the next.'"[50] And many thought this is what made the stories so good — Gibson didn't just write the stories, he lived them.[51] Many ideas would come to Gibson as he typed. He remembered one incident when he was typing in such a fury that he did not notice the large copper bowl that was sitting beside the typewriter. At each keystroke, the carriage of the typewriter slowly slid the bowl closer to the edge of the desk. Eventually the bowl fell to the floor with a resounding gong, the sound that could appear in Wang Foo's hideout.[52] With each succeeding lesser character, readers were getting to know the Shadow. Soon the lesser characters became less important, and, Gibson admitted the "stories, themselves were getting stronger, because cumulative plot facts were more frequently evident.... Thus though I didn't recognize it, I was becoming an experienced fiction writer."[53]

When writing the synopsis, Gibson would often pause in between chapters to collect his thoughts for the next chapter. But when writing the actual story he would always stop in the middle of a chapter, or sometimes even in the middle of a sentence. In this manner it was much easier for Gibson to get back into writing when he returned to his typewriter. Such a style of pausing for breaks may have well been introduced to Gibson at a time when he was being called on by some friends. He remembered that "'once some friends busted in on me and wanted me to go out. "When I get to the end of the page," I told them. When I got there I was in the middle of a hyphenated word. I stopped at the hyphen. When I came back I never picked up at an easier place.'"[54] It was at the end of a page that Gibson would often stop his writing, regardless of whether he had finished the sentence or not. In writing, the hardest part is producing the first page. Gibson would not even worry about this, but simply start writing with the intention of going back to correct things after completing the story. But the best way Gibson found to

©1974 FRANKLYN E. HAMILTON

Walter Gibson

·THE MAN·
·BEHIND· ·THE· ·SHADOW·

After fleshing out the character known as the Shadow in 283 novels, Walter Gibson can arguably be dubbed the creator of this crime-fighting mystery man. Paper and ink illustration by Frank Hamilton.

begin a new story was to start immediately following the completion of another. "'When I can I plan a light day for the last one on a book, and as soon as it's done start another while I'm under power. That way I get into it easiest, and the second-day pick-up isn't something to worry about.'"[55]

There was no time for relaxing in between stories. A restaurant on Juniper Street near the *Ledger* syndicate building acted as the first office space where Gibson wrote some of the original Shadows. Gibson would often take his portable typewriter along with him on trips and type on the train. He would even type in the midst of a party. Gibson recalled a trip he took to Michigan to attend a party at Harry Blackstone, Sr.'s summer home. Deadlines were quickly approaching and Gibson needed to finish the next Shadow story, so he set up and wrote during the party, to the great amuse-ment of the guests. As soon as he was finished with a page his friends would snatch it up and read it and would be anxious to read each succeeding page. "'That only spurred me on,'" said Gibson.[56] His fingers pounded faster as the images came quicker. Gibson would have never known his abilities to produce such a massive out-put if there had not been the demand for it. This is a fact that points to a personal conviction of Gibson's: "namely, that many writers who think they've approached their output limit, are only kidding themselves.... Output means money. If you don't write stories, you can't sell them. *So write them until it hurts. Then Write More.* Maybe you'll find that pain will help them."[57] After producing the first 2,000 words, Gibson would approach his peak of progress around 3,000 to 4,000 words, and he would be good through 5,000 words. It was only after reaching this peak point in a story that he would quit for the day. Granted, he would take long pauses for meals and to see a show or attend a party, but he did so with the intent to return to his typewriter. In this manner Gibson would return from his break, even if the break itself was unjustifiable, with an increased zeal for his work.

Gibson produced the novels so rapidly, and was so far ahead of his deadlines, that he enjoyed reading the novels himself when they were published. "'As I read, I'd be mystified myself,'" admitted Gibson. "'I'll remember the general synopsis, but for-get which alternative I chose in dealing with a situation.'"[58] Because of Gibson's hec-tic writing schedule he had little time to read much else than his own work. Yet this habit was good for him for sometimes he would find fault with his writing or think of how he could have done it differently. This only improved his future writings. Gibson would write maybe ten hours a day with a half-dozen packs of cigarettes on hand to calm his nerves.[59]

The constant thinking of plots and names was always on Gibson's mind. There was no time for him to tarry over names, due to the busy deadlines of the pulp mag-azines. "'Somebody writing for the *Saturday Evening Post* might spend a week try-ing to think up a good name,'" thought Gibson. "'Whenever I traveled I checked the timetables. I remember reading the Seaboard Airline timetables in Florida [where he'd often spend the winters writing], and noticed that some of the branch lines were named after people. Those were some of the names I used.'"[60] Sometimes people would accuse Gibson of using their names and question him: "'Why did you use me

Walter Gibson sits writing another Shadow novel. He smoked incessantly to calm his nerves during this intense time of high demand for his Shadow stories. From the collection of Robert Gibson.

for the villain in that story?'" Gibson would quickly respond, "'Because you happened to be the third stop on the Winchendon line.'"[61]

Plots would come to Gibson from any number of places, newspaper articles, a paragraph in the encyclopedia, anywhere. Unlike many pulp writers, Gibson researched his stories meticulously to make sure they were in the realm of plausibility, often studying guidebooks and traveling to various cities across the country to study the locations for future stories. The localizing of certain Shadow stories was on the suggestion of the publisher so that the company might publicize the magazine in those areas. The Shadow has traveled to Philadelphia, Boston, Chicago, Miami, and New Orleans. Gibson said, "'I liked to do stories in real places, mainly Florida, the Carolinas, New England … I preferred Shadow locales I was familiar with, though others were well researched.'"[62] One locale was taken from a camping trip Gibson had made through the Timagami Forest Reserve in Canada as a sixteen-year-old. He had chronicled the trip in his Keewaydin logbook issued by the Keewaydin camp. He recalled the details of the surroundings, but changed some of the names of lakes and places. "'Once I got the tempo of pulps I would suddenly get a new idea, like getting up a new trick. If an idea came up in the course of a story, I'd lay it aside for another story. I had a backlog of incidents. For example, I was doing research into castles in England and came across a description of the Golden Arrow train. I began to think of some murders taking place on this train.'"[63] One story, *The Masked Lady,* came to Gibson when he went to a nightclub called Leon & Eddies': "'I took Steve Fisher along. They had a review in which girls appeared in costumes and masks. They'd come out and sit on the customers' laps and so on.'"[64] In Gibson's story one of the performers shoots a customer and returns to her dressing room. It turns out it wasn't the performer at all but the mobsters attempting to blame this murder on that masked lady. Gibson's nephew Wendel recalled cab rides with his uncle in New York City which turned into plots in *The Shadow Magazine*:

> In those days there was such a thing as a Desota taxi with a sunroof ... and it was called a Sky View. Desota Sky View Cab.... We were on Sixth Avenue ... and we stopped under the "L" and we're looking up and instead of seeing the sky we're seeing the underneath of the elevator. "A person could just get up on the roof of this car and in no time he could be up there," [observed Gibson]. And The Shadow did just that. Lamont Cranston "escaped" from the car; and he got on the train to chase down the criminal he was tracking.
> The other one: It wasn't too uncommon to see people handling plate glass with these big suction cups. They had a truck ... and two guys get out, one on each end and they'd walk over and put the sucker right in where the window was broken. Cement it and in no time the thing is good as new. So Walter said, "there's more to it than that. You could put suction cups on your knees and in both hands and you could walk up any building." And The Shadow did just that in the next Shadow story. That thing was picked up on and used as a theme in a lot of other writing.[65]

Gibson further explained his rationale for the Shadow using such suction cups to scale buildings:

> Before 1900 acrobats were performing as human flies—using rubber suckers to walk upside down on ceilings. They were real human flies.
> The cups work on a simple scientific principle. A concave disc of soft rubber is attached to the bottom of each of the performer's shoes, and the edges of the discs moistened.
> Each time the foot is pressed against the surface of the ceiling, a vacuum is created, so that the air is ejected from within the concave disc, and the edges stick tightly, preventing the air from returning when the foot pressure is released.[66]

Dan Goodwin, a stock exchange clerk from San Rafael, California, known as the "human spider," used this same technique to climb the tallest buildings in North and South America. He climbed the 100-story Hancock Tower in Chicago, scaled the 1,362-foot northern tower of the World Trade Center in Manhattan, and conquered the world's tallest building, the 110-story Sears Tower in Chicago.[67] Such a story as this makes the Shadow's devices plausible. The Shadow used this device in many adventures—*The Black Falcon* of February 1, 1934, was one such:

A batlike shape was clinging to a wall which projected at an angle from the set-in fire tower. Invisible in the darkness, this hidden creature seemed other than a human form.... The batlike shape was moving away from the fire tower. Past the angle, it crept with sidewise, crablike motion along the extended wall. The glow of city lights revealed the figure dimly. Like a huge vampire, The Shadow was sidling across a vertical surface!

Hands and feet were pressing against the wall. Each was equipped with a large concave disk of rubber. Each pressure of a suction cup gave its wearer purchase upon the wall. Each twist released one of the supports. The Shadow had become a human fly [pages 41–42].

All the Shadow's mysterious abilities were in the realm of possibility.

In the *House of Ghosts* of September 1943, the Shadow uses a magical device that he had frequently used before:

The Shadow produced a small tin box with two sections, dipping his thumb in one, his forefinger in the other.

A burst like a reporting gun went off ... along with a flare of flame. Those special chemicals had served The Shadow often, but never more dramatically than this.*

(The editor of the magazine supplied the following note: *Because of the danger connected with this explosive formula, we do not give its components here. It is a device often used by the Shadow in his exploits against crime — Ed.*)

Though his weapons were quite sophisticated, the Shadow still remained in the realm of possibility. One of Gibson's inspirations was a favorite author he had read as a child, John T. MacIntyre. MacIntyre wrote mysteries and a popular detective series in the early 1900s featuring a character called Ashton Kirk. One of MacIntyre's best known books is *Steps Going Down*, which was a best seller and won an international prize for writing. Gibson was fortunate enough to meet MacIntyre during his time of writing the Shadow. MacIntyre passed along this advice to Gibson: "'Don't get the stories too good! Keep within the patterns, whatever they are, and stay with it. Don't try to get the stories too sophisticate....'"[68] Yet Gibson did make his novels sophisticated to a degree. He thought that readers would grow with the Shadow. Large words were defined within the context of the sentence. Nanovic often wanted Gibson to be more cautious about his plot twists, for once it is written it is hard to backtrack in the future to explain various character traits of the Shadow. But Gibson found that "'The Shadow had such avid readers that I had to work hard just to stay a jump ahead of them.'"[69] Like in his magical performances, Gibson loved to lead his readers down the garden path, where the answers to the mystery appeared obvious. "'I would just blow it up in the reader's face halfway through the book and then start a new twist.'"[70]

"'I have always written for readers, and have found it valuable to continue that policy. It keeps a writer from going stale, enables him to follow any trend, and sometimes to start a new one.'"[71] And who knew that this writing would lead to what today is well known as the double-identity superhero. The Shadow knows!

7

Who Knows the Shadow?

"Have you ever seen the Shadow?" … "I don't know." "Does he live here in New York?" "I don't know." "What is his purpose in life?" "I don't know." "Is he a crook?" "I don't know." "Is he on the side of the law?" "I don't know."
— *"The Living Shadow,"* The Shadow Magazine,
Volume 1, Number 1, April–June 1931.

"Who knows what evil lurks in the hearts of men? The Shadow knows!" And who knows the Shadow better than his creator Walter B. Gibson. Gibson described the Shadow as:

> A weird crime fighter who invariably emerged from the blackness of the night to pluck helpless victims of black-hearted villains from the brink of doom. As a character The Shadow was as nebulous as the swirling fog (a favorite habitat of his). But as the story progressed, he took on substance. It was formula writing…. Still, from his first appearance The Shadow captured the imagination of hundreds of thousands of readers, and of millions of radio listeners. How The Shadow managed to do this I don't know. Not even now. But he did. And I am grateful. For it happened in the days of the depression, of unemployment, of breadlines. And I was then a hungry young writer, even as writers have always been.[1]

Gibson's lengthy association with Street & Smith allowed him to become good friends with the editors, especially John Nanovic. Gibson was grateful to be able to work with this talented editor, probably the only other individual that "'had come to know the Shadow as closely as I did'" he thought.[2] Nanovic commented that Gibson "'had mystery and magic in his writing…. He had the newspaperman's knack of giving you enough facts so that you wanted to read on to the next paragraph, and enough of the magician's flare to flash things before you long enough to intrigue you, but not give his point away.'"[3]

In the days of the pulp magazines they were not called by this name, but rather character magazines, or category fiction. Pulp magazines covered western, science fiction, detective and romance stories. The pulps gained the market from dime novels and were the forerunners of paperback thrillers.[4] Pulps were printed on lesser quality paper than the "slicks" of the time, such as the slick-stock magazines the *New Yorker* and *Harpers,* and featured less advertisements.[5] Pulp writers were never considered great writers by the literary world. "Pulp," writes William Dunn in his article "Dashing off a yarn" that appeared in the *Detroit News* on February 24, 1980, "to literary elitists, has come to mean mass-produced hack writing, usually of the sensational variety. But to the millions of fans of category fiction, the word 'pulp' means action-packed stories written by dependable journeymen." Gibson stated about writers in this genre, that "'we didn't associate with other writers, but we had our own literary circle, and we got together whenever we could — Lester Dent, who wrote Doc Savage; Paul Ernst, who did the Avenger; and all the rest. We were eager to meet each other. We were a very self-satisfied group — we were reasonably young, we were fast writers, and we were happy.'"[6]

Lamont Cranston, the Shadow's alter ego, was created in the second novel, *Eyes of the Shadow.* Cranston was a wealthy adventurer and for such a character Gibson wanted a name that portrayed distinction. Two family names of two syllables seemed to combine nicely to ring the bell of distinction, such as Rudyard Kipling or Woodrow Wilson. So Gibson did his research and combined the last name of Wall Street financier Thomas Lamont with the last name of Baillie Cranston, a Scottish theatre owner associated with Houdini, to create Lamont Cranston.[7]

Yet Gibson added a twist to this association by revealing in the third issue of *The Shadow Magazine* that the Shadow only assumed the identity of Cranston while the real Cranston was traveling. For years Gibson hinted at the Shadow's true identity. It was finally revealed in *The Shadow UnMasks* on August 1, 1937, six years into the Shadow's continuous adventures. In reality the Shadow is Kent Allard, a famous aviator who reportedly had disappeared into a tribe of Xinca Indians on the Yucatan Peninsula. Allard only assumed the role of Cranston while the millionaire was away on frequent world trips. The Shadow lurked in the disguises of many characters. He would sometimes

In the Shadow novels, Gibson was the first to popularize the concept of the double-identity superhero. The Shadow, who assumes the identity of Lamont Cranston, is in reality Kent Allard (*The Shadow Unmasks,* August 1, 1937). From the collection of Marc Sky, retouched by Jennifer Ann Shimeld, reproduced with permission from Condé Nast.

appear as Fritz, a janitor at the police station, in order to eavesdrop on Inspector Joe
Cardona and Commissioner Ralph Weston. Gibson drew from his childhood memories of his home in Germantown, Pennsylvania, when he invented Lamont
Cranston's mansion.⁸ Cranston's wealth allowed him to acquire such modern con-
veniences as an autogiro, a predecessor to today's helicopter. For approximately a
year, Kent Allard would appear quite frequently in the novels. By the 1940s, due to
the popularity of *The Shadow* broadcasts, Allard appeared less frequently and
Cranston made more regular appearances. Gibson remembered:

> As soon as the War hit, I couldn't have any of those fantastic spy rings or anything
> because they were in reality. And we went into whodunits. Whodunits were fitted
> perfectly for Cranston around the Cobalt Club and having some peculiar crime in
> New York. And we wanted to use Margo[t] Lane occasionally because of the radio
> tie-in and she fitted into stories as long as Cranston played that debonair part....
> Also, many people thought of him unless they read the Allard story. That was one
> difficulty that got worse and worse as we went along.... So we just figured that since
> the people were sold on Cranston, we might as well play along with it.⁹

Gibson never considered the radio version of the Shadow to be the same Shadow
he had created. He did not listen to the program on a regular basis.¹⁰ The Shadow
radio broadcasts aided greatly in the promotion of Gibson's writing for the magazines. Though Gibson never wrote for the radio shows, a look at the Shadow's radio
history is important.

The Shadow's sinister voice scratching across the airwaves is how many people
remember the Shadow. The voice, produced by a carbon filter microphone that gave
the speaker's voice a "fiercely metallic" tone, was played throughout the years by a
number of talented actors.¹¹

Frank Readick, Jr., had played the improved Shadow character on *Detective Story*
and the *Blue Coal Radio Revue*.¹² In January 1932, the Shadow began a series of his
own on CBS. The series moved around from one station to another, finally disappearing completely during the 1934–1935 season. Street & Smith wanted to promote
Gibson's writing on the air, yet Blue Coal, the sponsor of the series, was content in
having the Shadow as the narrator of a variety of mystery stories. It would be two
years before the Shadow's eerie laugh reappeared on the airwaves as the most famous
fictional character in America at the time.

Ruthrauff & Ryan Advertising Agency wanted to revive the Shadow program in
1937; Street & Smith insisted that they base the stories on Gibson's Shadow character. Gibson never wrote for the radio program, but he did work with the original
scriptwriter, Edward Hale Bierstadt, who had written for the Warden Lawes program, *20,000 Years in Sing-Sing*, to make sure the radio program followed Gibson's
creation as closely as possible. Gibson recounted his first experience with Bierstadt:

> The place was stacked with Shadow magazines and Ed ... [*sic*] told me that he not
> only had read them, but had liked them. That marked the beginning of a warm and
> lasting friendship, particularly as I liked the script when he read it to me. He had

featured a death-row scene, something that he was closely familiar with, and he had captured The Shadow's mystique as well. His experience as a criminologist had given him an insight into the ways and wiles of small-fry crooks that showed clearly throughout the script and caught the tempo of the earlier Shadow novels.[13]

Gibson continued his account of the first radio script in the *Starlog* of April 1986:

> That first script followed The Shadow pattern pretty well.... But Ruthraff & Ryan insisted on changing it to suit their particular ideas. So, Hale went in and they read it to him and when they got through, they said: "What do you think?"
> He said, "I think it was written by an imbecilic child who was dropped on its head at the age of six weeks," Gibson recounted laughing in obvious agreement.[14]

The Shadow of the radio show was never Gibson's Shadow and he never identified with it.

The Shadow on the air could never match the complexities of Gibson's character for it would be too confusing for radio listeners to identify the various voices as disguises of the Shadow. So the Shadow was given just one alter ego: Lamont Cranston. Many of the other main characters on the air would be based on Gibson's creations, such as Harry Vincent and cab driver Moe Shrenitz, but the famous Margot Lane was created specifically for the broadcasts in order to offer a voice contrast to the dominant male voices. The original radio script included Harry Vincent, but producer Clark Andrews replaced this character with Margot Lane. Andrews' girlfriend, Margot Stevenson, an actress on Broadway in "You Can't Take It With You," was the inspiration for the creation of Margot Lane. Ms. Stevenson would later play the role of her namesake opposite Orson Welles.[15] The radio program's popularity eventually forced Gibson to add Miss Lane to his characters in the magazine. In the radio broadcasts, Margot Lane saved the Shadow as often as he saved her, thus "'around the office' Gibson laughed, 'the old joke used to be, 'Who knows what evil lurks in the hearts of men? *Margot* knows!'"[16]

Edith Meiser was hired as story editor for the 1937–1938 season. She had produced and edited the radio broadcasts featuring Sherlock Holmes. As a result of her feminine influence, these scripts featured a less cliched female character and are thus thought to be some of the best scripts of the Shadow broadcasts.[17] On September 26, 1937, the twenty-two-year-old Orson Welles played the Shadow on the debut of the program over the Mutual and Yankee networks. Clark Andrews and Martin Gabel produced and directed "The Death House Rescue." The story featured the voices of stars that would shine even brighter in the future. They include Agnes Moorehead who played Margot Lane and who would later appear on television as Endora on *Bewitched*; Ray Collins as Commissioner Weston who would become Lt. Tragg on *Perry Mason*; and Bill Johnstone in a supporting role who would later supply the Shadow's voice and even later act as Judge Lowell on *As the World Turns*. Frank Readick's voice as the Shadow filled listeners' hearts with a thrill at the commencement and conclusion of the show; Welles supplied the Shadow's voice during the radio drama.[18] Welles juggled his busy schedule to be the Shadow, often sending assistants

Richard Wilson and Bill Allard to read and to mark up the script for him during rehearsals as he attended to other projects.[19] Welles would stay with the show for twenty-six episodes with sponsor Blue Coal and twenty-five episodes with sponsor Goodrich Safety Silvertowns before leaving the series to produce his own program, *The Mercury Theatre of the Air*.[20] By the time Welles left, the Shadow was the highest-rated program on daytime radio.[21]

The next season began on Sunday, September 25, 1938, and featured Bill Johnstone. Johnstone had supplied supporting voices for Welles' Shadow and also Readick's Shadow of the early 1930s. Johnstone kept the Shadow's voice alive for five seasons, during which the Shadow became a friendlier character, and Margot Lane became the "cliched damsel in distress" after the departure of Edith Meiser. Marjorie Anderson replaced Agnes Moorehead as Miss Lane when Moorehead left to be in Orson Welles' classic film *Citizen Kane*. In the 1940s the Shadow was now more than a popular radio voice and magazine character. He became an American institution.[22] The Shadow appeared in comic books, newspaper strips, Big Little Books. *The Shadow Magazine* was printed in seven different languages and had a monthly distribution of 750,000. The Shadow Club had well over 1,000,000 members. In 1942 C.E. Hooper reported about the radio broadcasts of the Shadow: "'since they first began rating daytime shows in Feb. 1938, no other daytime commercial program has ever attained as high a rating.'"[23] In the 1940s listeners could tune into the Shadow on about 300 stations around the country. In March 1942, the Shadow broadcasts held 55.6% of the listening audience captive, earning a Hooper rating of 17.2.[24] Thus, as Anthony Tollin observes, "The Shadow had become the *first* of what is today referred to as a 'multi-media phenomenon.'"[25] The popularity of the Shadow would continue for the full eighteen years it was in print. As Robert Sampson observed, "the Shadow was part of American life, familiar as Fords and the Flag."[26]

Bret Morrison appeared as the Shadow for a season, and would later return in October 1945 to play the Shadow for more episodes than all other actors combined.[27] People often associate Morrison with the Shadow for he "sounded exactly like the Shadow looked in our mind's eye...."[28]

During Morrison's "hiatus" from the role of the Shadow, John Archer provided the voice for 30 episodes beginning in 1944. Judith Allen provided the voice of Margot Lane. Steve Courtleigh replaced Archer, who left due to his conflicting schedules, in the fall of 1945. Laura Mae Carpenter performed as Margot Lane. Courtleigh left after playing only six episodes, opening the role for Morrison to return to it.

The Shadow laughed his final sinister laugh on December 26, 1954.

Throughout the 1940s, Gibson would write for various radio programs including *Nick Carter, Chick Carter, Blackstone, Frank Merriwell, The Avenger*, and others. He later scripted and hosted his own show about psychic phenomena, called *Strange*.[29] The creation of the Nick Carter radio program came about when Gibson requested more work after Street & Smith cut down *The Shadow*'s output from twenty-four a year to twelve. Gibson accepted the job receiving little compensation for his work, with promise of higher rewards when the program gained sponsors. Street & Smith made this deal with Gibson informally through a letter. The *Nick Carter* program was soon taken away, along with a spin-off of the program, *Chick Carter*, for which Gibson also wrote. A radio director claimed these and evolved them, yet Street & Smith did little protesting. The move left Gibson out of that job, but he could still continue with the magazines.[30]

Women played a small role in the adventures of the Shadow. They often were present as people to rescue, or sometimes appeared with the criminals. But in the early years it was best to just have women characters with walk-on roles. It was not until the introduction of Margot Lane that a woman became a regular character in the magazine. Gibson explained:

> Of course with Margo[t] Lane, when I put her into the stories, a lot of readers began to scream. In fact, a lot of them said she was a troublemaker. That's true, that was the comic relief. She initially met The Shadow as Lamont Cranston on a cruise ship, and she looked him up when she got back to New York. She found The Shadow instead. She never knew the difference. So that satisfied readers.[31]

Gibson did not offer readers much sex appeal in his Shadow stories, he was more of the traditional mystery writer in the style of Arthur Conan Doyle, only adding Ms. Lane by pressure. Another chronicler of the Shadow, Ted Tinsley, did add some sexual aspects to the stories.

To grab more attention, Tinsley added sexual elements to his stories: more women, light sex, and dresses getting ripped. The artists took advantage of these scenes and depicted them on the covers and inside graphics. Towards the final years of *The Shadow Magazine*, Gibson touched lightly on such sexual subjects. In fact in 1939 in *The Smugglers of Death* the reader discovers a naked lady, Myrna Elvin, swimming ashore from an island, who gets mixed up in matters and ends up wearing the Shadow's clothes. This scene is depicted on the front cover, piquing the readers' interest for it looks as if the Shadow is *a woman*! Sex in the pulps was always clouded by innocence so they would not lose the younger readers but could retain the older ones.[32]

Yet the Shadow's fame need not be kept by such tricks of the trade. The writing and adventure were good enough to keep the readers. So good, that even in the face of imitators the stories still gained fame. The Shadow being the first multi-media creation, many publishers wanted to cash in on Gibson's creativity. Thus Gibson's writings inspired the inception of such pulp-heroes as the Spider, Wu Fang, Operator 5 and the Phantom Detective. The Shadow's imitators never threatened Gibson. Gibson related, "'Babe Ruth — they asked him one time which pitchers bothered him the most. He said, "They all look alike to me." So all the imitations of the Shadow look alike to me. They were interchangeable; I never paid any attention to them.'"[33] In 1932, even Street & Smith decided to imitate the Shadow with the *Doc Savage* series. At first they wanted Gibson to write it himself, but the demand for *The Shadow Magazine* pushed it up to a twice-monthly publication, leaving Gibson too busy. Lester Dent got the job. Street & Smith required him to read *The Shadow Magazine* and to even write a story for it (this story, *The Golden Vulture,* was retained and restructured by Gibson and published six years later on July 15, 1938).[34] The Shadow radio narrator was successfully imitated by *The Whistler* and *The Mysterious Traveler.* Gibson's Shadow inspired the creation of Superman and directly influenced the creation of Batman. Gibson always saw Batman as simply a "clowned-up version" of the Shadow. Actually Gibson scripted for the Batman series later in his life; in fact, his last published fiction writing was in March 1981 as the text story in *Detective Comics* #500 for the story "The Batman Encounters Gray Face."[35] Gibson got $300 for the 4,000 word Batman story: "would have been $40 back with S&S," Gibson admits in his 1980 diary on August 19. Will Murray notes in "Remembering Walter B. Gibson", "It was as if every time Walter Gibson hit a typewriter key, the hammer struck a responsive chord in a new writer or editor. And he hit billions of typewriter keys."

The Shadow is the country's first good hero. Gibson's creation was used as the prototype to develop such characters as Superman and Batman. Gibson is often credited with developing the first double-identity super hero. But in fact, the Shadow had numerous disguises.

In his article "Fore Shadowings" that appeared in the *Xenophile* in September 1975, Bill Blackbeard challenged the originality of the Shadow:

> The idea ... of an individual like the Shadow, securely settled in society in his true and respected identity, masking himself in order to selflessly right wrongs without personal gain, and by methods outside the law for private citizens, is a wholly novel one in literature, unheard of before the 1910s, and is uniquely an outgrowth of Americans in the early decades of this century. It is a significant, important, and widely appealing concept, particularly when combined with the exactly right name and physical image as occurred in the instance of the Shadow, and it is simply not one likely to have emerged from the conservative and practical creative sources employed by Street & Smith.[36]

Blackbeard continues to cite instances in history where the Shadow appears as a character. The first instance, Blackbeard notes, of a shadowy character is in 1879 in the detective mystery *Watch-Eye — the Shadow,* by Edward L. Wheeler. Then in 1913, Arthur Stringer wrote *The Shadow* which features a derby hat-wearing character. H. Bedford-Jones wrote a novel by the same name in 1930. "The Freshest Boy" feature story of the July 28, 1928, issue of the *Saturday Evening Post* also uses the Shadow. Blackbeard explained this character:

> While the author and creator of the Shadow as a dual-identity character, even to the capitalized "The", was Francis Scott Key Fitzgerald, symbol of the keynoting "jazz age" literature of his decade, and himself the most avidly-read writer of the twenties. Nor was Fitzgerald's Shadow confined to this one story; he appeared in several more written around the same period (most notably in "The Captured Shadow," in the *Post* for December 29, 1928), thus giving Fitzgerald the additional credit of having first established the Shadow as a series-story character.[37]

Fitzgerald's Shadow was the manifestation of his teenage character's, Basil Duke's, "thriller-fed imagination" as the "gentleman burglar that's called the Shadow." It is noted that Fitzgerald's Shadow is more similar to another pulp-fiction hero, the Spider, and not Gibson's Shadow. These Shadow characters had limited, if any, popularity. It is Gibson's creation that thrills the world.

Walter Gibson received no monetary rewards for the radio shows for they were a product of Street & Smith publications and they had all rights to the Shadow character. In 1946 Gibson walked out on a contract from Street & Smith requesting that they relinquish creator's rights of what was now truly Gibson's creation. For two years Gibson pursued other projects until Street & Smith begged him to come back to save the failing series. He returned and soon Street & Smith discontinued the Shadow's adventures in pulps and comics in order to pursue other projects,[38] like its slick titles such as *Mademoiselle*.[39] Nanovic approached Gibson to create another pulp series based on the adventures of radio and television private eye Martin Kane. Gibson wrote the first novel, but the series was never accepted.[40] The Shadow would forever more be the creation that Gibson is known for. The pulps never lasted much past the 1940s due to the popularization of television, the gaining market of paperback novels and the wartime paper shortages.[41] In 1952 Gibson, along with friend and Street & Smith staff writer Ed Burkholder, wrote the entire contents of *Fantastic Science Fiction* under pen names. Gibson edited only two issues. Gibson was never bitter that he lost out on the financial advantages of spin-offs and merchandise that would accompany the Shadow if it had been developed later in the century. Simply look at the massive market that Batman and Superman have possessed throughout the years. But Gibson has no regrets about the Shadow, having produced 283 of the 325 Shadows from 1931 until 1949. "'I thoroughly enjoyed writing these stories,'" admitted Gibson, "'and am pleased to have made a lasting contribution to the evolvement of the super hero in American literature.'"[42]

Gibson had dropped out of magic almost completely during the years that he wrote for *The Shadow Magazine*. This writing occupied much of his time, and the lack of journals during these years proves that he was busy. Gibson later acknowledged this, and that the sheer monotony (at least activity wise) did not warrant him to record over and over again: "worked on the Shadow today." In 1946, Gibson had quit the Shadow and worked with Blackstone.[43] Gibson's connection with magic always stayed strong. In fact, Gibson wanted to create a series featuring a detective magician. Thus was born *Crime Busters*.

Gibson approached Street & Smith's then general manager Ralston with the idea of producing more character magazines. Ralston was hesitant about the idea for fear of failure. Gibson suggested putting out one with three characters in it to see which one went the best. Street & Smith ended up using five or six characters and asked its writers to write the stories under their own names, except for Gibson — he would write under his Maxwell Grant pen name so Street & Smith could advertise the new magazine within the pages of *The Shadow Magazine*. Gibson created the character Norgil the Magician, who was a composite character of magicians Harry Blackstone, Sr., John Calvert, Russel Swan, and Joseph Dunninger. Gibson explained this creation: "'Norgil was modeled somewhat on an earlier Harry Blackstone, typical of the vaudeville acts. Miriam Laymond was a typical leading lady of the show.'"[44] Gibson modeled Norgil's show after magician Bill Neff's show:

> Bill Neff's company had two men, himself and three girls. I traveled with him briefly. He put on a popular midnight spook show. In his regular act, he'd do 30 or 40 minutes of magic, with some weird stuff such as burning a girl alive. He'd put her in a coffin-like thing and set it afire, and her arm would flop out. He'd put it back in. At the end, there was a skeleton in there, and its arm flopped out.
>
> For the spook show, the lights would be out and ghost-things would be flying around on fishing rods; balloons would shoot out; and puffed rice was thrown onto the audience like "fairy fingers"—it felt like spider webs on your face.[45]

Gibson's outlines for the Shadow novels read like a comic strip with snippets of dialogue. It was inevitable that the Shadow would creep into the comic book realm (*The Shadow Comics,* No. 2, 1940). From the collection of Thomas J. Shimeld, retouched by Jennifer Ann Shimeld, reproduced with permission from Condé Nast.

Norgil appeared in *Crime Busters* from November 1937 through September 1939. Norgil's adventures continued in the *Street & Smith's Mystery Magazine* until November 1940. Gibson, a lover of puzzles, adored playing with names. He revealed that Norgil's real last name was Loring, an anagram of Norgil. Gibson never revealed Norgil's full name, but it was planned on being W. Bates Loring, an anagram of Walter Gibson's own name. Gibson didn't want the W to stand for Walter, so a good friend, Will Murray, suggested using his first name. Gibson liked the idea, only adding an S to the name to stand for Williams. Williams and Bates were two colleges that Norgil's family had attended.[46, 47] The magician's exploits would later be republished in book form by the Mysterious Press in 1977.

Gibson created other magician characters such as Gerard, based on a post-war nightclub type magician, for *The Saint Detective Magazine.* For Vital Publications' *Current Detective* Gibson wrote two stories, one featuring a magician detective named Ardini and the other featuring a mind-reader named Valdor.[48]

As if the Shadow didn't keep Gibson busy enough, he could not rest his creative mind. At one point while Gibson was writing a synopsis in Maine, some of his cousin's children were visiting and enjoyed reading Gibson's synopses. "'One of the kids, who was a very smart kid, said: "Why don't you publish these instead of the stories?"'"[49] And why not indeed? A synopsis of Gibson's read much like a comic book, so why not publish them as such. Gibson approached Street & Smith with the idea in 1937, but they rejected it. It was not until after they saw Superman's success that Street & Smith decided Gibson had a good idea after all and launched *The Shadow Comics* in April 1940 which ran monthly until May 1947 as the first and longest running successful comic book of Street & Smith.[50] In order to keep himself "established" as Maxwell Grant, Gibson wrote some of the scripts for these comics and received no pay. Street & Smith began compensating his work at $2 a page and gradually increased this amount to $10 a page. According to Gibson's interpretation of the clause in the contract, he should have been receiving this rate, which was equal to that of his Shadow magazine writings, for *any* extra work he completed for them. Yet Gibson was determined to nourish his brainchild at any expense.

There was a drawback in depicting the Shadow visually in the illustrations in the comic books: he is often unseen to his enemies. Gibson came up with the solution in printing the Shadow's image as a blue surprint to make him look invisible.[51] *The Shadow Comics* were also made as a newspaper strip at the same time and were distributed through the *Philadelphia Public Ledger* syndicate. These newspaper strips appeared in papers from June 1940 through June 1942.[52] Gibson was one of the pioneers in the comic book industry and would later contribute to *Super-Magician Comics, Red Dragon Comics, Crime and Punishment, Crime Does Not Pay, Detective Comics, Racket Squad in Action, Space Western, Strange Adventures,* and over a dozen commercial comics.[53]

The Shadow enveloped Gibson's entire being. Even when away from this writing, Gibson's creative mind never rested. The Shadow, which brought Gibson much joy, may have been the darkness that often shaded his eyes from his loved ones.

8

Shadows of the Shadow

But apparently the present fact is this: Street and Smith are depending upon two words "The Shadow" to prove their title to a character. I am depending upon fifteen million words to prove my right to be known as Maxwell Grant, creator of that character.

— *Walter B. Gibson, personal papers*

Gibson's creation has been rediscovered by each succeeding generation and every decade a resurgence of interest in the Shadow emerges from the dark past. Gibson convinced many publishers that his words written on a number of subjects were timeless, and reprints of many of his books appeared. In 1963 episodes of the original Shadow broadcasts re-aired around the nation, and publishers released paperback novels of the Shadow. New comic book series and reprints of books would follow during each succeeding decade.[1]

Gibson became a popular lecturer in his later years, speaking about the Shadow and his association with Houdini and other magicians, and also demonstrating his skills as a magician. The pulp magazines that once were sold for $.10 went for $70 plus. Gibson remarked, "'I had boxes and boxes of those old magazines. If I had [known] what they would be worth, I would have kept them. But I used to sign them and give them away as souvenirs.'"[2] Doubleday and Pyramid Books re-issued some of the Shadow novels which promised Gibson a full plate of speaking engagements. "'Do I mind? Heck no,'" admitted Gibson; "'That's what keeps me going. I love it.'"[3] Gibson was finally getting the publicity he deserved. When Condé Nast bought out Street & Smith, Gibson retained no rights to his work. On Sunday, July 29, 1973, Gibson wrote, "Heavy what hangs over — The Condé Nast deal … it makes you say — 'Shove over Watergate' — But I go on — and on —" They eventually reached a deal that would give Gibson fifty percent of the reprint royalties to the Shadow. Gibson worked with Condé Nast in producing reprints. Although Gibson was excited about the reprints of the Shadow, he wished he had retained more rights to his work: "But to fight it out with Condé Nast at this late hour is sad indeed…."[4] On Tuesday, November 27, 1973, Gibson reported, "Took early train & had 10.30 appointment with Condé Nast ... temporarily flagged Pyramid deal."

Bantam reprinted six novels from 1969–1970. Bantam then relinquished rights to Pyramid books. Pyramid produced sixteen Shadow paperbacks from 1974 until 1977, when a merger with Harcourt Brace Jovanovich continued the series under Jove Books until 1978 producing seven more paperback books. The cover art for this series was provided by Jim Steranko. Doubleday's Crime Club had produced two books, in hardcover, each containing two Shadow stories in 1975 and 1978. Gibson recalled that on Thursday, January 17, 1974, he "rode in to see Larry @ 10.30. He said 'How do we make out the contract?'— and the Shadow was in!" He reported that the deal was all set by March 4. They wanted an introduction for the Shadow replica edition so he worked on it during the end of May. On May 18 and 20 Gibson wrote: "Having lots of fun (?!) reconstructing old Shadow days," and "Banged away on Shadow intro—but slow. Hard to think back to those days." Dover Publications produced a similar book containing two of the Shadow's adventures in 1975.

Gibson wanted his name to be recognized and connected with the Shadow. On August 8, 1974, he reminds himself: "Must push use of my name with the Shadow." He was particularly concerned with the Pyramid book series. On Tuesday November 5, 1974, Gibson writes, "The first Shadow is out but does not list me as Max Grant — So I called Goldfind who said it would appear later." Yet when the second issue in the series published by Pyramid appeared, Gibson wrote on Tuesday, December 3, "Picked up Shadow #2 —*without* my mention, which I must check." The series never did connect his name with Maxwell Grant.

Gibson continued to enjoy reading each of the reprints that appeared. He continued to read copies of the old *Shadow Magazine* too to get ideas for future reprints. At one point, on February 3, 1975, Gibson records in his journal, "Read old Shadow 'Hand in the Dark': Great! Maybe I should get back to it!" As of Friday, August 1, Gibson was trying his hand at a new Shadow story.

On Wednesday, May 5, 1976, Gibson got the contract for *The Shadow Scrapbook* from Harcourt Brace Jovanovich. On August 17, Gibson reported that he had "set $4,500 as price for Shadow Scrap Book with 6% royalty." *The Shadow Scrapbook* appeared in 1979 as a history of the famous personage and those involved in the magazine, comic, radio and film adventures. The book sold out quickly. On July 22 Gibson wrote, "we'll have to wait for a new printing!" No more Shadows could be reprinted due to the pending release of a feature film about the Shadow. The popularity of the Shadow was growing once again. As Otto Penzler wrote in *People Magazine*, Gibson "doesn't have to write any new Shadow stories—he stays busy enough just signing contracts for reprints. The Shadow insists 'The weed of crime bears bitter fruit. Crime does not pay.' In Gibson's case, the Shadow's mind is the one that's clouded."[5] When Gibson was asked in an interview in 1980 if anybody knew about his prolific writing for the pulps Gibson replied with an eerie laugh, "'The Shadow knows! Heh, heh, heh!'"[6]

Gibson loved this era of renewed interest in the Shadow. He always felt good about creating "*the* most recognized characters in all of literature."[7] In July 1973, Gibson reported his joy in digging through and reading copies of his old *Shadow Magazine* to find appropriate ones to suggest for reprints. In reading them he found them still "quite good."

On Saturday, March 29, 1975, the ring of the telephone woke Gibson. He reported that "Charley MacDonald called from L.A.—he's interested in Shadow T.V." Through the years there were a number of movies devoted to the exploits of the Shadow. As early as 1931, just weeks after the magazine started, *Burglar to the Rescue* appeared as the first of six two-reelers. The stories were enacted in the style of the first radio shows of *The Detective Story,* the Shadow appearing as a silhouette to introduce the stories. The first major film, *The Shadow Strikes!,* appeared around 1936–1937; it was put out by Grand National Films and starred Rod LaRocque as the Shadow. A sequel to the movie, *International Crime,* appeared on the big screen the following year. In the 1940s, Monogram released three films, *The Shadow Returns, Behind the Mask* and *The Missing Lady* starring Kane Richmond. During the same decade Columbia released *The Shadow,* starring Victor Jory. This was Gibson's favorite film version of the Shadow because it was consistent and based on his novel *The Lone Tiger.* Republic released the *Invisible Avenger* a.k.a *Bourbon Street Shadows* starring Richard Derr, based on the radio broadcasts. A Shadow television pilot was made with British actor Tom Helmore in 1955 but never aired.[8] The Shadow was gaining popularity though. A Gene Tycher wanted to start a Shadow Nite Club in Chicago and there was talk of a "Shadow Story Game."[9]

In the 1950s three television pilots were filmed. One starred Tom Helmore and Paula Raymond, the other two starred Richard Derr. The Shadow never made the transition to television, but these three television pilot episodes were later edited together and produced as two films: *The Invisible Avenger* and *Bourbon Street Shadows.*[10] In 1963 Gibson was approached to revive his creation. He wrote *The Return of The Shadow* published by Belmont Books. This was the first book that purposely gave Walter B. Gibson credit as the author and not Maxwell Grant. This book was meant to be a segue into reprinting the original stories but Condé Nast, and literary entrepreneur Lyle Kenyon Engel, wanted to produce a series of books written by Gibson that would provide the Shadow with some new adventures and reprint some of the original stories too. The contract did not last and they replaced Gibson with author Dennis Lynds. Under the name of Maxwell Grant, Lynds wrote eight novels. The books were controversial among pure Shadow fans. Cox points out that "Gibson himself did not approve of them and was known to surreptitiously rip pages from copies he found on newsstands."[11] Gibson wrote, "I feel peeved about a scrawny pulp-fan mag, 'Echoes' praising the phoney 'Shadows' done by Belmont." Will Murray recalled, "The only time I ever heard Walter swear was when he referred to that particular packager. It was a long time before he was willing to have anything to do with the Shadow again."[12] It would be at least another decade before Gibson became involved with that mysterious figure that looms in the darkness.

Gibson didn't make a public appearance as the Shadow's creator until probably

July 5, 1975, as a speaker at the Comic Art Convention in the Commodore Hotel in New York on a panel that included his longtime friend and editor John Nanovic. Gibson enjoyed the attention of such fans. He told stories and signed his special double X autograph combining his name with Maxwell Grant's in which the W of Walter and the M of Maxwell intermingle to produce a double X. He recorded in his 1975 diary that he received a plaque as the guest of honor and "[Frank] Hamilton gave me a painting of a cover he reproduced using real gold leaf for The Golden Pagoda."

The Shadow book presentation plate with the "double X" signatures. Signed to magician/actor John Calvert. From the collection of William V. Rauscher.

After this initial lecture, Gibson made appearances at various conventions. He was twice the guest of honor at Pulpcon. Gibson recalled one Pulpcon held in Akron. He received airline tickets along with a letter on June 24, 1976. On Friday, July 9, Gibson was in Akron and "found big displays of pulp mags with Shadows selling @ $20+ per issue. Talked, autographed, listened to a talk on magazine collecting & turned in." The following day Gibson wrote: "…John [Nanovic] & I did a panel in P.M. So by banquet time I only had to make a brief 'overall' talk which I topped off with some magic including Hindu Wands." The Shadow enthusiasts wanted Gibson to return for the Pulpcon in October. Gibson had truly reembraced the Shadow and was now basking in the newfound light away from the shadows. Murray observed that Gibson had "reconciled with the Shadow so firmly that he began wearing a girasol ring,"[13] the ring the Shadow wore. Gibson continued going to pulp conventions and comic shows. At one on Saturday May 26, 1979, Gibson recalled "Autographed & talked too much so I felt woozy during the panel discussion that followed. Steranko & Will Murray were on panel — also to NY." At another Pulpcon in November 1980, Gibson received another plaque. In the late seventies, also Gibson's late seventies, he felt content with the final recognition of his having created the Shadow: "'I feel like Rip Van Winkle,'" reported Gibson. "'I'm up in those Catskills, you know, where he went to sleep, and I come back after all these years.'"[14]

It has often been said that "television was the only villain to get the best of the Shadow,"[15] but it didn't get the best of Gibson. He used television much to his advantage. Gibson wrote novels adapting the television scripts from *The Man from*

U.N.C.L.E. and the original *Twilight Zone.* He wrote two books of *The Twilight Zone,* collecting short stories based on the television scripts and added some of his own original stories.[16]

Gibson wrote 283 Shadow novels for *The Shadow Magazine* and 149 Shadow scripts for *The Shadow Comics,* not to mention numerous comic news strips. As Morris N. Young, M.D. points out, "This unqualifiedly establishes the hero, Lamont Cranston, and the author (WBG) as America's Sherlock Holmes and Arthur Conan Doyle. Uncannily, Walter met Sir Arthur at an annual S.A.M dinner in the New York City McAlpin Hotel."[17] In June 1922, Houdini had introduced the two authors. Gibson recalled that Houdini had introduced him as "an up and coming magical writer." "That was Houdini's way, to flatter people when they deserved it. In return he expected people to flatter him when *he* deserved it. Houdini was truly reciprocal...."[18]

Gibson remembered that "through those [15] years I had come to know The SHADOW quite well, or perhaps *he* had come to know me. It was hard to tell which was the true case."[13] Those years, Gibson recalled were "hard and hectic" but looking back he found that he remembered "mostly the fun and excitement of those hectic years."[19]

Just at the commencement of the hectic years of the Shadow, Gibson's personal life took a number of stomach-churning peaks and valleys. According to the legal papers "Walter B. Gibson the Respondent, on the 25th day of September, 1927, at the County of Philadelphia, in this Commonwealth, did willfully and maliciously desert and absent himself from the habitation of the injured and innocent libellant, without reasonable cause, and has continued to be so absent himself for and during the term and space of two years and upwards." Charlotte and Gibson's divorce was finalized on October 23, 1933. Wendel often heard Gibson say at age 87, "'The only reason she married me is because I had a car!' This is high school, when they got out of high school. Charlotte wanted to be able to get around ... and she was a good lookin' gal."[20] The marriage took Charlotte away from high school.

Charlotte was a beautiful woman, often described as "flamboyant" and "the life of the party." She was very different from Gibson. Dr. Robert Gibson, their only son, reflected on his parents' marriage:

> My own kind of thought about it was the things that would have attracted them would probably not be things that would lead to a lasting relationship because she was very, very different than he was and he was much more occupied with other kinds of things. She much more wanted to socialize and be involved in parties and things of that sort.[21]

Their different personalities led them to each discover their own lovers outside the marriage, lovers that were more compatible. This state of affairs led to a most unusual situation.

Charlotte had become interested in her former dentist, Russell Locker, who was married himself with a child. An affair began between the two. Dr. Gibson remembered:

I had some memories that, in retrospect, kind of would suggest an involvement or affair going on for a period of time. My guess would be that it was not something that particularly disturbed my father. He was sort of off into his thing, by then he was writing the Shadow.[22]

This seemed a typical Gibson trait of being overly involved in his writing. The deadlines were continuous and Gibson would always manage to meet and even exceed them. It was not that editors pushed him, it was more the fact that he had this inner drive to write. Gibson once was questioned about his enjoyment of being an author. He responded, "I'd rather do any of a thousand other things. But whatever job I took, I'd spoil all the fun of it, by wanting to write. So there it stands."[23] Dr. Gibson explained simply that writing was "just something that he needed to do."[24] So it would be quite easy to image that Gibson did not discover (or even care?) about his wife's affair.

Though the circumstances surrounding it are unknown, Gibson soon began his own affair with Julia, affectionately known as Jewel, who had been married and had her own child, Margaret. Charlotte and Gibson had both found their own loves and an amiable separation would thus ensue, yet there was a one-year waiting period before one could divorce, so they waited in a most unusual situation.

Dr. Gibson recalled:

I remember when I was eight years old we were living in Lansdown [Pennsylvania]. So at that time, this was in the summer, I remember that was probably the first that I became conscious of Jewel, … that my father was seeing her and had a relationship with her, and that my mother was seeing Russell, the dentist, and had a relationship. So we were living in Lansdown and I remember there was a rather short period when I, I can remember, Russell's son coming over and staying with me in my room and Jewel's daughter coming over and staying with my father and Jewel who were living together, and we were all living in the same house. So, Lansdown, where I'd grown up and where everybody knew everybody. So then, my assumption … they decided, "well we probably better move a little bit away," because I was probably going to continue in Landsdown. So we moved out to a town called Springfield which was about ten miles away. We then moved to a real big, big house. And my father and Jewel lived there together. My mother and Russell lived there together. My step-brother and step-sister, that's Jewel's daughter, and I all lived there together. And so we lived there together as a very compatible, happy group for six months…. And we ate dinner together…. There was a table for four which the two couples ate at, and then we had another table that my step-brother and step-sister-to-be all ate at. And nobody was divorced as yet because they had the waiting period. And we went out and did things together. Everybody seemed to feel fine about this. There was no animosity. Of course, everybody had decided what they were going to do when the divorce took place and who was going to marry whom, and that we were going to move back to Lansdown because that's where Russell's practice and things had been in the city. And my father, their plan at that time was Jewel's father lived in Florida and they were going to … go to Florida and spend time there.[25]

As a child, Dr. Gibson saw nothing unusual about this situation. Reflecting back he imagines that the Depression had made the living arrangements more tolerable for all, since Russell was not doing well financially as a dentist, and Gibson was making a great deal of money for the time through the Shadow.

The two couples' situation may have caused much strain in them mentally. Dr. Gibson recalled, "we had this Christmas there which would have been my ninth birthday... 1933.... It must have been out of some sort of sense of guilt, you never saw any three kids get so many presents in all your life. This Christmas was something beyond belief."[26]

After the divorces were finalized there was some antagonism between Charlotte and Gibson over the amount of time Gibson could spend with their son. They came to the conclusion that Gibson would get Robert during the summers, otherwise he would live with his mother. It would be a couple of years before Robert got to see his father regularly, since Gibson and Jewel had gone to Florida, and then returned to Germantown, Pennsylvania, to live on Philellena St. with Gibson's mother. Gibson spent many winters in Florida for a number of years, up until about 1957. He wrote some Shadows there. Gibson thought Florida had some excellent locales for stories. He often used familiar Florida scenes but changed their names, such as a scene in Pomelo Springs which in reality was Silver Springs. Gibson would stay in hotels, like the Angebilt Hotel, and apartment houses. He recalled one winter when:

> My wife and I rented a bungalow out near Maitland on a citrus estate for $15 a week. We had a sleeping porch, two more bedrooms, living room, dining room, refrigerator, wood for the fireplace, all the orange and grapefruit we could pick, plus the use of a boat on the lake.[27]

Robert got to see his father often when he was in New York, but it would not be until Gibson built his cabin in Maine that the two would get to spend more time together.

It was just a mere week after the divorce was finalized that Gibson married his second wife, Julia Helen Martin (born on October 3, 1897, in Philadelphia, she was known as Jewel to her loved ones), on January 19, 1934, at Norristown, Pennsylvania. Joseph D. A. Wolfe, justice of the peace, married them. Jewel had been divorced from her first husband, Harold D. Kindt, since August 10, 1933. She was a well-educated woman, holding a graduate degree in archaeology. Jewel was well read and could hold her own in conversations with Gibson. Robert remembered that "their conversations were on very esoteric levels about almost all kinds of topics in the world."[28] It seems that Gibson found someone who could relate with him. The two newlyweds lived together for four months in Solebury, Bucks County, Pennsylvania, with Gibson's brother Theodore (until May 1935). Due to Gibson's increased need to be in New York City, the two moved into the Gilford Apartments on E. 46th Street. After approximately a year at this residence (May 1936), the two moved back to Pennsylvania and lived at 19 W. Philellena St. in Philadelphia for the next six years (till May 1940), just down the street from his childhood residences of 703 W. Philellena and 707 Westview Avenue. They moved back to the New York area where they took up residence for six months in Crestwood, New York (Nov. 1940). They then returned to Philadelphia and lived in a large, fancy house on Juniper and Chancellor Streets for about a year and six months (May 1942), then lived at the Hotel Des Artistes at 1 W. 67th St., New York, New York. All this moving around did not give Gibson sufficient time with his son. It was not until they settled in a cabin in Maine that father and son could spend a greater amount of quality time together.

Gibson had always been drawn to Maine. As noted earlier, his mother's family grew up in the state. He also spent many summers there attending camps as a boy around the Rangeley Lakes and Casco Bay (the Casco Bay camp was run by Donald MacMillan, a noted Arctic explorer). [29] "'I always wanted to live in Maine from the time I was a young boy and spent summers there,'" admitted Gibson. "'It was a wonderful place, and I found it ideal for writing.'"[30] In 1934, Gibson began vacationing in Maine. He would often visit his cousin Carlton Eaton (Gibson's mother was the sister of Eaton's mother) who lived on Little Sebago Lake in Gray, Maine. Gibson loved the area and he bought the last plot of land a few plots up from Eaton's. Gibson's second wife, Julia, was instrumental in this decision to move to Maine. Gibson was so busy in New York with other projects always coming in, that he needed to get away, and Maine was the place to where he would retreat.

Gibson initially built a log cabin on Little Sebago Lake, which was finished by 1936. One would follow a path that was overgrown with brush that opened up to the campsite. It was during the construction of this cabin that Gibson had a specially crafted pine wood desk built, a desk that would serve him well throughout life. Gibson recalled:

> We bought more wood than we needed [to build the cabin]. In those days we got what was called "unsorted" lumber, and if you had any ends that were too knotty, you just cut them off, used them for tent platforms and that sort of thing. I had the carpenter make up this desk [with them].
>
> It was designed just as I wanted in working on the Shadow manuscripts. It had slots over to the left where I kept the paper and carbons, and on the right I had a special square cut out so the finished pages could drop down into it — no time for rewrites in those days![31]

When Gibson first arrived in Maine, he came so early in the season that he had to complete a Shadow novel while the carpenters were still working on the cabin:

> Picture me sitting at a desk, put together out of leftover lumber in the middle of an empty room, largish and not quite finished, with carpenters banging and nailing all around me, or carrying two-by-fours in and out through the room. That old desk I still have, and use, and it remains as sturdy as the Maine pine from which it was hewn.[32]

The cabin was the ideal womb to nourish the thoughts that would grow into the adventurous Shadow novels. Gibson would sit at his desk in a corner of the large central room with vaulted ceilings and type. To ensure his privacy, Gibson wanted no telephone communication with the outside world. He had a private line that ran to Eaton's neighboring cabin. Thus all calls could be screened by Eaton and relayed to Gibson if important.[33]

In his cabin in Gray, Maine, Walter wrote many of the Shadow stories on this pine-wood desk constructed out of some leftover wood after the cabin was built. Walter designed the desk and placed finished work in the tray on the left. Here Walter hands Litzka some finished pages of writing. From the collection of William V. Rauscher.

Though the ideal hideaway for a busy author, this cabin served another purpose as well. During the summers, Gibson's son would come live with them for eight weeks; this was the specific reason for having the cabin. Robert Gibson spent seven summers with his father in Maine which brought him closer to his father and leaves him today with warm feelings for him.

Around the main cabin were a number of nice, 8 × 10 tents, complete with floorboards and cots that acted as spare bedrooms. That summer of 1936, Robert shared one of these tents with his cousin Wendel Gibson. Though Wendel was ten years older than Robert at age 21, the two had a great time together and both have fond memories of being at the cabin in the summer. Wendel recalled playing "King of the Raft" out on the lake in which a person would claim the raft and others challenged the king to a wrestling match to see who could remain the king without falling into the lake. He remembered that his uncle would originate and teach the kids such games: "he was terrific at that," recalled Wendel.[34]

There would be games every evening. Gibson loved to get a game of Monopoly going, yet he never wanted to see anyone losing money at it, so he would encourage everyone to help out the one in need. The game would thus go on for hours. This demonstrates Gibson's noble mind, yet also his lack of business savvy.

Gibson loved to invent games, or spin-offs of existing games, such as "Camelot," a cross between checkers and chess, and his own version of charades which the children simply called the "Game." There would be two teams of five to six people on each and members of the teams would write down movie, book and play titles, famous quotes, etc. The other team would have to act out what was on the paper. There were hand gestures for the category and for the number of words. One evening, the other team indicated the category of a play with a long title of thirty plus words. The other team knew it would take forever to act out each word, but Gibson sat still, counting on his fingers, and soon yelled out the correct title before any of the acting had begun.

Though Gibson loved playing games each night, when he was under the spell of writing, he would never give it up. Another favorite game of the children was "Sardines" in which the lights are turned out and one person hides and the others must find him and upon finding him must pile in together in that hiding place until all the hunters are packed together like sardines. The last one there loses the game. One night the children all wanted to play this game, yet they were hesitant to disturb Gibson by shutting the lights out since he was typing at his typewriter. The children slowly approached Gibson and said, "Well, you know, we were thinking about playing 'Sardines.'" Gibson immediately retorted, "Go ahead, it doesn't matter." So the children turned the lights off and enjoyed a couple hours of Sardines in the pitch black. The noise of laughter mingled in the air with the clickty clack of Gibson's typewriter as he spewed forth chapter after chapter of the Shadow in the darkness![35]

Gibson often attributed his ability to write in all sorts of hectic situations to his days as a newspaperman, since one needed to write in the midst of the bustle of the newsroom. Robert recalled that his father could go a day or so without doing much, but then something would possess Gibson and he would rush to his typewriter. There he would sit, sometimes for hours, disregarding meals and sleep to transform his thoughts into words. Robert:

> ...something would start to happen in the middle of the afternoon, and he'd be typing along and just keep going, could barely bother to have anything for dinner. And I would go to bed and I'd come up in the morning and he was still sitting there, unshaven, cups of coffee ... Christ! [he would have] forty or fifty pages typed.[36]

Gibson's writing was driven. It all came naturally and he would see the details and pour them out onto the page.

Wendel and Robert also recall at night beautiful melodies gliding across the water. These pixie land notes came from a flutist named Kinkade who was the first flutist with the Philadelphia Symphony Orchestra.[37, 38] Kinkade was considered one of the greatest musicians in the world at the time and the Gibson family was fortunate enough to hear his sweet notes as he practiced in the evenings.

That fall of 1936, Gibson purchased a house in the town of Gray, five miles from the cabin on the road that leads to Poland Springs. The white house on the corner of Shaker Road and Gray Park was an old farmhouse that was modernized and expanded. The cabin then turned into his summer place, as the winters were spent at the house. Gibson's nephew Wendel recalled spending time up at this house after graduation from high school.

> And I went up there and I put wall to wall bookcases up [in three rooms] with them — not with him, because Walter, he couldn't even swing a hammer without hitting his thumb first. He's not mechanically inclined, believe me....[39]

Wendel continued to relate a typical day with his uncle:

> Walter worked, and worked, and worked. And when we went out to dinner he'd
> make dinner last a couple of hours, and then he'd go back and started working. So he
> got up late in the morning and we'd sit at the breakfast table and Jewel [Julia] would
> bring out tomato juice in glasses ... and Walter sips tomato juice — he was very ner-
> vous. He was always looking ... and blinking ... he'd drive you crazy. He just had a
> mind that was so full, and it was hard to deal with. -Then he would start writing. He
> would take eight-and-a-half by eleven yellow sheets. If you were going to make a
> carbon copy it would always be on yellow paper in the old days, before computers....
> [Tapping noises with two fingers demonstrating how he typed] That page is done,
> double-spaced so it doesn't take long to finish a page. S-h-h-u-u face down [mimes
> turning paper, tapping noises].... Then he'd get up and check a reference or some-
> thing and then come back.... Along around 9:00 he'd say, "Well, let's have dinner."
> So we'd go out some place for dinner. We wouldn't get back from there until 12:00.
> And then he's got to do some research. All day long, it would wear you out. And then
> at breakfast, we could sit down and have a nice breakfast and a half-hour later we
> could all be doing something constructive. Instead, *two* hours later we're still sitting
> around, Walter's telling stories and we're all on the edge of our seats listening.[40]

Gibson's hectic lifestyle often kept him up late into the night. The light showing from the house was often a beacon call for unexpected visitors. People would call

Gibson wrote many of the Shadow novels here in his Gray, Maine, home. Gibson's nephew Wendel remembers putting up wall-to-wall shelves in this home to store the vast collection of books
Gibson was accumulating. Photograph by Thomas J. Shimeld.

on him to use the phone. Gibson once had a long talk at 2 A.M. with a Native American who was selling arrowheads. There was also an elderly lady who would often wake up in the middle of the night; she knew Gibson would be awake so she would often call him for a friendly chat.[41]

For ten of the fifteen years Gibson wrote many of the Shadow novels in Maine, thus he became a bit of interest to the local people. Gibson spent much time commuting back and forth to New York. Wendel remembers the club car on the train which "had living room chairs and they were on a swivel base and they had foot stools."[42] When news of Gibson moving to Gray, Maine, was heard, a local paper headlined "The Shadow Comes to Maine." After a brief time, Gibson's home was reported to be listed as a tourist attraction in several Maine guidebooks.

A town historian, Gerald M. Kimball, remembered in an interview on July 8, 1997, that Gibson's home was next door to Earl Wilson, the funeral director. For the birthplace of many of the mysterious adventures of the Shadow "I mean that's an ideal place," jokes Kimball.

Kimball remembered Gibson as "a very jolly person." "This was a great novelty for the local people to have a *real* magician who has been associated with Harry Houdini. We knew who Harry was. Then we soon learned who Walter was." Gibson would give magic performances now and then in town, often with the assistance of his son, and Eaton's children, Tony and Jane. Robert recalls building illusions for his father with Tony, one of which, called a "Doll House" Jane would appear out of in an elaborate dress with flowers, looking twice as large as the doll house from which she had appeared.

Gibson enjoyed sharing his magic with Robert, who became quite proficient in sleight of hand with cards. On-stage, the two would perform "the Six Card Repeat" together. Gibson would explain to the audience that his son was not too bright in math, he thought six minus three was six! Robert would demonstrate that it truly was as he discarded three cards from the six he had in his hand, only to end up counting out six. This was repeated a number of times to the amazement of the audience, making the "not-too-bright" Robert look like a genius.

When Robert was older (and taller), Gibson used to perform a magical exchange with him on-stage. Gibson would don a "monk's robe" with a hood that partially obscured his face. Robert would stand behind a curtain that had holes in it for his head and arms. Gibson would hand a donkey mask to Robert who promptly put it on. Gibson then would joke with the donkey, having it wiggle its ears. Next, Gibson would walk behind the curtain, his hands visible the entire time; he emerged from the curtain and got the donkey to wiggle its ears some more. Then the magic. The robe would be thrown off to reveal Robert in his father's place. All eyes were drawn to the donkey, who was revealed as Jane. Gibson himself would bound down the aisle, appearing from behind the audience, to accept the applause.

Many of the Shadow's adventures in Maine are greatly significant for they show historians the life of the people of the 1930s and 1940s. Some Shadow stories set in Maine include *The Isle of Gold* of August 1, 1939, *Vengeance* Bay of May 1, 1942, and

Crime Over Casco of April 1946. Gibson often used unspecified Maine settings in his writings. He remembered that "'Maine proved an inspiration for me. It was a fantastic rock-bound realm — half land, half water. I loved every minute I spent there and really was impressed by the people who were famed for their individuality and salty humor.'"[43] Gibson had to stay in constant contact with Street & Smith in New York, taking frequent trips there to go over plot outlines and story ideas. The onset of World War II made travel more difficult, so Gibson moved to New York City to a small apartment. He later moved to a larger apartment in a hotel for artists and authors called the Des Artistes. Gibson recalled "'Fannie Hurst [novelist and short-story writer] had the biggest place in the building and I had the second biggest.'"[44] Robert recalled the grand apartment:

> You came in and there was a very large living room which went up two floors. So it was a double height, and there was … full windows that went the entire height. So that was what was the living room. Then there were [3 or 4] bedrooms up above that literally looked out down on to this; they were on the second floor. And the first floor, the lower floor, also had a dining room and a sitting room as well as this great living[room].[45]

Unfortunately, the owners were turning the apartments into condominiums and Gibson and Julia had to decide if they would buy or sell. Robert recalls that they could have bought the place for $6,000 — it would be worth $1 million today. Yet with much of Gibson's business dealings, he did not have the foresight to invest in such an enterprise. He did not see what the future could be; all he could see was the Shadow of the present moment. It cast his eyes shut. So closed were they that he could not even foretell his wife's dissatisfaction and her desire to leave.

A new tenant was to take possession of their apartment on October 1, 1946. Julia began packing her bags and on October 1 she moved out with her daughter while Gibson was making the rounds at the magazine offices. She had given no indication of her desire to separate from him. He returned at 4:00 to discover his wife and her daughter gone. A couple of hours later a friend told Gibson that Julia had left him and was not coming back. Gibson called a mutual friend, Margaret Narmington. She told him that Julia was living at his stepdaughter's house. The following day the stepdaughter showed up at the Des Artistes and collected together some of her mother's things. She told Gibson not to worry, that her mother just needed some rest. She didn't want Gibson to contact her directly; she could relay messages he had for her. He soon received a phone call from Julia. She told him that she definitely was not returning. She was tired. His work had been grueling and that this lifestyle was too hectic for her. Gibson moved to 3909 W. Pine St. in Philadelphia until December 1948 after leaving the Des Artistes.

Gibson frequently returned to New York. On one occasion, on November 4, 1946, he met Julia in Penn Station, New York. She wanted to get back together but Gibson did not give a definite response to her wishes. The two stayed in contact with each other through occasional letters. By June 1947, Gibson had made up his mind.

He wanted her back. They dined together and Gibson asked for her to return. She said no, but Gibson still hoped that they would reconcile in the future. They met again in a restaurant in New York. They were cordial to each other but they did not make up. Their last intimate talk was in September 1948.

By December 1948 Julia and Gibson were divorced. On March 24, 1950, Julia signed the quit-claim deed in which she released the rights to their Maine retreat: "remise, release, bargain, sell and convey, and forever quit-claim unto the said Walter Gibson, his Heirs and Assigns forever, Two certain lots or parcels of land situated in the Town of Gray, County of Cumberland and State of Maine, on the shore of Little Sebago Lake, and being lots numbered 5 and 6...."

Wendel commented on their relationship. "He and Julia had a parting of the ways. They lived at the Des Artistes; she left and went to Florida where she had relatives.... Walter didn't know what to do. And a lifestyle was gone. When you get involved in that kind of a lifestyle, or any one, and all of a sudden it breaks off, you're a lost soul. You know what he did? He ran off with the Blackstone show. He talked Harry into carrying him as a member of the staff. He wrote for Harry, he made magazines for Harry, he was a promoter and he did great for the Blackstone show."[46]

9

Harry Blackstone, Sr.— Lighting the Floating Bulb of Friendship

In those days [of the 1940s through the 1960s] for thirty rail tickets you could have the use of a ninety-foot baggage car, so he [Blackstone, Sr.] found it cheaper than shipping to buy forty-five tickets, which allowed one and a half baggage cars for Blackstone equipment. As a result, there were many traveling companions. A frequent favorite was Walter B. Gibson....
— Harry Blackstone, Jr.,
The Blackstone Book of Magic &
Illusion, *Newmarket Press, 1985.*

Gibson was devastated and shocked by Julia's departure. He did not see it coming. Robert explained his wife's views of Gibson: "He is just sort of in a world of his own to a certain extent that he doesn't really often quite grasp what is going on with the other person."[1] This self-absorption of Gibson's increased with age. Robert recalled that his father was never reliable:

He was always sort of notorious at being completely unreliable if we were going to go anywhere. I remember one time ... we were to go somewhere [with Jewel and her daughter, Margaret] at a certain time and he showed up about an hour late. Finally it turned out he had gotten back from wherever he was about a half an hour early but he had gotten into a conversation with the guy who handled the baggage at the front of the hotel and talked to him for an hour and a half.[2]

With no time to prepare mentally for a break-up, Gibson plummeted into a depression. To further add to Gibson's dilemmas, the Shadow, which had stood by his side as a constant companion for nearly two decades, was beginning to fade; it had now become a quarterly magazine. Gibson's annual income of $12,000 had steadily declined with irregular work. The six months leading up to the separation Gibson earned $4,000. Life has no guarantees.

For support, Gibson leaned on his son, Robert, who was now married to his first wife and attending medical school. For two to three months, Gibson lived with his son and daughter-in-law in their apartment. He was moderately depressed and it pained Robert to see his father in such a condition. Gibson's productive life had fallen apart.

Over these months, a good friend of Gibson's, magician Harry Blackstone, Sr. (1885–1965), frequently visited Gibson at Robert's apartment. Robert had remembered Blackstone from his youth. He recalls once Blackstone visiting them when he was around six years old, and the house they lived in at the time was so small that Blackstone had to sleep in Robert's room. Knowing what a master magician Blackstone was, Robert feared, as he went to bed that night, that he would be made to disappear during the night! Yet Robert's early memories of Blackstone proved him to be a caring individual. Blackstone once offered to wash the young Robert's hair, a grooming necessity that Robert detested, yet in the hands of this master magician, Robert was at ease. It came as no surprise to Robert that Blackstone offered Gibson his kindness and support. Blackstone had sympathized with Gibson's first failed marriage. In the original letter owned by David M. Baldwin of New York City, Blackstone writes to Gibson on I.M.C., Kalamazoo, Michigan, stationery[3]:

July 12, 1931

Dear Walter:

So your magical romance is busted. So is mine. But I am still alive and able to tell the story and may God have mercy on your soul. I know what the feeling is and the thoughts that are racing thru your mind at the present time. And I bet the next issue of tricks [in the *Seven Circles* magazine] will be lousy. We can't think of women and tricks at the same time. I have tried it! Although some women are happy tricks.

Speaking of tricks, there are three tricks at the house right now. Billie, Mildred Mansfield and Miss Gerard. And I have an extra pair of overalls for you out here. So grab that funny bus of yours and come to Colon. But, before doing so, get your arm around an armful of cash. The doors of the Bank are still closed.

We open August 23rd at the State Theatre, Kalamazoo, Michigan. With four more weeks in Michigan on the Butterfield time. I O.K.d the indebtedness at Three Rivers by giving a personal ninety-day note. Regarding Hanna, tell him not to worry. Tell him that starting in September he will get $25 or more a month. That's when the business of Magic is going strong. He is a dandy chap and I am for him and I want to do all I can for him.

Walter Harris is sweating blood. He is worse than Hot Tamale on Opening night, waiting for you to send him the tricks for the next issue.

Come early and avoid the rush and help Harris get some odds and ends off his chest.

As B-4
[Signed] Harry B.

So Blackstone once again invited Gibson to join him; a get-away to bring magic back into his life.

Gibson almost apologetically announced his decision to join Blackstone on the road. Robert recalled him saying, "'Well, Blackstone has invited me to go with him and I'm going to,' he said. 'That's easy for Blackstone because he always has the suite and so I'll just stay with him in his suite.'"[4]

Blackstone offered Gibson a position in his shows selling souvenir books in the lobby and acting as a "listening post" to hear the audiences' reactions to the show. Gibson often would ask people, "'How do you like the show?'"[5] Blackstone knew the magical touch that would lift Gibson's depression. Almost every week Gibson would write to Robert telling him of his adventures touring with his famous friend. He would tell of the people they met and the towns they visited. He wrote of the inevitable functions that Blackstone would be invited to where he and Blackstone were both the center of attention: the author of the Shadow alongside a master magician was certainly a spectacle. "With each letter that I got," recalled Robert, "I could see that his depression was lifting. And it really, I think, might have saved his life." Robert's eyes began to tear as he continued: "'Cause I was very concerned about him at the time.... I thought this was a magnificent act of friendship [on Blackstone's part], because he knew, he could tell what was happening." In an emotion-laden, wavy voice, Robert said, "It just turned his whole life around. Um, um, I'd say I'm sorry but there is no reason to be sorry [referring to his tears]. It's just the way I feel about and the admiration I had for what Blackstone did. 'Cause he didn't need to do this."[6] Theirs was a friendship bonded with magic.

In 1929, after completing Thurston's autobiography, Gibson began work for another great magician, Harry Blackstone, Sr. Gibson saw Blackstone as the most colorful and sensational illusionist of the time. He was original and always sought perfection in his performances. He carried two carloads of equipment and approximately forty assistants. Despite all the grand illusions, Blackstone was always ready to perform at the slightest provocation.[7]

Born Henri Bouton in 1885, Blackstone toured the United States performing escapes similar to those of Houdini's. Blackstone often performed one escape in particular that Houdini would do for challenges. It was an escape from a box in which the escape artist would be locked and the two would be thrown into a river. Houdini would miraculously escape, yet the box was never retrieved. Blackstone outdid Houdini by designing a box that could be retrieved after the escape.[8] Yet Houdini went on to make escapes encompass his entire act while Blackstone used them as part of the publicity for his magic show. Blackstone was quickly becoming popular with his elaborate stage show. As Blackstone's name grew in recognition, he also came to Gibson to have him ghost-write books.

The year after Gibson finished his work with Thurston he began his work for Blackstone. Gibson first met with Blackstone in 1929 in Philadelphia. The two were introduced by a Chicago astrologer by the name of Professor Alfred Francis Seward. Prof. Seward had arranged for Gibson to ghost-write a number of books for him. In 1930 the first book was self-published by Seward, *Facts about Brunettes and Blondes and How to Read Them*, a psychological text "based on the theory that success, happiness, and a thorough understanding of others can be achieved only through a study of racial differences and national ideals."[9] Several years later two other books appeared under Seward's name: *Periodicity or Cycles of Destiny* and *How to Be Happy*.[10] And soon Gibson wrote his first book for Blackstone, under the Blackstone name, the *Blackstone's Annual of Magic* published by Cooper Printing Company in 1929. It was designed to be a program book that included magic tricks and the short story "The Man of Mysteries." Gibson would go on to write and publish seven more books for Harry Blackstone. The books include programs and full trick books. One of special note is *Blackstone's Magic: A Book of Mystery* published by Shade Publishing Company in 1930. It was within these pages that Gibson wrote a little bit about everything in which he was interested. One notes that the pages contain details of simple tricks, methods of wonder workers, escapes, hypnotism, the methods of mediums and mental magic tricks. This book also contains a biography of Harry Blackstone. Gibson must have been very proud of this small 64-page book, for he was able to discuss all his interests within one single volume.

The last book Gibson wrote for Harry Blackstone appeared in 1948, published by Permabooks. It was called *Blackstone's Tricks Anyone Can Do.* It resembles Thurston's books of 200 tricks. This book and many others of Blackstone's have been reprinted and still can be found in bookstores and libraries today. Gibson did work under the Blackstone name again, but this was with Blackstone's son, Harry Blackstone, Jr. in 1980.

In the early 1930s, Gibson contributed some tricks to the magazines *Popular Mechanics* and *Seven Circles* under Harry Blackstone's name. The articles range from impromptu magic, to manipulation magic, to mental magic. He also wrote a syndicated feature called "Revealing the Trickery of Fake Hypnotists" for the *Philadelphia Sunday Ledger Magazine* in 1930.[11] These articles that Gibson wrote for Blackstone were written on a fifty-fifty basis. Gibson became great friends with Blackstone. Their working relationship was very pleasant, and the two remained good friends until Blackstone's death in 1965. According to Gibson, Blackstone was much easier to work with than Thurston. Blackstone was very helpful in his participation on the books.

In 1941, Gibson had a wonderful idea of making Blackstone "the world's only living comic book character."[12] At the time Gibson was working for Street & Smith publications writing *The Shadow Magazine*. Gibson sold the idea over the phone to this publisher. His idea for the *Super Magic Comics* would feature fictitious adventures of Blackstone around the world. (In reality Blackstone only toured the United States and Canada, and only once left in 1931 to perform in Bermuda. Robert Gibson recalls the fuss around the house about his father taking a plane to Bermuda with Blackstone.) Gibson gave Street & Smith such a wonderful sales pitch the company could not resist. Gibson offered the publication to the publishers as a one-shot deal — if successful, it could become a regular monthly publication. A minimum run of 200,000 copies was agreed to, but to make the deal even more enticing for the publisher, Blackstone promised to buy 50,000 of them for half the cover price (5 cents a copy) to give away

Walter B. Gibson made Harry Blackstone into a living comic book hero in the *Super Magician* and *Blackstone* comics. Here Blackstone is shown performing his signature piece, "The Floating Lightbulb" (January 1946, volume 4, issue 9) From the collection of Thomas J. Shimeld, retouched by Jennifer Ann Shimeld, reproduced with permission from Condé Nast.

to children in his matinees. This would work out perfectly for Blackstone, for it would not cost him a cent. He would have the theatre managers cover the bill for the comics and they in turn would raise the price of a ticket 5 cents in order to cover the promotional comic book give-aways. Street & Smith were convinced that it was a perfect deal; they only needed a copy to run. Gibson wrote the first issue on the train from Boston to New York. When he arrived in New York and showed Street & Smith the script, they loved it, and it went to the comic book artists, and then to press. Once the issue was printed, Blackstone arrived to pick up his 50,000 copies and was shocked to hear that the issue had sold out! Street & Smith asked Gibson to write more, and the publication ran successfully for five years under Street & Smith publications, with only a simple change of the title to *Super Magician Comics*. Street & Smith published these comics successfully until February 1946.

The comic book then changed publishers to Vital Publications and its name changed to *Master Magician Comics* and later to *Blackstone, the Magician Detective* which ran until September 1948. The idea was extremely popular among the children of America. Gibson reported that "'sometimes, kids would know Blackstone was in a theatre, and they'd sneak into the backstage area, and it would turn out they wanted to see if he had any extra issues of the comic book in his dressing room.'"[13] The popularity of Blackstone as a comic book character inspired Al Capp to create the character "Whackstone" in 1949 for the comic strip "Li'l Abner."[14]

Gibson wrote some radio material for Blackstone and often appeared on air with him during interviews. The Blackstone comic book series eventually led to a fifteen-minute radio program called *Blackstone, The Magician Detective*, beginning in 1944. Gibson scripted the shows and a series of seventy-eight were recorded and later sponsored for two years by a washing machine company named Blackstone located in Jamestown, New York. Blackstone appreciated the interesting tie-in and performed a show in Jamestown to express this. Blackstone often commented that Blackstone was *the* name in magic and *the* name in washing machines![15]

Gibson's friendship with the Great Blackstone allowed Gibson's nephew Wendel the wonderful opportunity to travel with the Blackstone show. Wendel recalled that while he was with the show, "Mary was the girl I went with. [After leaving the show] whenever Harry Blackstone was in the New England area I'd rush down to see him in Lowell, after they performed at the Lowell High School, I met them at the train station as they were going back to New York, and Mary came up to me and said, 'Wendel, Wendel, Wendel, so glad to see you. Do you think you could get your uncle to make my hair a little bit lighter...?' She was in the comic strips. Her hair was real dark blonde and she wanted to be [light blonde]. Naturally I said, 'He's not a hairdresser, he's an author, but I'll see what I can do.' She was often disappointed because the four-color printing was a hazardous thing, [and] you never knew how the colors are going to turn out.... The color they had for her hair was horrible. I started laughing along with her and she was laughing along with me because it was extremely doubtful whether anybody could do anything."[16]

Gibson and Blackstone where great friends. Not only did Blackstone's kindness and the magic of his show save Gibson from his depression, but Gibson traveled with the show now and then throughout the years. In fact, Blackstone, Jr., observes in his book, *The Blackstone Book of Magic & Illusion*, that from the 1940s to the 1960s "...for thirty rail tickets you could have the use of a ninety-foot baggage car, so he [Blackstone] found it cheaper than shipping to buy forty-five tickets, which allowed one and a half baggage cars for Blackstone equipment. As a result, there were many traveling companions. A frequent favorite was Walter B. Gibson...."[17] Gibson remembered many interesting stories resulting from their traveling together.

Wendel Gibson, Walter's nephew, assisted in the Blackstone show for a number of years. Here he stands (left) with Harry Blackstone, Sr., holding Harry Blackstone, Jr. between them. From the collection of Thomas J. Shimeld.

One time a group of us were on the road and the car ran out of gas…. No one seemed to be able to flag down a passing car for aid. Blackstone, wanting to help, stepped onto the road and began plucking cards out of the air. A car stopped and the driver leaned out and asked, "Why, Blackstone, what are you doing here?" It was someone who had been to the show.[18]

Gibson recalled another time when Blackstone was appearing at the Rajah Theatre in Reading, Pennsylvania, in 1933 during the Great Depression, and at the time of the bank closings in Philadelphia. The show was a record sellout because people wanted to escape from their everyday existence into the fantasy world of magic. For this show in particular, Blackstone was paid $3,000 in cash. After the show, Gibson and Blackstone drove together to Philadelphia and when they arrived, Blackstone began cashing checks for all of his friends until the banks reopened. Thus the Great Blackstone magically produced money and turned the city of Reading into the Bank of Philadelphia.[19, 20]

Blackstone last traveled with his entire extravagant show in 1947. America mourned the loss of this great magician in 1965 after his death. Fortunately, the tradition of magic presented in this extravagant style was kept alive through Harry Blackstone, Jr.'s performances of his father's signature magic tricks such as the dancing handkerchief and the floating light bulb. Blackstone, Jr. found a name for himself in the world as a wonderful magician. His name is known around the world thanks to his international appearances on television. Blackstone, Jr. performed until his death in May 1997.[21]

Gibson's association with these three famous magicians—Thurston, Houdini and Blackstone—often sparked comparisons between the three. For example, they all attempted extravagant escapes. As mentioned before, Houdini and Blackstone competed for a while with escapes, but Blackstone focused more on magic in his shows. Toward the end of Houdini's career, he attempted a large-scale magic show. Thurston speculated that Houdini would soon reach a point where he couldn't carry such a show. Houdini always tried to outdo himself and as a result each show was different. Thurston would never put himself through such an ordeal. In fact, Thurston did invent an escape to use in his act. It was a glass coffin, which was patented to him by James Wobensmith. Yet, Thurston would hypnotize a Hindu assistant and put him into the coffin to avoid any strenuous maneuvers on his own part. Gibson described Thurston as being smart this way. And he was also smart about his money. Gibson remembered Houdini as being "very good" but he insisted that Thurston was definitely "the greatest magician of his time." Gibson thought Thurston was just so far ahead of his time in his productions. His productions were grand. Gibson said that "'Thurston was so much bigger than Houdini there was no comparison.'"[22] Thurston traveled with almost thirty assistants and two baggage cars of illusions, while Houdini had a couple of key assistants which he paid regularly. When Houdini performed his magic show at the Hippodrome he would simply take a cab from his brownstone in upper Manhattan and perform. Gibson estimated that Houdini made around $1,800 a week after introducing the subtrunk in 1913. Thurston made anywhere from $75,000–$100,000 a year gross profit. Thurston would take home approximately $20,000. Blackstone often grossed $240,000 a year with a profit potential of $80,000, but this was when times were good; some weeks were slow which would decrease this estimated gross profit. Thurston had the ability to get around problems of slow weeks—he would only play the biggest theatres in the country. Blackstone, on the other hand, played many theatres that were close together. Gibson recalled his time traveling with the Blackstone roadshow. "'By the time the dates were up, the theaters weren't big enough to bring the crowds, and the one-night stands were murder. You'd have to load and unload the trucks, and the [stage hands] were run ragged. It was hell economically. But Thurston rigged it so his people had it easier. Thurston was beyond all from a business standpoint.'"[23] He was even beyond that great publicist Houdini. Houdini tried to be a successful road magician like Thurston, but he wasn't cut out to be a good magician. He was only good in his specialties up to a point. From 1913 to 1922 Houdini stopped traveling and stayed in one spot in the Hippodrome, and did well financially. From there Houdini added spiritualism and made movies. Gibson said, "'I think Houdini was honest about starting the movie company. His ego was so big he thought he could go into financing and making movies himself. But his movies flopped.'"[24] Houdini then had a vaudeville act and got into spiritualism in his last years of life (he died in 1924). Gibson is further quoted as saying that Houdini was more of a showman than a magician: "'He was a good lecturer, with a powerful physique and a strong personality,' he said. 'But his knowledge of magic was less than [that of] either Thurston or Blackstone.'"[25]

Gibson's simultaneous work on the Shadow and writing magic books was certainly an exhausting feat. From 1946 to 1961 Gibson wrote mostly about true crime and wrote some books. But from 1961 on, Gibson's writing talents were used almost exclusively for books on a wide range of topics, yet always with a spice of the mysterious, the unexplainable and the bizarre.[26]

10

Psychic Phenomena and Mental Magic

Mr. Gibson's life story is as remarkable and diverse as his characters'. He has been a magician, ghost writer, crime reporter, occult investigator, comic book scripter, radio host and, of course, The Shadow's confidant and raconteur. At the core of his work is an interest in the mysterious, the magical, the unexplained.

— Bernard A. Drew, "Walter Gibson's Magicians,"
Attic Revivals, 1982.

Throughout his life Gibson had always been drawn into the shadows. He had a fascination with the mysterious and the magical in life. Gibson had been interested in fortune telling from a young age. On January 1, 1913, at the age of fifteen, during his vacation from school, Gibson purchased some fortune cards. He reported that "the fortune cards are pretty classy." Gibson had always known that there was some force, something greater than the comprehension of the human mind. A force, seemingly beyond him, had always guided his mind. Characters came alive and danced their adventures in front of his mind's eye. Many may think that Gibson's fascination with psychic phenomena was due to ignorance, yet as Gibson was a magician, he learned to be skeptical. Gibson believed magic was very educational. "'It is very healthy. It shows people to have open minds, to look for the trick.'"[1] Although taught to be skeptical by the nature of the magician, Gibson looked at the world with curious eyes and an open mind; he believed that the hand is not quicker than the mind's eye.

There were many unexplainable incidents that occurred in Gibson's everyday life. For example, one day he had been reminiscing about his old friend and roommate Ed Burkholder. Gibson stopped off at a newsstand to pick up a paper and scanned the obituaries—Burkholder's name was listed.[2] Such stories as this Gibson enjoyed recording in his 1973 diary under the "month's expenses" page of the book. One such occurrence Gibson noted on May 16, 1975:

Yest'd'y, I tuned in on CBS-TV just in time to catch my old friend Jack Tebbel — one of those odd chances that happened both with Wismer & Dunninger.... He was talking about the early days of radio & gov.t. regulations.... Just as I added the word "Magic" to "It's Magic" [in today's entry], J.Y., referring to radio censorship problems, said "If the situation could have been solved by some *magic—*"

Quite a coincidence — the sort that has happened often before with names ... which I've been typing when somebody spoke them on TV. This could prove how common coincidences are, as we deal in thousands of words daily. Still it could be an inkling of premonition.

A further story is recorded on January 15, 1976:

I wanted to hit N.Y. [from Baltimore] by 12 noon to see if I could contact someone before lunch. It proved an odd hunch because a young man spotted me coming from the train & introduced himself as editor of the *Conjuror* in Calif. Had come to Phila., met a girl & just missed the train to N.Y. so took the metro. I was *one person* he had wanted to see!

Further such entries include that for February 11, 1981:

Big fire @ Hilton Hotel in Las Vegas * * Around 6 A.M. I began thinking about [John] Scarne — wondering if he'd be going to Las Vegas on Tues. Tho't I might hear from him for some reason. First thing on TV (7am) was Hilton fire! That's where he would stay!

Such coincidences (?) of Gibson's later years had a well-researched background.

In 1927, Gibson took his first romp through the realm of the occult when he wrote the *First Principles of Astrology* under the name Wilber Gaston. George Sully and Company of New York published this 186-page book as a guide to using astrology in everyday life. Cox reports that this book is "a good, workmanlike job with no flamboyant style of writing ... a model for the handbooks and other self-help manuals which Gibson wrote in the 1950s and 1960s."[3] This work was the first Gibson wrote under a pseudonym that was not based on a real person or persons, and this was the only time he used this pseudonym. Sully published three other of Gibson's books that year so maybe they suggested he use a penname on this work. Proving its timeless fascination, the book was reissued in 1959 under Gibson's own name under the title *Astrology Explained* (New York: Vista House).

Gibson had always been fascinated by psychic phenomena. This led him to continue to write a number of books on the subject. He ghost-wrote a book for David Hoy, a professional mentalist, called *Psychic and Other ESP Party Games*, published by Doubleday in 1965. Gibson also worked with Litzka, his third wife, a magician in her own right who had been married to the world-traveling magician the "Great Raymond," on writing a few books. The first of these was Gibson's "most ambitious book to date" filling 403 pages with the history of psychic and mystic phenomena. The book, Walter B. Gibson's and Litzka R. Gibson's *The Complete Illustrated Book of the Psychic Sciences*, was published by Doubleday in 1966. Editions of the book appear in British, Spanish, Japanese, and Italian.[4] Litzka R. Gibson's and Walter B. Gibson's *Mystic and Occult Arts: A Guide to Their Use in Daily Living* appeared in 1969 thanks to Parker Publishing. Litzka and Gibson returned to Doubleday to produce their *Complete Illustrated Book of Divination and Prophecy* in 1973 with a British edition being produced the following year and a paperback edition in 1975. At least one translation was published in Brazil in 1978.[5]

Gibson's fascination with the bizarre led him, in 1955, to host, produce and author a radio show called *Strange* on the ABC network. The show was arranged through Cavanaugh Radio and TV Productions, Inc. and controlled by Bernard A. Young, Dr. Morris N. Young's brother (Dr. Young collaborated with Gibson on writings on Houdini). The show ran for a number of months and featured five fifteen-minute enacted stories a week, each based on a true incident.[6] Some of the scripts from *Strange* were included in Gibson's books on *The Twilight Zone*.

In 1948 Gibson wrote a historical article for *American Weekly* about the 100th anniversary of the "rappings" of the Fox Sisters that acted as the leap-off point for the era of "Modern Spiritualism."[7] People were fascinated with spiritualism and sought the advice of mediums. Many of these mediums preyed on these innocent souls seeking out their loved ones and took advantage of them financially (and some note cases of mediums taking advantage of their clientele physically). Many stood against the mediums, yet none more adamantly than Houdini.

An interest in magic, mystery and the occult would be the connection that bound Houdini to Gibson, and Gibson to Houdini. After the First World War, mediums were in popular demand because people wanted to contact their dearly departed soldiers. Houdini even had a particular fascination with mediums after his mother died. In his later years Houdini traveled around exposing false mediums and hoping to find a real one through whom he could speak to his deceased mother, though he never found one. Houdini's life of mystery has fascinated the world for decades. Everyone has wondered what means Houdini used to accomplish his feats of escape. Sir Arthur Conan Doyle, creator of Sherlock Holmes, hypothesized that the escapes were accomplished through spiritual and psychic powers. In "The Riddle of Houdini" Doyle writes, "'Who was the greatest medium-baiter of modern times? Undoubtedly Houdini. Who was the greatest physical medium of modern times? There are some who would be inclined to give the same answer.'"[8] In a letter to Dr. W. J. Crawford, lecturer in mechanical engineering at Belfast, Ireland, on June 24, 1920, Houdini writes on mediums: "Sir Arthur [Conan Doyle] tell[s] me he thinks that the power comes from the womb, it certainly is a wonderful affair and there is no telling how far all this may lead to."[9] Despite Houdini's discounting any supernatural powers, many people, Doyle included, thought Houdini did have such powers.

As a result of Houdini's fascination with spiritualism, he vowed that if it was at all possible, he would escape the bounds of death and return. In honor of Houdini's memory, friends and family attempt to contact him beyond the grave on each anniversary of his death, Halloween. Gibson often attended such séances. One such incident on October 31, 1974, in Niagara Falls, included a rather spooky occurrence.

During the séance event, the guests discussed their old friend and the Amazing Randi paid tribute to Houdini by performing the Milk Can Escape. Anne Fisher conducted the séance and as she made contact with the spirit of Houdini a book mysteriously fell from a shelf. This excited many people. Yet Gibson recalled the night's events in his diary through a different perspective. Randi and Sid Radner, being two individuals "in the know" of the art of magic, rigged the book to fall from the shelf at the appropriate moment. The spirit hand that unshelved the book chose one of a particular sort: one authored by Walter B. Gibson!

Gibson often said that the plots and characters during the time of the Shadow seemed to take on their own personalities and the stories would simply write themselves. Gibson wrote the final issues of *The Shadow Magazine* in an apartment at 12 Gay Street in Greenwich Village, an old section of New York dating back to the 1700s. Gibson lived there with Street & Smith staff writer Ed Burkholder. On Halloweens this home was the site of a number of annual séances to contact Houdini. After Gibson had moved out of this apartment, there were many reports that the home was haunted, but not by the ghost of Houdini. Rather it was haunted by a more mysterious figure: Lamont Cranston.

Hans Holzer in his *Yankee Ghosts* describes the house as a "typical old townhouse, smallish, of the kind New Yorkers built around 1800 when 'the Village' meant *far uptown*." He continues by relating a brief architectural history of the house. "In 1924, a second section was added to the house, covering the garden which used to grace the back of the house. This architectural graft created a kind of duplex house, one apartment on top of another, with small rooms at the sides in the rear."[10] The tenant history of the house is sketchy. Prior to the 1930s, Mayor Jimmy Walker owned the home. The tenant who rented the apartment seemed to have been Walker's lover and many of the house's records disappeared during this time. After this a sculptor owned the home. Holzer seems to believe that this gentleman was "fond of bootleg liquor" and cites the trapdoor in the ground floor of the newer section of the home as a possible hiding place for the gentleman's liquor cabinet. Of course Gibson lived in the home during the latter part of the 1940s. A real-estate broker, Mary Ellen Strunsky, was the owner of the house who sold it to Frank Paris and T. E. Lewis in 1956. At the time of the publication of Holzer's book in 1966, Paris and Lewis lived in the upstairs apartment and found the downstairs apartment suitable for a workshop and studio for their little theatre where they performed puppet shows. Holzer discovered that 12 Gay Street was haunted during an interview with reporter Cindy Hughes of the *New York World Telegram*. Hughes took Holzer, along with medium Betty Ritter, to the home on May 30, 1963. Holzer was careful not to tell Ritter the location of the house; he also removed her from the room "out of earshot" while he questioned the people present, so their comments would not influence Ritter's psychic abilities. Holzer's interviews revealed some mysterious happenings in the house. Paris reported that he and his dog had smelled "a strong odor of violets" around 3 A.M. while working downstairs, yet Lewis, who was also present in the room, did not detect this odor. At night the two roommates heard footfalls going up and down the stairs, yet they never found anyone on the stairs when they investigated the noises.

They explained a further haunting incident after they had their dog put to sleep — but over a year later they could still feel the "dog" poking them in the leg with his snout "— a habit he had in life." The owners were entertaining two friends at the time of the visit, Richard X. and Alice May Hall. Miss Hall, one of the older guests present, recalled an experience she had had in February of 1963. She had been relaxing in a chair in the spacious living room when she looked toward the entrance door that led to the hallway and stairs. "'There was a man there, wearing evening clothes, and an Inverness Cape — I saw him quite plainly. He had dark hair. It was dusk and there was still some light outside.... I turned my head to tell Frank Paris about the stranger, and that instant he was gone like a puff of smoke.'"[11]

Paris had not believed Miss Hall, but a week later, at dawn, he saw the same ghost "'wearing evening clothes, a cape, hat and his face somewhat obscured by the shadows of the hallway ... he was a youngish man, and had sparkling eyes. What's more, our dog also saw the intruder. He went up to the ghost, friendly-like, as if to greet him.'"[12] After these stories were shared, Ritter was summoned, and the group took a tour of the house with her.

Ritter's psychic powers discovered that a crime had been committed there. An argument had ensued between an Oriental named Ming and a woman. Ritter continued to describe "a gambling den, opium smokers, and a language she could not understand."[13] Ritter's psychic abilities were proven in the eyes of the onlookers when she correctly stated that a close friend to Paris named John had passed away and he had trouble with his right eye. She also told Lewis that a Bernard L. was with him. Bernham Lewis was his father. She also discovered that Richard X. worked with books (as an editor).

Later, on a continued tour, she saw government documents and felt a former tenant named Mary Ellen had lived there. She also psychically discovered the presence of a "well known government official named Wilkins or Wilkinson." Ritter was not even told the address of the home prior to bringing her there, so the possibility of her researching the history of the house was ruled out in the minds of the group that day.

Ritter's impressions of 12 Gay Street sound like the plots of crime stories, which very well could relate to the Shadow. Gibson explained that the "ghost" that Paris and Hall saw could have been what Tibet lore calls a *tulpa*, an "'unintentional by-product of a powerfully conceived idea.'"[14] "'They're seeing what we call an after-image psychic projection, not a ghost,'" said Gibson.[15] It was in this very apartment during the summer of 1949 that the Shadow completed his final adventure for Street & Smith in the novel *The Whispering Eyes*. Gibson wrote it there under the editorship of Daisy Bacon.

Though the days were busy during the fifteen years Gibson wrote the 283 out of the 325 total adventures of this mysterious crime fighter the Shadow, he still found time for other pursuits. One such pursuit was aiding an old friend, Joseph Dunninger (1896–1975). Dunninger started out demonstrating a propensity for sleight of hand

Lamont Cranston, the alter-ego of the Shadow, is depicted here in front of Gibson's residence at 12 Gay Street in New York's Greenwich Village. Gibson is silhouetted in the window, intensely writing. His concentrated mental energy is thought to have left behind a psychic imprint of Cranston whose ghostly form was often seen by later residences. Paper and ink illustration ©1977 by Frank Hamilton.

at the early age of five; it was a skill that his parents encouraged. By age seven, he had performed at a Masonic Temple as "Master Joseph Dunninger, Child Magician." It is reported that Dunninger never did too well in school, but somehow always did well in mathematics. The teacher accused him of cheating, but Dunninger explained it was telepathy.[16] By age sixteen, Dunninger had become a competent magician and mentalist. Gibson recalled his first meeting Dunninger at a young age. He was in New York visiting his aunt Florence Stowell, who was head of the shopper's service department at Wanamaker's. Gibson had shared with her his beginning interests in magic and Ms. Stowell introduced him to a *real* magician, Joseph Dunninger, who was working in the advertising department in the store. Dunninger was only around twenty years old but demonstrated a remarkable dexterity in the tricks he showed Gibson. "He showed me tricks, things I had never seen before," recalled Gibson, "and invited me to see his show." That evening Dunninger was engaged nightly for a year's contract at the Eden Musee on 23rd Street. "Our friendship, begun that day, was to last for 60 years," mused Gibson.[17]

Dunninger had performed on many of the vaudeville circuits. At seventeen years of age, Dunninger had performed at the homes of Theodore Roosevelt and Thomas Edison. Gibson proudly scribed in his journal on June 11, 1914, "...am acquainted with 'Mysterious Dunninger,' one of New York's best magicians." Through the years, Dunninger's show became larger, eventually acquiring fifty members. He presented a full evening show featuring magic, mentalism and escape artistry as "Dunninger, the Master Mind of Mental Mystery." And during the wars he treated patients in New York hospitals with hypnosis. In the 1930s Dunninger was establishing himself as a psychic entertainer. Gibson helped Dunninger in this pursuit by ghost-writing some books for him about psychic phenomena and spiritualism. *Inside the Medium's Cabinet* exposed the secrets of mediums in 1935; it was published by David Kemp and Company. The companion volume, *How to Make a Ghost Walk*, appeared the next year.[18] A year before Dunninger's death, Gibson produced *Dunninger's Secrets* published by Lyle Stuart. The book was in the style of the Blackstone and Houdini books he had written before, giving the reader biographical information while spicing up chapters with exposés of the mental magic Dunninger performed.

Dunninger also entered the radio world thanks to Gibson. Gibson made spare time during his hectic days writing the Shadow to create some scripts for Dunninger. The stories "ran the gamut of the weird, the ghostly and strange, authenticated experiences of a telepathic nature."[19] Gibson had suggested that a broadcasting of Dunninger's act would be of interest to the listening public. An audition record was made featuring both Dunninger's question-and-answer act and a dramatic portion on which Gibson worked. The program was successful, yet the sponsor thought broadcasting Dunninger's act would be more interesting to listeners so the dramatic sequence was dropped. Dunninger tried hypnosis over the radio and also acted as a psychic detective, yet neither of these shows did well. Finally on September 12, 1943, the first broadcast of "Dunninger, the Master Mind" aired. Gibson provided many of the scripts for the Dunninger shows as well as for Blackstone at around the same time. Dunninger became involved in two other radio series and also worked in television for two years beginning in 1948. Paramount motion pictures even consulted Dunninger as the technical advisor for the movie *Houdini* starring Tony Curtis in the title role and Janet Leigh as his wife.

Dunninger's unique talents raised him high in the eyes of the public. There were so many other writers interested in writing about Dunninger that there wasn't much room for Gibson to add anything new. In his personal papers Gibson recalls, "so many feature writers were becoming Dunninger-conscious that it resembled a stampede. I don't go in for mass competition. Like Dunninger, I believe in finding an unusual field and topping it."[20]

Like Houdini, Dunninger

Since their youth, Walter Gibson and Joseph Dunninger had been good friends. Dunninger became known to the nation through his radio show highlighting his study of mentalism. From the collection of Maxine Dunninger Hohneker.

was a leading psychic investigator of his time. To help establish this in the public's mind, Gibson used Dunninger as a character in one of his Shadow stories, *The House of Ghosts*, which appeared in September 1943. The summary of the story states: "Stanbridge Manor was haunted — haunted by ghosts that shot guns, crushed people, and otherwise acted like a bad bunch of humans. So the Shadow, aided by the great Joe Dunninger, ghost-breaker extraordinary, smashes mystery and crime in one telling blow."

Dunninger is called in to investigate the spooky happenings of Stanbridge Manor. Margo Lane is quite excited to find out that "The [ghost] hunt was to be handled by a psychic investigator named Dunninger, long famous as a ghost breaker" (29). The reader finds the ensuing conversation between Margo and Cranston to be quite flattering to Dunninger:

> "I've heard of Dunninger!" expressed Margo. "Why, he's the man who has offered a huge award for any spirit phenomena that he cannot explain or duplicate!"*
>
> "An award that no one has ever collected," added Cranston with a calm smile, "and probably never will."

(The editor of the magazine supplied the following note: *This offer still stands. No one, to date, has been able to meet his challenge.— Ed.*)

(Dunninger had also set up a challenge in Niagara Falls, Ontario, Canada, at the Houdini Magical Hall of Fame. Dunninger, chairman of the Universal Council for Psychical Research at the time, specially prepared a box two years after Houdini's death to test psychic phenomena. The box contained a pencil suspended on an elastic band over a blank pad of paper. The directors of the museum had placed a $31,000 reward for anyone claiming psychic powers who could produce writing on the pad. No one claimed this prize either.) When Margo finally meets Dunninger she is quite impressed: "There was something about Dunninger that promised results. He was a tall man, with dark eyes that fixed steadily on everyone he met.... When he spoke, his tone was firm, direct" (30). Dunninger carried with him an investigator's "kit." Gibson explained the content of this kit and their purpose:

> First there was a steel measuring tape, for checking the exact dimensions of rooms and passages, the initial step for uncovering secret hiding places in old houses. Along with the tape went balls of string and sticks of varicolored chalk, to aid the same general purpose, since measurements could be made with string, particularly around corners, and chalk marks used to identify the points of measurement.
> There were some heavy fish weights, by which the string could be transformed into a plumb line, for vertical measurements. Another very useful item was a carpenter's level, Dunninger explaining that in certain houses, a slight tilt of a floor could account for a considerable space at the other side of the house.
> To illustrate this, Dunninger used a pencil and a sketchpad, also part of his equipment, to make a long V lying on its side, one arm of the V representing a down-slanting ceiling, the other an uptilted floor above it. He had run across just such an arrangement in another old house that he had investigated.
> Next, Dunninger produced a flask of mercury and poured the silvery liquid into a small bowl. Apparently the mercury was to serve as another agent for determining levels, but Dunninger explained that it had an added purpose. Placed anywhere in the house, the mercury could be watched for tremors. Should it show any, it would indicate that someone was moving along the floor in that vicinity, thus making the mercury vibrate [31].

Gibson demonstrates Dunninger's knowledge in "psychic phenomenon" when he writes about a situation involving Margo Lane, Jennifer Stanbridge, and her planchette. Gibson first explains within the context of the story what a planchette is. He writes, "The object was like a tiny table itself, a heart-shaped contrivance mounted on three small wheels. From its center a pencil pointed downward to a sheet of paper that bore numerous scrawls" [13]. The planchette works like a ouija board in which the operator places her hands on the mechanism and receives a spiritual message. Miss Stanbridge challenges Dunninger with the planchette:

> "Come Miss Lane, let us place our hands upon the planchette and learn if Mr. Dunninger can explain whatever happens...."
> "I can explain what happens beforehand," declared Dunninger. "Whatever the planchette writes will be the expression of your subconscious thought. Without realizing it, you will let your hand guide the wheeled pencil"[37].

And sure enough as Dunninger begins to explain that noises in old homes are often caused by ... "RATS" thinks Margo and the planchette moves to write her thoughts.

During the investigation, Gibson reveals some more about Dunninger personally. At one point Margo catches Dunninger examining the antique furniture in the Colonial Room of the house. "Wondering what the furniture had to do with ghosts, Margo soon learned that the answer was nothing. It merely happened that Dunninger was interested in antiques and was taking a short recess from his ghost-hunting activities" [36]. Dunninger's initial investigation of the home revealed that the happenings were caused by humans and not apparitions; it was then up to the Shadow to discover who these people were and what motive they had. Dunninger's keen senses detect the presence of the Shadow despite his attempts at disappearing into the shadows. The two correspond and Dunninger leaves after laying down the groundwork for the Shadow to continue the investigation.

Gibson once reported about his friends Dunninger, Kreskin and Jeanne Dixon that he did not know if they were truly psychic. He knew that they relied on some amount of trickery, for even a gifted psychic could not rely on his or her gifts to work all the time, especially on demand. Gibson recalled:

> Dunninger was remarkably gifted at following a person's eyes and guessing their thoughts by how they reacted. And he was also a good hypnotist. I think he did have the ability to get an audience concentrating so hard that a mass state of partial hypnosis was induced and people actually became confused by what he said.[21]

Although Gibson was a skeptic himself, he had no patience with magicians who claimed they could duplicate psychic phenomena, thus "proving" that it could not possibly exist. "'That might be true with physical phenomena, but there is a lot more to being psychic then bending [a] spoon.'"[22]

In 1975, Gibson was in close contact with Dunninger's wife, Billie, about her husband's health. On January 13, after talking to Billie, Gibson reported that "Joe is not too well." Dunninger was to receive the Master's Fellowship in March. Billie was afraid he would not be able to make it, yet Dunninger was determined to accept the award in his wheelchair if need be. But he began to get a fever and by February 27 it was arranged for Gibson to accept the award for him. On Saturday, March 8, 1975, the day of the awards, Gibson wrote in his diary:

> This was the big day. Got some work done [on a rented Olympic typewriter] — then went over to Mark [Wilson]'s & had a hairdo — all rigged in rented tuxedo. Went to the hotel. Dinner — sat with Mark at corner table. Fine show — Ballantine produced a "famous TV personality" who proved to be Cal Worthington [earlier on March 6th Gibson wrote: "Up *real* early, as I am still going on N.Y. time. Saw early TV of a personable chap with a bit hat named Cal Worthington, who sells 'acres of used cars,' walking around his car lot singing, 'I'll do anything at all to make a deal. I'll stand right on my head 'til my face is turning red, I'll do anything at all to make a deal."] Gen. Grant was there for an award — Mark got magician of year — I picked up Joe's Master Award — told how he had subbed for Houdini.... Show was good with "Mr. Electric" & "Dante."

On March 9th Gibson wrote "In the eve Mark picked me up & we went to The Magic Castle for a gourmet dinner in the Seance Room. 13 of us around a big table — lecture followed with 'spook' effects climaxed by the table rising in the dark. I told Bill L.[arsen] 'your father would like this place' — & he said, 'My father is here every night.'"

On Monday, March 10, 1975, Gibson had an urge to watch the *Today* show on television. "Tuned in on the *Today* program & by another amazing 'coincidence' … I heard Frank Blair announce "Joseph Dunninger —" & of course I knew" Dunninger was dead. On March 12 Gibson attended the funeral in New York. He reported that "We went to the funeral home thru a light rain. I talked about Joe — I said we were honoring one of the most remarkable men of our time. I repeated what I had said when taking the award & I read the plaque & gave it to Billie."

After Dunninger's death, Gibson worked with another mentalist, Kreskin (1935–). George Kresge, Jr., in the "tradition of Blackstone, Houdini, and Thurston" worked with Gibson in his home at Eddyville, New York, to produce *Kreskin's Mind Power Book* in 1977 published by McGraw-Hill. Kreskin had a television show in Ottawa, Canada, and invited Gibson to make an appearance on it in 1973. Gibson refused the initial $300 the program offered him for the appearance; he accepted their offer finally at $400. He left Tuesday, January 30 from Albany Airport, for Montreal, stopping once at Burlington, Vermont. Gibson watched the first show on a television set at the studio, and then at 9 P.M. Gibson went on the program to talk about Houdini and Thurston. Kreskin did the mailbag escape. The two friends had dinner after the show and talked about magic until 2 A.M. Gibson was up at 6:45 to catch his plane the following day. Gibson's spot on the Kreskin show went over so well that the producers offered him another $400 to return on August 24th.

In 1976 Gibson worked with Kreskin to put together some ideas for television related to the *Strange* radio program that Gibson had hosted. The following year Gibson worked on a book for Kreskin which Gibson wrote on April 7 was going "slow & tough." By May 9 the material was complete and Gibson felt "like 'school is out' after delivering K's stuff." When Gibson received the proofs of the book on August 1, "All hell broke loose…." There were changes that Kreskin had made that didn't show up in the proofs and Gibson didn't understand what Kreskin's changes had been. Kreskin became upset and wanted the book canceled, but finally he dictated the changes over the phone and everything was all right.

Gibson truly believed in "'psychic experiences, [and] special powers of the mind.'" He thought that ESP was "'an extension of the mind beyond our present physical concepts. It's not something supernatural, just a power we have but don't often realize.'"[23] Gibson was skeptical about spiritualism, believing that the supernatural is simply a fact of life that we just don't comprehend yet:

> If a person was on a polar expedition for years and came back and saw television for the first time, he would think we were faking it or that it was real ghosts there.
>   Somebody said that all mystery is the effect of novelty upon ignorance. I used that in my stories to create mystery, something we don't understand.

> Sometimes when I started writing, characters and things came so fast. I
> didn't understand where they came from or why. It was so fast, it was hard to get
> them down. I didn't understand our minds transcend our normal abilities to use
> them.[24]

During the creative and imaginative process of writing, Gibson often found
himself entering "'a timeless sort of dimension'" where he could "'get out'" of his
surroundings to receive ideas, some of which, Gibson believed, could be extrasen-
sory. "'It is almost as though time stands still,'" stated Gibson.[25] It was as if a psychic dimension took over as he wrote. As Gibson told reporter Claire Huff in 1976,
"'Memory does not only contain things we remember from the past. It contains
events of the future as well.... Often when writing mysteries I picked up ideas psychically of things that really did happen in the future.'"[26] For example, Gibson had
written a story about a group of people suspected of murder who were trapped in a
building along with the sheriff. Someone began killing the people one by one. The
conclusion of the story revealed that it was actually the sheriff who was the murderer.
Gibson explained:

> I had picked the locale as a place in Maine that I was familiar with. Quite a long time
> afterward, I was in that town and learned that the local sheriff had, indeed, been
> arrested and convicted of a crime.[27]

In one article Gibson was noted as having predicted the atomic bomb, guess-
ing the exact element, in the comic strip of 1942 "Bill Barnes, America's Air Ace." In
the strip a Dr. Blannard asks a high American official, "You want an earthquake as
a weapon and you want me to supply it?" Barnes replies, "We're asking you for the
trigger that will start one. Can you do it?" "Yes," comes the reply. "With U-235!"
The doctor in the strip dispels the belief that U-235 can't be separated for he has
already separated ten pounds of it. Dr. Blannard hypothesizes that it will take a year
to build a plant capable of constructing the "world's most tremendous explosive":
eleven pounds of U-235 is equivalent to 30,000,000 tons of TNT.

After the comic strip appeared, government officials contacted Gibson asking
him to no longer hint at such a possible device. Gibson of course complied "'in interests of war security.'"[28]

One day when Gibson was living in Putnam Valley, New York, he was in Manhattan to close a book deal with Grossett & Dunlap on his *Stories from the Twilight
Zone,* an anthology of the radio and television program. Gibson recalls in the article "Memories that will not fade" by Mikhail Horowitz in the November 22, 1983,
Freeman:

> I met the man from the ad agency at the Barclay [Hotel] for breakfast. He'd been par-
> ticularly impressed with one of my stories, and told me how much he enjoyed it.
>   The story, entitled Back There, was about a man who goes to Washington, D.C.
> on a stormy night and finds his way to a private club. His clothes are drenched, so he
> changes into the only garb available — a period costume from the Civil War.

He has an accident, blacks out, and winds up going back in time to the moment when Lincoln was assassinated at Ford's Theater. Upon awakening, he imagines it was all a dream — and then finds the ticket stub from the theater in his pocket.

So we'd just been discussing that story, and I went over to pick up a ticket to Minneapolis, and it happened! JFK was shot! I was wholly in a state of confusion, exactly like the man I had written about![29]

Many of Gibson's Shadow stories have been noted to have a prophetic value. Such as his story of August 1, 1933, titled *The Black Hush* in Volume VI, Number 5 of *The Shadow Magazine*. The summary of the story on page three states: "Out of nowhere comes a deep, an enveloping blackness, hiding nefarious work, making helpless all means of defense. The awful ray searches out easy wealth — but it finds the Shadow, too, and the Shadow tracks it to its lair!" The story features a special spotlight that casts darkness onto buildings, a darkness so black and thick that no light can escape, no electricity can work, no sound can escape. On Thursday, July

Many of Gibson's Shadow creations turned out to be predictive of future events, like this story of *The Black Hush* (August 1, 1933) which Gibson was reminded of during the blackout in New York City on July 14, 1977. The city stood still and crime lurked in the shadows. From the collection of Marc Sky, retouched by Jennifer Ann Shimeld, reproduced with permission from Condé Nast.

14, 1977, such an impossibility occurred with the New York blackout, which brought the city to a standstill and allowed crime to reign. Gibson wrote that day:

> Today, NY Blacked out!!! I learned of it by turning on radio to check weather & sports — I'd waked up very uncertain about the trip & definitely deciding *not* to stay in N.Y. over tonite ... no trains were running into N.Y.! Had a call from Morris. Naturally our meeting was called off — he & Ginny were 16 floors up without water — they watched the lights blackout district by district — we set meeting for Thurs July 28th.

On Friday the blackout continued. Gibson wrote:

> Trains still not running right today. Tony Tollin [Shadow historian] called — said he was rereading the "Black Hush" — my old Shadow story — over again. All talk today about the blackout — this time the looters were ready — more than 3,000 were jailed....

The mysteries of existence brought Gibson through life with a child's fascination for the world in which he lived. The mystery of love was one with which Gibson tried and tried to reconcile. It seems his third union remained the love that lasted.

11

Litzka Raymond Gibson — A Uniting Force of Magic

Today was our 31st wed[ding] anniv[ersary]— so we celebrated with hairdos — back then [in 1949] we were working together on the palmistry book — so the literary angle seems to figure all thru the years!
— *Walter B. Gibson, 1980 diary, August 27th entry.*

It was during Gibson's break–up with Julia that he found a light of happiness in Litzka, a friend of many years who was married to the "Great Raymond." Robert recalls his father going to New York often to see Litzka sing and play the harp with her constant companion China Boy, a Cochin bantam rooster, at her side. These encounters with Litzka's graceful singing and beautiful presence would always have a positive effect on Gibson's mood, lifting him up, even for a moment, from his depression. Litzka's positive essence would embrace Gibson for the rest of his life.

Litzka was a devoted wife who was constantly attending to Gibson; he often called her Angel — to him she was certainly a gift from above. The two shared a life of magic and a love for the mysterious. Litzka was born Pearl Beatrice Gonser in Mount Carmel, Pennsylvania, on January 11, 1901. Her father, William, was a clergyman and her mother, Elizabeth, was a music teacher. She was the only child of her mother, and her father's fourth child, he having had three other children from a previous marriage. Elizabeth taught her daughter from the early age of three years old how to play the piano. Later her mother bought her a harp. In 1993, Litzka confided in Rauscher that she would love the world to remember her for her music and, especially, her harp: "She said, 'That was my first and last interest. I feel I owe everything to my mother. She taught me everything in music.'"[1] A family friend, upon his return from Europe, dubbed Ms. Gonser "Pearlitzka" in order to give her name a more "exotic, Bohemian touch" for the stage. She liked the Litzka part and kept that, yet she often signed her name as "Pearl Litzka Gonser."

While studying music at Emerson College in Boston, Massachusetts, an agent heard Litzka's voice and music lessons and offered her a contract to play her harp on tour. Her voice instructor at Emerson knew Litzka would do well at singing while accompanying herself on the harp. The Williams Agency of Boston helped Litzka establish herself in the Boston area. Her musical talents quickly established her in other locales, namely the New York area playing the Chautauqua vaudeville circuit. William B. Feakins, Litzka's agent in New York, scheduled her performances on the Chautauqua circuit. During the summer of 1921, Litzka performed as "Miss Pearl Beatrice Gonser, Harpist, Soloist, Reader and Pianist," presenting a variety of entertainment, including readings of poems and stories. Rauscher writes that "She had a striking personality, and it was said that when she joined her soprano voice with the rich tones of the massive harp in a soft lullaby, the beauty of the combination was thrilling."[2]

During 1921–1922, Litzka's talents were displayed at the National Lyceum in Washington, D.C. Also on the bill was a speaker by the name of Lieutenant Colonel Frank S. Evans. Evans was a British Royal Artillery officer who had spent three years in France. In June 1917 he was honored with the Distinguished Service Order, but by September 1917, Evans had been wounded and after a lengthy hospitalization he was honorably discharged in April 1918. Evans began making public appearances to "help maintain support for the war effort." He was soon booked to speak in America. He continued his speaking engagements after the war ended, speaking on inspirational topics. Rauscher relates that "although disabled, Evans was attractive and a distinguished young man who had a refined English manner and could relate the horrors of war in a dynamic way. He was an effective speaker who created strong emotions with tales of his experiences."[3] Evans became Litzka's first husband, but the marriage was short, ending after only two years when Evans died.

Litzka continued to establish herself as a talented musician and vocalist, playing for the Royal Conservatory of Music in Brussels, giving solo performances with the Boston and London symphonies, and performing at the Queen's Hall and Albert Hall in London, and at Carnegie Hall in New York. Her reputation reached the ears of a world-traveling magician, the "Great Raymond," who wanted to add a talented musician to the already numerous talents in his magic company.

Morris Raymond Saunders (1877–1948), a.k.a. the "Great Raymond," had an uncle who performed as Addison the Magician. Raymond joined his uncle's show at the age of nine when one of Addison's assistants contracted typhoid fever and could not tour with the company in the summer of 1886. After the three-month tour Addison went into the photographic business. Raymond, at age fourteen, convinced his uncle to give him his unused equipment. Raymond then joined a circus with his act. Gibson states in his book *The Master Magicians*, "since travel seemed the proper antidote for Raymond's mania for magic, his grandfather, who was going on a business trip to Europe, decided to take him along.… In London, he so amazed his grandfather's friends [with his magic] that they arranged for him to present a series of programs as a 'boy magician.' The highlight was his appearance at a lawn fete held by Queen Victoria."[4]

The Great Raymond (1877–1948). From the collection of William V. Rauscher.

This performance led to another command performance before the Prince of Wales, who would later become Edward VII. Among those present at this engagement was a gentleman named Charles Bertram, an accomplished magician and master card manipulator who was tutoring the Prince in sleight of hand. Raymond, attempting to impress these two onlookers, sprang his deck of cards from one hand to the other. In his haste, he ended up springing some of the cards onto the floor. Gibson explains the situation: "While Raymond stood frozen in consternation, Bertram arose from his chair, stooped and gathered up the fallen cards. He spread the cards between his hands, showing them to everyone including his royal patron. Then, raising his eyebrows in a manner of real surprise, Bertram remarked: 'Why, I was positive that these cards were all strung together, but none of them are! [And then he uttered his catch phrase] Isn't it wonderful…?' Soon, Raymond was springing the pack perfectly while he acknowledged Bertram's courtesy with a grateful smile."[5]

On Raymond's return to his home in Ohio, he finished school and studied medicine at Western Reserve University. Hypnotism gained popularity in 1892, and Raymond began to perform magic again featuring hypnosis in his act. He became so busy with magic that he left school to pursue a magical career. Gibson explains, "The world was an oyster for anyone willing to pry it wide, and young Raymond, though not yet twenty-one, was eager to have a try. Major Pond [a well-known producer in the entertainment field] won over the family, so Raymond packed the best of his equipment — including some of Addison's old props — and with his father as his business manager, started out on his first world tour."[6] Raymond was in great demand, and he often booked shows for passage on a ship. On one such passage Raymond had the great opportunity to meet Mark Twain, who was on a lecture tour around the world arranged by Major Pond. The two seemed to hit it off and Twain wished to announce the young man's show. Gibson describes the incident:

> That evening, as the liner glided through a calm tropical sea, Mark Twain arose before the assembled throng, gestured to the smiling young man who stood beside

a velvet-draped table holding a wand in his hand, and spoke in his most serious tone.

The ship's passengers were most fortunate, Mark Twain said, to have with them that evening the Great Raymond, a true master of mystery and more ... he went on to describe Raymond as handsome, clever and gifted with a wonderful personality. They would find that every word that Raymond uttered literally sparkled with humor and wit.

There, Mark Twain paused, while Raymond, overwhelmed by the introduction, swelled with pride. And then:

"In short," summed Mark Twain, "he is the Mark Twain of Magic."[7]

Raymond's first world tour ended abruptly in Buenos Aires in 1898 when he was forced to return to the United States due to the Spanish-American War.

During the next six years, Raymond toured the United States assembling a diversified company of many talents. Gibson found that "Raymond's program was so diversified that he could switch to any form of mystification; handcuffs, mind reading, hypnotism or straight magic."[8] Raymond had gathered together an act that would become the largest to travel the world. And that he did, once again, starting in Cuba. Raymond's first world tour gave him the necessary skills of speaking the various languages of the countries in which he performed, a capacity that audiences loved.

He gained a true menagerie of animals from parrots, to a cheetah, to a dwarf deer, and even an armadillo and anteater. A few other world tours followed, in which he performed for royalty around the world. Gibson explains that Spanish speaking audiences began to recognize the words *rey* and *mundo* in Raymond's name, meaning "king" and "world." "Where magic was concerned," admits Gibson, "Raymond was indeed 'King of the World.'"[9] At one of his command performances in the Palacio Do Necessidades, Raymond was knighted by King Carlos. Raymond was so proud of his decorations that he often wore them while performing, especially when performing for royalty.[10]

When Litzka was a young girl she got the great opportunity to see this world-famous magician perform. From Litzka's childhood home she could look out the back door and see the back of the Mount Carmel Opera House. She loved to watch the performers enter and exit through the stage doors. Her parents took her to see some of the shows. One such show was a performance given by the "Great Raymond." She was only eight years old but "in later years she often said in all seriousness she knew when she saw Raymond for the first time that one day she would marry him!"[11] Years after Litzka saw Raymond perform, Raymond saw Litzka perform. He wanted to highlight the talents of a musician for his show, and requested an audition from Ms. Gonser. Litzka was undoubtedly thrilled to perform for this magician who had so infatuated her many years before.

At the audition, Litzka opened with "Ave Maria" by Schubert. Her talent and delight touched the listeners, who hired her immediately. She was amused with this whole incident for she recalled her first seeing Raymond onstage. Rauscher quotes her as saying:

I fell in love with my first stage hero. I was eight years old. He was godlike to me. He pleased my father and mother because we all went backstage and talked to Raymond and he patted me on the head. It was a matinee, and that evening I told my mother I was going to marry him. That is why I laughed![12]

For the first week Raymond treated Litzka like any other assistant, only really speaking to her to give instructions for the show. She worked as the musician and primary female assistant. Yet soon their relationship grew beyond their work and Raymond eventually proposed to her.

In 1926 the two were married in Lisbon, Portugal. There was a legality problem with the marriage since neither Litzka nor Raymond was a resident or citizen of Portugal. Though marriage is truly only governed by the heart, the two established the legality of their marriage when they stopped on the *American Legion*, an American mail ship stationed seven miles off the coast of Montevideo, Uruguay. The United States recognized the ceremony conducted on the ship as legal since the ship was considered American soil. Thus Captain C.E. Hilton legally married Litzka and Raymond on January 28, 1927, at the ages of twenty-six and fifty respectively. They honeymooned at the Arquiza Theatre. The two had a third wedding ceremony, a religious one, at the American legation in Asuncion, Paraguay.

Litzka's roles in the show increased. Litzka played her music and sang her songs around the world touring with the show. Litzka recalled that at one stop on their tour: "'I was sawed in two in Lima, Peru, with the president of Peru holding my hands and the American ambassador holding my feet.'"[13] She collected a number of harps from stops in various countries, each being added to the show with the appropriate costume to match the origins of the harp: an Irish costume accompanied her Irish harp, a Peruvian costume for the Peruvian harp, a German and French one for the German and French harps, and a formal gown for her concert harp. Litzka simply adored her regular harp: "'It's gone over the Andes by cable, been carried on camel back and elephant train, crossed oceans, and lugged on more carts and trucks than you can imagine.'"[14]

It was while Litzka was with the Raymond show that

Litzka (on the right) assisting the Great Raymond. From the collection of William V. Rauscher.

Raymond encouraged her to take up palm reading. He saw a natural intuition in Litzka on many occasions, which he felt often saved them from various hassles. For instance, she refused to take a boat in South America, and they later found that the boat became shored; or Litzka arrived with the show in Lima, Peru, a day early and ran into Raymond by a chance meeting. Raymond arranged for Litzka to be taught by Cheiro, the world's most celebrated palmist.

Litzka had taken good care of Raymond, yet his health was declining; she could see his lifeline shortening, and on January 27, 1948, Raymond died.

Litzka continued presenting her act in vaudeville. Wendel remembered that "when Raymond died, I can still hear Litzka's voice, 'He [Gibson] pestered the daylights out of me. And he promised me that he'd build a place and he'd have the Raymond Show on exhibit for all the magicians in the world to see.'"[15]

Litzka Raymond plays her Lyon and Healy harp as her rooster China Boy looks on. All three traveled the world and appeared onstage alongside Litzka's second husband, the Great Raymond. From the collection of William V. Rauscher.

Throughout the years that Litzka was with the Raymond show, Gibson was a good friend to both of them. Litzka found Gibson fascinating and would spend hours with him talking. Gibson was a good friend who consoled her after Raymond's death. Soon a love affair grew between the two, and they were married on August 27, 1949. The two were able to meet coming down separate, yet very similar and busy paths. It was a match made in heaven to be sure. In keeping with his promise, Gibson collected the Raymond show together to store it. The collection of the props cost what Gibson reports as $2,000.[16] Unfortunately, the Gibsons never had the opportunity to give these props the display they deserved. For years they occupied a barn on the Gibson property.

The love of magic and intellect is what bound Litzka and Gibson together, for after traveling around the world with an extravagant magic company, Litzka had picked up a trick or two. In fact, it was during a matinee performance in December 1938 in Los Angeles with the Raymond show that Litzka debuted her solo magic performance, although it was a performance about which Raymond knew nothing. The children were so excited about the first act of the Raymond show that they demanded

Oil painting by Sally Bouchard of Litzka performing her Chinese magic act assisted by the rooster, China Boy. This painting, which hung in the Gibsons' Eddyville, New York, home, is now housed in Ray Goulet's Mini Museum of Magic in Watertown, Massachusetts. Photograph by Edwin E. Fitchett.

more during the intermission, so Litzka, elegantly draped in a Chinese costume, entertained the children by magically producing popcorn and candy, and concluding with the production of a live rabbit.

Gibson relates that "the excitement brought Raymond from his dressing room to find his stage taken over by a Chinese wizard. Far from having misgivings over such a rivalry, he suggested that Litzka add more tricks to the routine. Gradually, it grew into a complete act of Chinese magic that Litzka presented as a regular feature of the Raymond show."[17]

Wendel recalls: "But on her own, when Raymond died, she was doing shows. And she did birthday parties. Her favorite party was out on Long Island at the home of the woman who later became Jackie Kennedy Onassis.... She [Litzka] was in big demand."[18] Furthermore, Litzka would also read palms at some functions. She read Robert and Ethel Kennedy's palms soon after they were married and predicted they'd have a football team of children. She further saw that there would be a great catastrophic disaster.

Through the years Litzka remained good friends with one member of the Raymond show: a rooster named China Boy. China Boy was a foot tall, two-and-a-half-pound Cochin bantam rooster Raymond had trained for the show. China Boy often appeared perched on Litzka's harp. Litzka loved China Boy dearly and took him everywhere she went, which attracted much attention. Litzka found that China Boy loved to travel in the subways, but detested buses, crowing his disapproval when on them. He also enjoyed informing people when the phone rang. China Boy went with Litzka everywhere. He'd accompany Litzka to the movies and to restaurants. Litzka refused to eat in a restaurant where the manager didn't graciously accept her feathered friend. In restaurants the rooster enjoyed eating salads and would crow if the waitress forgot the salad dressing.[19] China Boy had toured the world with Litzka and the Raymond show. At one point, the Chicago Railroad Fair awarded China Boy a medal for being the "World's Most Traveled Rooster."

China Boy was not only a famous traveler but a literary hero as well. Gibson used China Boy as the main character in a story, "China Boy in 'A Trip to the Zoo,'" in 1948. The story was one of four (a second story being "Blackstone and the Gold Medal Mystery") Gibson wrote for a set of six comic books in the Carnation Series that sold for $.10 with a label from Carnation Malted Milk.[20] Gibson used China Boy's name as the inspiration of a pseudonym under which he wrote a detective story for Walter Annenberg's *Official Detective* magazine. The byline to the story cited C.B. Crowe as the author.[21]

Litzka was so attached to China Boy that after his death she had a taxidermist preserve his physical beauty. She kept him on display on her bedroom bureau. China Boy was placed in a copper-lined box and buried with Litzka when she died.

Litzka took care of Gibson like he was her son. She would organize the finances and even got Gibson to quit smoking. Gibson

Litzka, Walter and China Boy. The rooster often accompanied the Gibsons to restaurants, carried in Litzka's handbag. He enjoyed helping Litzka eat her salad. From the collection of William V. Rauscher.

was a chain smoker, often lighting up one cigarette from another. He, at one point, reportedly smoked four packs of cigarettes a day. One article on Gibson rationalizes his smoking behavior: "Walter Gibson was a highly nervous man — who wouldn't be, turning out 100,000 words a month!"[22] Gibson gave up smoking entirely late in 1949 due to Litzka's positive influence.

During his later years with Litzka, Gibson's writing pace slowed since he was no longer writing the Shadow, but he certainly kept busy. In 1950 Gibson wrote for *True Detective* and other factual crime magazines until this market declined. He would visit towns throughout New England to gather facts about murders and other major crimes. Gibson played detective by perusing the local papers, and interviewing local personalities and the police. In the magazine articles that Gibson wrote, he would reconstruct the crime, often highlighting overlooked clues to make the case more interesting by adding suspense. One of Gibson's stories led to the conviction of the true killer in a case of someone murdering a woman by strangulation. The defense lawyer reopened the case on behalf of his client who had been convicted of the crime. By following Gibson's clues, the real murderer was found and confessed to killing the woman.[23] Gibson also edited *Mystery Digest* in 1957.

Yet it was still magic that Gibson loved and that kept him and Litzka together.

Will Murray describes Gibson's performance style in his later years: "he'd play the part of a slightly befuddled old magician and pretend to have blown a trick. You'd be momentarily embarrassed for him — then he'd pull a trick within a trick and show he'd been in control all along."[24] Such tricks, known to magicians as sucker tricks, Gibson simply adored, and his writing style for mysteries reflected them.

It was the love of magic and writing that Gibson and Litzka could share. Litzka was the first woman to be inducted into the Magic Hall of Fame by the Society of American Magicians. Robert reported that the giver of the award had said to Litzka:

> Now it should be recognized that you are the first woman to be inducted into the hall of fame and I guess that you probably hope that there will not be another woman to be inducted in to the hall of fame. Litzka at that point responded, "No, I certainly hope there will be many women inducted into the hall of fame. But I doubt that there will be another woman inducted into the hall of fame who has been married to *two men* who were in the hall of fame." Her reference being to Raymond and Walter Gibson.[25]

The Gibsons, having both lived very full lives and now in their sixties, needed a place to live to store their vast collection of memories. They had moved out of New York to Putnam Valley in 1959, and then finally settled in Eddyville, a suburb of Kingston, New York, in 1966 in a twenty-four room Victorian mansion overlooking Rondout Creek. This was not a home in the traditional sense but acted more as a private library and magic museum. Located on Creek Locks Road, the central portion of the home is a 1757 stone house.[26] It was reported that the turrets and gables made the home resemble a library, [27] and this it certainly was. Upon moving in, an eighteen wheeler was seen in the driveway, full of books. It is estimated that Gibson's library contained well over 9,000 books and thousands more articles on all subjects. All these books were stored on wall-to-wall bookshelves that Litzka installed. Litzka fixed up each room of the house, one at a time. Their home contained magic memorabilia of all types, and old and unique posters hung on the walls, including the Miss Undina poster mentioned earlier. Gibson stored 125 crates of the magic equipment of the Great Raymond in the barn on the property; many remained unopened for nearly sixty years until they were sold in 1994. Each room in the house contained books devoted to a particular subject of research. There was the "Occult Room," the "Crime Room," the "Magic Room" and, of course, the "Shadow Room." Gibson had a total of nine typewriters and writing tables scattered throughout the house; he often worked simultaneously on different books at different typewriters. He often enjoyed working in the "Crime Room," dragging along the research material he needed from the other rooms.[28] For an article of 1974, the writer observed Gibson at his home in Eddyville. He reported that Gibson's writing pace had slowed down since the 1930s, but he was still a prolific writer on a variety of subjects. The reporter writes:

> In his "upstudy" for example, opened books, scattered notes, and partially completed projects are literally swirling around the room. It looks like chaos, but upon further

One of the numerous libraries in the Eddyville home. Each library was housed in a separate room and had a separate theme: the occult, the Shadow, magic, etc. In this manner Gibson would have the research for a particular themed book easily accessible. He often worked on more than one book at a time, rotating himself from library to library, typewriter to typewriter as needed. From the collection of William V. Rauscher.

> examination, one sees that one project is being written on pink paper, a magazine article is being written on white paper, and another book is being completed on green paper.[29]

Despite the wealth of material Gibson had acquired through the years, he still had a keen sense of where everything was. Wendel reports that his uncle would be speaking about a particular passage in a book and would be able to get up, walk over to a book shelf, instantly retrieve the appropriate book, and immediately open it to the exact page on which that passage was written.

As good friend William Rauscher writes in his book: "Their house, with its many varied libraries, was a testament to an intellectual world, a productive and varied life, with friendships all over the globe. The time came when travel was no longer possible, but as Walter observes, 'I do not travel around the world now. Now the world travels around me.'"[30] Rauscher continues saying that "... stacks of paper accumulated, because someday the information therein might be necessary for an article. Every room was filled with books. There were no soft chairs in which to sit and relax. Straight chairs were more serviceable, since this was now a place to work more than

The Gibsons' Eddyville, New York, home where they spent the remaining years of their life together. The tower on the house reminded Walter of where the Shadow kept his radio sending set. Photograph by William V. Rauscher.

a place to live." In every room there was a typewriter, and often a bed, for, Gibson admitted, "'I used to have a habit of going to sleep wherever I happened to be working, but my wife got tired of changing all the sheets.'"[31] His regular bedroom was on the first floor, just off the kitchen. Litzka slept in the bedroom directly above this one.

From 1963 to 1970 Gibson, often along with Litzka, appeared on various television shows such as *Today*, *The Pierre Burton Show* in Toronto, *Alan Burke*, *Merv Griffin*, *Long John Nebel*, *Barry Farber*, *Ben Grauer*, *To Tell the Truth*, a John Keel television special, the *Alan Spraggett* television series, *The Unexplained* in Canada, Kreskin shows from Ottowa, Tom Snyder's *Tomorrow Show* from Hollywood. Also throughout his later years Gibson accepted many requests for radio interviews in person and over the phone from around the country. Gibson often appeared on Mary Margaret McBride's radio show on WGHQ in Kingston, New York, where he was often on three times a week as a special guest.[32] The topics of conversation were numerous. Gibson reported that they discussed witchcraft, Houdini, and divination: just a few topics covered from February through September on Mary Margaret's show. Listeners often heard Gibson on WELV as well. Other radio and television engagements were continuous. Various organizations also enjoyed Gibson's lectures. He once lectured to a class at Roosevelt High School that was studying detective stories, "So I started with Poe, Doyle &c ... [*sic*] one kid said he could pass the course just on what he had heard."[33] He sometimes would give lectures with Litzka. On one occasion he spoke to a group at Mohonk. He began with the Shadow, then moved on to ESP an hour and fifteen minutes later. This was a subject that Litzka also addressed in her discussion on palmistry while Gibson set up for a ten-minute magic show.

The Guinness Book of World Records was interested in Gibson's output during the Shadow years. Yet on June 14, 1975, Gibson wrote that he had received a "Letter from Guinness. Thinks they may reject my records, maybe not, who cares?" He did not end up getting in the book. It is impossible for anyone to come up with an exact total to his output. He has written so much, under a variety of different names. Gibson was noted for offering a reward to anyone who could make a complete bibliography of his work; but he knew no one could ever claim it, for even *he* could not verify if it was complete.

Litzka was very important in Gibson's hectic life and was often mentioned in his diaries. Gibson wrote on January 14, 1977: "TV all hopped up about Carter's appointments — we are in a crazy world of mistrust & c... Two things count in our life Litzka & myself.... [*sic*]" On the following day Gibson added ".... [*sic*] I should have said '3' the cat-" Gibson always kept young at heart playing with his cat, whom he would refer to often as "the cat" or sometimes "Baby." The cat was a wonderful companion, especially when Gibson wasn't feeling well. The cat would let himself in and out through a window that was always left partially open for this purpose. Gibson reported one evening, on September 25, 1973, "Cat monopolizes my bed at night, driving me into Litzka's room."

Gibson loved recording cat stories in his diaries. The following is from January 13, 1973: "Home for dinner —& Bango! A *Bat* busted in on us. We battled it & killed it. Puss cat may have prodded it out of the attic. He looks concerned. Hope it wasn't Dracula Jr." The added joy in life that this beloved cat brought Gibson did not last, for on Monday June 20, 1975, Gibson wrote:

[Puss cat] moaned a little & groaned later, so we contacted vgt, who came @ 3 P.M. & found tumors & swollen

Walter and Litzka still enjoyed performing in their later years. Photograph by William V. Rauscher.

bladder — he had moved to familiar spots during the last hour — so it was a quick needle. He looks beautiful in death — soft — furry — peaceful.... But OH!!!

The following day Gibson continued:

Today we consigned the angel to his grave. Stephen [a friend] dug one by the forsythias where baby & mama pusscat had a happy haven six summers ago & Litzka hopes to plant a dogwood thereon — or perhaps a pussy willow! So back to work in an empty, empty house where every cranny is haunted by a presence that owned & loved it.

Throughout the following weeks, Gibson often noticed the absence of Baby. Yet on Thursday, November 6, 1975, Gibson and Litzka found a stray cat in Rhinecliff "*exactly like* dear baby, we picked it up & it purred all the way home — in the house it took over where baby left off!" The cat later became known as Doll Baby, and was often nicknamed Dolly or even "Dali." The cat's favorite spot was in the upstudy.

In his seventies Gibson was a busy man. He writes in his 1973 diary, "Up at 5 A.M. ready to knock the whole world cockeyed — which I can still do." Gibson was constantly on the phone and took trips to New York once a week to go over book deals, often running from Doubleday to Pyramid delivering and picking up Shadow books. He was constantly at work, juggling a number of projects at once, rarely taking time off; not even major holidays would stop his writing. He and Litzka did enjoy dining out together, usually every night. They had there runs of favorite restaurants, such as Roberto's in 1973, and Beekman Arms in 1974 and 1975. In his diaries Gibson, as he had done ever since he was a child, would always list the weather. He also categorized what he ate at meals (especially good meals) and listed time schedules of trains, noting if they were late and by how many minutes. He still, as always, enjoyed visiting antique bookshops and purchasing books for later reference. His days were long — he often got up early and stayed up late. He often napped after a busy couple of days to catch up on his sleep.

Gibson always kept a sense of humor. On December 9, 1974, he wrote: "coined a new word: Stinkler. Anyone who is a stickler and/or a stinker.... We are living in a *super* world: superficial." Another entry, on July 7, 1977, after a plane trip to a Shadow convention, reads:

Caught plane nicely & had seat up front facing lady & a boy named Bob — while alongside was a boy named Phil. When we got above the clouds, Phil said, "They used to think there were angels up here." I said, "Maybe they're hiding in the clouds" — soon we were going thru some clouds & when it got bumpy, I said, "We must have hit some angels" ... [*sic*] So we counted angels for a while.

In his 1976 diary Gibson listed 51 different anagrams under the "This book is the property of:" page. It could almost be a page listing the different personas Gibson had played throughout his life. He checked off seven of the names that were of particular amusement to him, such as "Wrestling Boa."

Gibson relied on Litzka to do income taxes and handle other financial aspects of their lives. "Unfortunately, his talent for writing far exceeded his talent for business, and once again Litzka had to take over, trying to save whatever money she could...."[34] Gibson had a habit of taking on everything asked of him. He wrote on January 6, 1974: "Sid [Radner] phoned yesterday — wants a gambling book! Things just seem to pile up. Will have to teach the cat how to type!" Gibson, in his late seventies, was working hard during this period: "A fine day workwise — inside — and gorgeous outside — but we never got out! Like the old Shadow days — or nites."[35] On January 30, Gibson "stayed home all day today plugging away — Now I know why I didn't keep a diary during the Shadow days. Life was so much the same except for work."

With the number of projects Gibson had going at once, it was a wonder that any of them got finished. Litzka pointed out to Gibson how long he had been working on one project in particular. Gibson wrote on November 26, 1974, "I went into a tantrum when Litzka said I'd been 8 years on the close-up book. Tried to choke myself & may have hurt my throat, as I have coughed all day. Found I made 2 news stories on Sunday. But still I am a bum. Got to work on it & will see it through. Hassle resumed after a nice fish dinner."

Once again, as if writing did not occupy enough time, Gibson still kept quite involved in magic, performing now and then when he got the chance. Of course, magic books appeared often from Gibson's typewriter. On July 24, 1973, he received "a call from Mark Wilson in Hollywood. He's coming east & wants me to cooperate in some way with his new magic show. Great!" It turned out that Wilson wanted Gibson to aid him in producing a course on magic. On Friday, August 10, 1973, Wilson arrived in town and met with Litzka and Gibson. After showing him their house, they took Wilson to eat at Beekman Arms for dinner. Conversation revolved around this course of magic. On September 12, 1973, Gibson got a call from Wilson offering $500 for the first lesson as a "binder" for the rest. On July 4, 1974, Wilson paid a visit to the Gibson household with his family to go over tricks. They worked from noon to 7:00; by then they had arranged the first lessons. The following month, Gibson flew out to California to work with Wilson and to tour the famed Magic Castle in Hollywood and to meet some of the great names in magic. Gibson continued his work on Mark Wilson's *Course of Magic* through 1975. With his new electric typewriter, Gibson typed out tricks slowly. He had difficulty typing so he would dictate some of the tricks. At one point he had to dictate some of the writing over the phone. He received his copy of the finished product on August 22, 1975; "Looks Good!" he commented.

January 11 was Litzka's birthday, and Gibson would always make sure he reported the day's events. In 1973 he wrote: "Today was Litzka's Birthday. I was singing 'Happy Birthday to you' at 2 A.M. or there abouts — Got up toward 7 or 8.... Roberto's for a birthday dinner. Tried frog's legs for a change. Good as usual." Just a few days prior to Litzka's 76th birthday, Gibson wrote, "I have spent the best of all days with the best of all persons — Litzka!" On January 11, 1981, he reported: "Litzka's Birthday ... would have dined at Martin's — if it hadn't burned down. Oh, Gawd!"

When Gibson was writing, he would concentrate so intently on his work that other things would just seem to fade into the background, including his tolerance. On one occasion he was working on a project of puzzles for Parker Brothers, a project that reminded Gibson of his "Puzzle a Day" column for the *NEA*. He would often wake up in the middle of the night to jot down ideas for puzzles, "like in 1922," Gibson remembered. All other projects became secondary to Parker Brothers' riddles and jokes. The jokes were aimed at an eleven-year-old level; often he thought up and wrote ten to a page, and completed more than 1,000 altogether. Gibson wrote on November 26, 1979, at 82 years old, "Thank God that after all these years, *somebody* (P.B.) appreciates me!" He was happy that a company was taking his work seriously once again. The following day Gibson wrote, "I am *happy* to be turning out material for somebody who wants it!" Gibson was on a high, feeling the excitement of his youth. "Seems like old days—hacking out material on the old mass production basis."[36] Of course he kept ahead of schedule in his writings. The work took its toll; he was not young anymore. He handed the job over to another writer in mid December. It turned out that Parker Brothers was "shelving" the riddles for the future, but still paid Gibson what was owed him. He wrote on November 29, 1979: "Tough day — but good. I piled up Parker material. I got angry over phone problems— Litzka to Marlene. Litzka won't forgive me for being stupid — which I always do when I get concentrated. However, I did pile up 50 items for Parker Bros. That is what *counts now*! [my italics. In diary the word was underlined three times].

Gibson's productivity was impressive, even into his later years. He was fortunately blessed with good health. In his 70s his health was great. His only struggle was with his weight. On August 13, 1973, he reported that he weighed 220 pounds and intended on dieting. By November he had lowered his weight to 205 pounds. His weight crept back up through the years and in 1975 the doctor recommended that Gibson go on a rice diet including fresh fruit and vegetables; "We celebrated with a spaghetti & clam sauce lunch — then for dinner had chicken with rice — I like rice (with fixings) so it shouldn't be so bad." Gibson called it "the Vietnam Diet."

In 1974, a cough was disrupting Gibson's health, and he napped with the cat most of the weekend of February 9. His diary entry for February 11 simply reads: "*Operation Emergency*!!!" He was in the hospital until February 27. He reported that he took notes of his hospital stay in another notebook, but this has not been seen by the author. On Gibson's return home he slept a lot but still forced himself to make business calls and to see visitors. His cough continued and greatly slowed down his writing. On March 4 he received some photographs of himself that Robert had taken of him while he was in the hospital; "I didn't look too good," admitted Gibson. On the 6th he reported on his health: "Puss cat occupied the foot of the bed last nite, but didn't exactly force me out, tho I did head into the other room, but came back after some coughing spells, which are all that really bothers me. Took a Bronkaid this P.M. & slept a while."

Gibson remained sluggish well into the next month. He didn't go out and was gaining some weight. By the end of March he was "itching to get out." On March 28

Gibson saw the doctor who prescribed some medicine, "otherwise I'm o.k. & can move around — go to NY after a few weeks. We went to Beekman for celebration dinner." He took it easy throughout April, although he went to New York to be on a television program. After the month of May, he seems to have been much better.

On January 25, 1975, in his late seventies, Gibson wrote "…it rained overnight & all was icy this A.M. I slipped going into P.O. & knocked back of my head, which left me a little shaky." "Regarding the P.O. slip. There were two packages there for me — both expected — otherwise I would have left it to Monday. I carried out the first & found I *could not begin* to cross the ice to the car, I brought out the 2nd package & shoved the two across the ice ahead of me — thinking I might use them for stepping stones … but I preferred to push the cartons ahead & crawl on my knees until I made it. What worried me was — what would happen to whomever [*sic*] else came along!" His vision began to deteriorate quickly then. He reported that his 20–25 sight had deteriorated to 25 in his right eye and 30 in his left after 3 years. In 1977 Gibson bought "a special gimmick … for reading phone numbers & dictionary words — a magnifier." In October he found that he was "having trouble reading, so work is going slow." Earlier, on April 25, Gibson wrote, "My real job is to ease the strain I'm under — which people don't seem to recognize. But it is telling on me & I know it." In October he complained of headaches due to his eyes, although his doctor believed it was his nerves.

After a hospital stay in January 1979, Gibson realized he must try to slow down. On February 3 he wrote: "Litzka has been handling big calls & all is well — today — Mark Wilson called — they want to give me the *Master's Award* on March 10. I'm sure I can make it easily — if I progress normally — & it's just the impetus I need to make magic my main job from now on." By the end of February, Gibson was attempting to do work: On February 22 and 23 he reported, "Moved work a little faster today, but at lunch, my hands began to feel uncertain, so I laid down awhile." "Did some work this morning & then got a bit shaky — so quit. Felt real moody." It seems that Gibson was getting discouraged at his body's inability to keep up with his mind. He often felt off balance in the ensuing months, and would often sleep most of the evening, "which seems to be a habit." In October he reported feeling heavy chest pains and the need to rest a lot.

On February 5, 1971, the Academy of Magical Arts presented Gibson with a Literary Fellowship for "'the high standards he has maintained over the years in his writing on the subject of magic.'"[37] Then in 1979 he received a Masters Fellowship. On March 10, 1979, Gibson received his fellowship at the Variety Arts Theatre in Los Angeles, California. Harry Blackstone, Jr. received the Magician of the Year award that year. This black-tie event gathers some of the most famous magicians and members of the Magic Castle from Hollywood, California. Bob Barker announced the night's events as master of ceremonies, and Tony Curtis was on hand to present the awards to the visiting magician of the year and the lecturer of the year (who were Frances Willard and Jerry Andrus, respectively). The fellowships are voted on by the board of directors from a list encompassing magicians from around the world who have devoted their lives to the art. After a show featuring Harry Anderson, David Copperfield and Doug Henning, among others, Irene and William Larsen, Jr. presented the Masters Fellowship to Walter Gibson:

> [The Masters Fellowship is] presented to that person who the Board of Directors feels deserves recognition for devoting a lifetime to magic in many fields. It has previously been awarded to Dai Vernon, Cardini, Virgil and Julie, Jose Frakson, Charlie Miller, Tony Slydini, Dunninger, Robert Harbin, Les Levante and "Dorney" Dornfield. This year it was my pleasure to award this great honor to Walter B. Gibson who came out as Mark Wilson's guest to receive it. A giant in our business.[38]

Gibson's star never shined brighter. And work as he may, it could not shine as brightly again. Time was taking its toll.

12

A Fading Shadow

I remember once when he [Gibson] was reminiscing about the joys and challenges of writing 24 Shadow novels a year, he paused and said very quietly: "Sometimes I wish I were still writing them."
— Will Murray, "Remembering Walter B. Gibson."
Echoes, 5 (February 1985)

On September 6, 1977, Gibson wrote: "Today was a great day — so Great! It began with a 'Birthday' card signed by all the Shadow's agents & c... [*sic*]" The Shadow was still Gibson's dear friend. His order of special stationery "Shadowgram" sheets arrived at his home on 21 December 1977.

In 1978 the Shadow still had quite a following. From Shadow secret societies to the reprinting of the original novels, "'The Shadow still lives,'" stated Gibson, "'but it fits into its own time frame. I don't have any plans to revive it with new Shadow books.'"[1] He didn't need to, he was too busy with other projects, even now as he was entering his eighties. Yet as many observed, he kept his youth through his productivity.

"'It seems like I'm always getting new ideas of projects to work on,'" Gibson told reporter Jim Detjen.[2] One writer observed that "Gibson is a big, cheerful fellow, who seems to find being an octogenarian amusing."[3] In 1976, reporter Claire Huff wrote about Gibson: "Gibson, who somehow manages to look like a mischievous little boy, is laughingly referred to by members of the Society of American Magicians as 'the ghost who walks and talks.'"[4] He was considered by many magicians to be the "foremost authority on magic in the world."[5] Gibson knew so much about the history of magic, for he lived through the first golden age of the art; no one would argue against his word, even if his word wasn't totally fact. Wendel recalled leaving a magic meeting in New York and confronting his uncle:

"Walter, you embellished that story more than you usually do." "Why shouldn't I? There's hardly anybody around that can contest it!" He is establishing fact right then and there because he's right. The guys who would contest it would be guys who got information and put it in their writings and they got it from a different source and it wasn't as reliable as Walter's. So I'd rather go with his. When he embellished it, he'd just make it sound more like a story. And it was great! It had an immediate impact on the listeners.[6]

Robert recalled attending a magic convention in 1977 of the Society of American Magicians in Philadelphia with his father who was to give a lecture.

> His session was to begin in the Grand Ballroom at midnight.... About 500 people were in the Grand Ballroom at midnight. So he was introduced.... So without any kind of notes or anything else he simply began to reminisce ... about Houdini and Blackstone and Thurston.... And here are all these young people there and my God here's a guy telling all his personal experiences with these people and they were just absolutely spellbound. As far as I can remember, not a single soul left ... finally about 4 o'clock, not a soul having moved and his just going on, seemingly endlessly the guy who introduced him came over and said, sort of very apologetically to the audience that we just shouldn't impose on him anymore. My father was a little puzzled ... so he went on to bed. I stayed there, of course, for the whole thing and God I collapsed. I was dead. At 7 o'clock in the morning my telephone rings and he says, "Are you ready for breakfast?"[7]

At 80 years old Gibson was still ready to take on the world. And he still could.

The Shadow celebrated his 50th anniversary in 1981. A friend of Gibson's, William Rauscher, gave Gibson a girasol ring, like the Shadow wore, to celebrate the occasion. Rauscher had a jeweler friend create two girasol rings. One he kept for himself, the other he gave to Gibson with the inscription: "To W.B.G. From Lamont Cranston." The Shadow's elusive arm still guided Gibson. On March 9 Gibson was rereading some Shadows to consider which to reprint, and he wrote: "Malmordo is fine on action — great surprise finish — but not much variance in crime sequences, as I did the last 80-odd pages in a day!" Not only were the books still of interest, but the Shadow was still struggling to develop into a television show. On July 20, 1981, Gibson received a call from California. The caller was interested in producing a show for which Gibson would write the pilot episode. "Sounded like Orson W.[elles] was behind it," wrote Gibson. The deal was turned down. Gibson received a number of calls from writers and producers wanting to start a Shadow television series, or a television animation series but Gibson was helpless in the venture,

A magic book presentation plate signed by Walter B. Gibson. Reproduced with permission from Robert Gibson.

having to direct all calls to Condé Nast. The pending movie of the Shadow attracted interest within merchandising companies. Shadow cards and a Shadow game were in the development. Jim Walsh of Milton Bradley was working with Gibson on the game in August and September 1981. On September 2nd Gibson "called Jim Walsh — he says movie won't be out until fall of 1983 — so no rush on Shadow game." A Shadow play was even on the minds of some people. On August 27th Gibson reported on a Saturday visit from an Ellen Bryson of New York. The two "spent all afternoon going over idea of an off-b'way [Broadway] Shadow play. Sounds good."

Universal Studios was interested in releasing a Shadow movie. They desired a new blockbuster character after their success with bringing Superman to the big screen. The script for the Shadow movie bounced around from one writer to the next. The original Shadow script, written by Leslie Newman (*Superman*), had some approval for some time. To quote Stuart Matranga about Newman's writing:

> She has infused the mysterious evil fighter with a brooding, almost poetic, nature. She envisioned Leslie Howard, an actor revered for his sympathetic and almost feminine sensitivity, while she wrote her interpretation of the Shadow. Frayard's *Fantomas*, a silent French serial character (1912–1917) also helped summon, "a dark romantic melodramatic world, full of calling cards, poison rings, secret passageways and figures in black, scaling walls...." To preserve a sense of mysticism, Leslie set *The Shadow* as far back as she could, in an age where "There was a willingness to believe in the possibility of clouding men's minds," which is an impossible concept. But if you set up a climate where people are ready to believe.... [*sic*]."[8]

Gibson was frustrated about it:

> I don't think much of it.... They tried to do it like *Superman*. They tried to go back to what The Shadow/Lamont Cranston/Kent Allard had done before he *became* The Shadow. With all the wealth of stuff they had to pick from in *The Shadow*, you would think they would have taken something *typical* of it. Why don't they read my Shiwan Khan stories?[9]

That script was rejected and many more were sorted through. Gibson understood that his character would have to be changed to some degree in order to best adapt it to the big screen; after all, he had adapted the Shadow to fit into the radio, comic book and comic strip genres.

The film bounced around from one writer to the next. Since 1980 the film idea continued its journey through a number of screenwriters, but no script seemed right. "They've just been acting like a bunch of damned fools," reported Gibson. "'They've been going on options and options and options and nothing's happening with it.'"[10] And no one ever inquired if Gibson himself would be willing to adapt his character to the big screen. Gibson admitted, "'I don't know of anybody who wrote more about one character and who was so completely ignored when people began to do something about it. It's the most incongruous thing you could imagine.'"[11] Gibson always had plans to resurrect the Shadow for television or the movies with some new writing, "'If I can first unload the 283 novels is [*sic*] [I] have already written to some

Walter Gibson sits in front of his popular magic books in his nephew, Wendel Gibson's magic shop. Reproduced with permission from Robert Gibson.

television producer.'"[12] Yet it was not the fact that he was being ignored that angered Gibson, it was the fact that he could not reprint any more of the Shadow novels until the film was released.[13]

Another topic of interest to Gibson was the actor who would play the Shadow. At one point John Travolta was considered to play the part. Gibson wanted someone else though. On November 28, 1984, Gibson decided on the actor he thought would be best to play the Shadow in the movies: Ronald Reagan. "'It calls for an active actor who has to be a daredevil crime-fighter,' Gibson mused. 'Then, as the Shadow's alter ego, Lamont Cranston, the actor has to play an urbane socialite at ease with both royalty and the rich. There is only one actor I can think of who fits that description to perfection — but Ronald Reagan won't be available until 1988[sic]!'"[14]

Although Gibson joked about this, it seemed to him that Reagan would have been able to play the part perfectly. Gibson is quoted as saying:

> In fact, I don't known [sic] of any other actor, dead or alive who would bring more to the Shadow than Reagan.
> The late John Wayne, for example, would have been too much for the role.
> He could have played the Shadow, of course, but not the part of the sophisticated Cranston, who wears evening clothes, a cape and a top hat.
> Orson Welles, who first had the part of the Shadow on radio in 1937, might play the sophisticated part but couldn't handle the action.[15]

Gibson was frustrated about the film. He wanted a cameo appearance in it. He thought it would be great if, while dining at the Cobalt Club, Lamont Cranston and Margot Lane pointed to Walter B. Gibson, a famous writer at a nearby table. This would at least allow Gibson a small bit of recognition and connection with his creation. The film changed scripters, producers and directors a number of times, and no one ever even thought to involve Gibson in the production to any degree. Gibson had figured that he would die before the release of the film; he was right.[16]

The pending movie featuring the Shadow was a constant stress to Gibson. It seems he was excited about it, but wanted them to do a good job at introducing the Shadow to a new generation. On February 6, 1981, Gibson received a letter from a friend reporting on the Shadow movie. He wrote how the movie writers "intend to botch the character." Due to the pending movie, all reprints of the Shadow were put on hold. Gibson was anxious to get more out. On March 22, 1984, he received a call stating that the "Universal [Studios'] lawyers gave 'go ahead' on Shadow books!!!"

On November 14 Gibson was visited by a friend, William Rauscher. "Bill brought along the 'Life size +' painting of The Shadow — copied by Woodbury artist from cover of 'Hidden Death' — Great!" The following day, Bill helped out around the house installing various items and hanging the Shadow painting over Gibson's bed. "Looks real weird!" admitted Gibson.

The cover of *Hidden Death*, September 1932 was always one of Gibson's favorite covers. He used to keep the original in a dark corner of his study: "It looked as though the Shadow was coming through a window." Gibson gave away all of the original cover paintings to friends, so he was delighted to have this reproduction that Rauscher had commissioned.

Although Gibson had once wanted nothing to do with the Shadow, he was enjoying the recognition now in his later years. Many people not only recognized Gibson as the creator of the Shadow, but often made *him* into the character. Gibson would often receive fan mail simply addressed: The Shadow, 12426 (his zip code). He would be recognized everywhere he went. Gibson loved to go out to eat and on Monday June 2, 1980, he had "a 9 P.M. dinner at the Capri, where the waitress was excited to learn I was the Shadow."

But in his 70s and 80s Gibson enjoyed other pursuits besides magic and literature. Being a historian and living in a historic house in Eddyville that overlooked Rondout Creek, Gibson became curious about the creek and its history as a canal. He joined the Delaware and Hudson Canal Historical Society founded by John Novi and his wife Rosalou, and he became involved with cleaning up and restoring the canal. The canal was originally built to transport coal from Pennsylvania into New York City. The idea for this canal was conceived

Gibson's favorite painting of the Shadow rendered in oil by artist Sally Bouchard from a cover of *The Shadow Magazine.* Gibson liked to keep it in this dark corner of his Eddyville, New York, home so it looked as if the Shadow was coming in the window. Photograph by Edwin E. Fitchett.

by Maurice and William Wurts who owned the coal mines in Pennsylvania. The D&H Canal Company was born in the spring of 1823 and soon it hired Benjamin Wright, chief engineer of the Erie Canal, to survey the land for the construction. The canal stretched 108 miles from Honesdale, Pennsylvania, along the Delaware River and ended at Rondout Creek in Eddyville, New York, and was in full operation from October 1828 until November 1898. The canal in some places is as wide as 32–36 feet at the water line and 24 feet wide at the bottom; it features 137 coach bridges, 110 locks and some aqueducts, or bridges that carry the canal over waterways. Some of the larger aqueducts are located at Lackawaxen, Delaware, Neversink, and High Falls. A towpath parallels the canal on one side where horses walked while towing a barge. Many citizens thank this canal for populating their towns. The canal provided a faster transportation than the traditional horse and mule-drawn carts.[17]

In Eddyville coal would be unloaded on a 14-acre man-made island in Rondout Creek. Completed in 1848, the "Island Dock," as it was known, was used to store the coal. Up to 95% of the coal that was transported along the canal was stored in Rondout.[18] The coal would then be transported to New York City, Albany and Boston. Furthermore, the barges were weighed on huge scales in Eddyville before unloading in order to determine the captains' pay.

Eddyville was also one of the sites where boats for the canal were constructed. The first boats held about 10 tons; by the 1850s some boats were able to hold up to 136 tons and traveled 3–5 miles per hour. These larger boats could travel up the canal and move directly down the Hudson River to New York which eliminated the need to unload at Rondout, thus saving money.

The canal began carrying passengers in 1829 for a five-cent-a-mile fare. This venture ended in 1851. Raw products, other than coal, were also transported via the canal. Such products included pressed hay, timber and cotton. Molasses, sugar, salt and liquor were even transported. The canal was quite successful, reaching its peak year for transportation of anthracite in 1872 at 29 million tons, and the D&H Canal Company became quite wealthy. But the canal eventually had to be abandoned when faster and cheaper modes of transportation appeared, such as the railroad. Furthermore, the demand for coal was not constant and the canal could only run during the warmer seasons. In November 1898, boat #1107 was the last to travel from Honesdale to Rondout. The lower end of the canal was used to transport cement up until July 26, 1901.[19]

Gibson was well known and well respected within the society. He would often perform magic shows at various functions. In December 1970, Gibson became the assistant editor of *Then & Now*, the bulletin of the society. At the 5th annual meeting of the society, on March 28, 1971, he ran for and was elected president of the society. The following year on March 26, 1972, at the annual meeting Gibson was again nominated and elected president for a second term. During this meeting the members participated in a game in which they had to answer questions about slides they were viewing. Kay Wagenfohr and Paul Sturges both won the game and received autographed copies of books by Walter and Litzka Gibson. Another member, Milt Wagenfohr, who took photographs for the *D&H Bulletin*, supplied the photographs for Gibson's book *The Complete Illustrated Book of Card Magic* published by Doubleday in 1969.[20]

Under Gibson's presidency the D&H Society established a Museum in April 1971 and celebrated its grand opening on July 17, 1971. On Sunday, March 25, 1973, at High Falls FireHouse, Gibson retired as president of the D&H Canal Society, only to become vice president for the next year. Litzka had served as a D&H trustee from 1973. Gibson continued the *Bulletin* for some time; in 1974 he was attempting to get someone else to take it over. In 1975 the D&H Society was worried about raising more funds for the opening of a new museum. Gibson worked with Sid Radner to make a picture of Houdini available to be used as a fundraiser. The plans were under way until October 1975 when Gibson found "they already had paid off the new museum. Good!" The Canal Museum was dedicated at 2:00 P.M. on Sunday, May 30, 1976, at High Falls.

On Sunday, October 2, 1977, Gibson reported: "Learned that Canal Museum is only opened on week-ends so it won't do for organizing the new S.A.M. Assembly that they want to name after me." The Society of American Magicians, Assembly #118, in Nashua, New Hampshire, bore Walter Gibson's name for years thanks to his nephew Wendel who lived there. The assembly currently holds both uncle and nephew's names in memory of their equal contribution to magic history.

Gibson still continued to be busy with lecturing at conventions. He often continued to speak at the Pulpcon annual conventions, and was honored by mystery conventions across the nation. He was honored by Murder Ink, an organization for crime and mystery novel lovers, at the Mohonk Mountain House in upstate New York. During his lecture there, Gibson showed a movie based on the Shadow, performed a half-hour magic show, and of course spoke on the hundreds of books he had authored.[21]

At Gibson's college reunion in 1977, he was initiated into the Mu Chapter of Delta Kappa Epsilon during homecoming weekend. Gibson had been involved with DKE for years through friends and had given financial assistance. In fact, after a visit to DKE in September 1975, where Gibson dined and learned songs, a friend, Bill Wilson, thought Gibson should become an honorary member

A 1979 oil portrait of Gibson by Sally Bouchard, commissioned by William V. Rauscher and now housed in Ray Goulet's Mini Museum of Magic in Watertown, Massachusetts. From the collection of William V. Rauscher.

of DKE: "that would be the day!" wrote Gibson on September 22, 1975. In the newsletter *Yon Clarion Bell* in January 1978 an article reports:

> One of the biggest events in DKE history took place when Mu initiated writer-magician Walter B. Gibson into the Mystic Circle on the eve of the 1977 Homecoming.... Brother Gibson was led up the front walk in the rain. Once inside he was blindfolded for the age-old ceremony. The magician seemed to be surprised and excited throughout the initiation which was somewhat doctored for the older participant, but well planned and executed by the Brotherhood.... Bro. Gibson was extremely pleased over the whole thing. It was a thrill he will treasure for the rest of his life, and it fulfilled a life-long dream of his Colgate classmates.[22]

At the DKE house, Gibson enthusiastically shared his magical mysteries with alumni and friends. The crowd enjoyed Gibson's magic so much that he continued to perform and even teach some card tricks throughout the evening after a dinner given in his honor. Bob Dawson wrote in the *Colgate Maroon*, "At the age of 80, Walter Gibson is still the showman he was at his undergraduate debut as a magician with the Colgate Glee Club."[23]

Gibson loved Colgate and often returned to visit. On one visit on September 15, 1976, he wrote: "Strolled around campus like old times & sat in balcony in Chapel watching Kreskin work on platform where I did my magic with Glee Club in 1919."

Throughout his life, Gibson was modest about his accomplishments. His work was something he enjoyed and not something for which he expected admiration. In fact on September 26, 1979, he pondered: "D[ouble]day interested in my memoirs—but why?" On September 29, he continued: "So Litzka & [I] talked over other prospects—& wound up in a super-dilemma. I'm a 'somebody' & she is a 'nobody'—tho' the opposite is *really* the case!"

By 1980, at 83 years old, it seemed Gibson had actually begun to slow down, although he was still quite busy by average standards. He blamed his lower productivity on watching too much television and would get angry at himself when he wasted a day. As the 1980s drew on Gibson found himself choosing relaxing in front of the television, watching a sports game, over doing work.

On June 15, 1981, Litzka took a fall and had to be rushed to the hospital by ambulance. This fall worried Gibson, for Litzka was his life. He visited her every day and still maintained a rather intense work schedule. Litzka had injured her back and was suffering frequent nosebleeds during her stay at the hospital. Litzka returned home on Saturday, June 27th. The housekeeper, Mrs. Walter, had stayed over the night before in order to receive Litzka since Gibson would be leaving for a trip that morning and returning on the 29th. When Gibson returned he found his wife slowly making it around with the aid of a walker. Gibson would wait on her at the sound of a big bell. Litzka's health slowly improved; her nose would bleed now and then, often warranting a visit to the doctor's office, but there was nothing too seriously wrong. Litzka's first real trip out of the house was on August 8th, when the couple dined at the Landmark.

Gibson was very concerned over Litzka's health. He depended on her help in many ways, including driving him around. After this incident, he reported every little cold and pain which Litzka suffered. The two were now both well into their 80s and Gibson knew he was getting old and would often reflect on the past, noting birthdays in his diary of his brothers and friends of long ago.

December 2, 1981, Gibson simply reported: "Eyes dimming … [*sic*]" In 1980 the idea arose of Gibson writing his memoirs, yet he was reluctant to do so. "Should I do my memoirs—rather than anything else?" he wrote on January 9th, hesitant to admit that his life was near an end. He still had other projects in mind, and current projects on which he was working. But by June and July Gibson was enthusiastically working on a memoir. He struggled through, attempting to write something, but it didn't work out well. Now in 1982, he was desperately fighting to write an account of his life. Yet his health often got in the way. "My hands felt wiggly & cramped, tho' typing seems to help them," he wrote on May 17, 1982. His "tired" eyes often prevented him from work. By December 1982 Gibson had his "first batch of memoirs [which] totaled 40 pages—maybe too long—or too short—which?"

He still struggled to write. On December 19, 1982, Gibson found it "amazing how I work well for a while—then flop completely—Wow!!" By December 1983 Gibson was not feeling well in general and his work slowed down, though it did not ever

Three generations of the Gibson men—Gibson's son, Robert, on the left, Gibson's grandson, Robert Jr., in the center, and Walter himself on the right—taken in the early 1980s in front of Gibson's Eddyville, New York, home. From the collection of Robert Gibson.

stop for any length of time. He always was working; he always was planning the next project. On January 29, 1983, he wrote, "So much happens that I can't keep it straight." In June 1984 he greatly slowed down. After a brief stay in the hospital, he wrote on June 27, "No use in trying to keep up on data. I'm just taking things as they come along…. [sic]" Yet throughout, he always kept his sense of humor.

During these latter years spent in Eddyville, Litzka and Gibson depended solely on Gibson's writing for funds on which to live. It was always a big deal to Gibson when he received a check in the mail from a publisher. He often noted such in his diaries. Because their daily lives depended on these checks, Litzka often felt angry when Gibson would accept a writing project for a small advance. Yet this was Gibson's way: he had little business sense, but simply wrote for the pure enjoyment of writing. On August 29, 1982, he dined at the Tea Garden with a few friends. This Chinese restaurant gave Gibson what he claimed to be a significant fortune cookie. He included the fortune in his diary; it read: "Your inclination to speak and act before you think may seem to get you into trouble at times." This could very well relate to his acceptance of so many writing projects for such little financial reward.

The year 1983 marks a severe decline in Gibson's physical health, yet his mental abilities throughout remained intact. He was in and out of the hospital for cardiac inefficiencies. Fortunately, Gibson had a good friend, Dr. Lew Neporent, who not only was his physician, but also a magician. Many times Dr. Neporent would come to the house to check Gibson and then the two would share card tricks. In January Gibson began complaining that his jaw creaked on the right side when he chewed. In May of the same year, he accompanied Litzka to her appointment with their doctor, figuring the doctor may be able to deduce the cause of his shortness of breath when climbing the stairs. The doctor checked Gibson first and discovered some heart palpitations that concerned him, and he checked his elderly patient into Benedictine hospital that same day, May 26th. Gibson wrote: "I was met by nurse with a wheelchair — rolled to intensive care dept — put to bed, given tests &c — with nurse on constant call." The following day Gibson continued:

> Slept well in a big crib much like earlier trip to hospital [in 1979]. I was given an oxygen breather — a pumping device — an intravenus [sic] attachment &c — nurses on job during night — by morning nicely settled…. [sic] In fact — during Thurs. P.M. they'd talked about The Shadow, so Litzka bro't a Scrap book to show them. During the day — which was monotonous at first — I was transferred to a room in another sector — before that Sister Mary Charles stopped by. She was going up to see Cynthia Lowry. Said she'd give her my regards.

The following day, Saturday, May 28, Gibson was moved to another room with a Bill Shunk (relative of the Shunks of Philadelphia that Gibson seemed to know). The two roommates relaxed and watched baseball on the television. The next day Gibson continued to relax. The big day's event Gibson reported in his diary: "Today they gave me a heavy recorder device — which I have to carry when I walk around — as I'm wired to it."

Then on Monday, May 30, 1983, Gibson recorded the following amusing incident:

> Last night I put the device on table & slept facing it (toward right). Later, woke up & shifted it to my left (on bed). Woke again, all snarled in the wiring which had been pinned to my gown — got it loose & the gown came off with it. Finally rang for nurse who finally got me rewired & re gowned .... [*sic*] This morning, Bill packed up & left — soon after, Litzka arrived & I packed up & left.

The day after Gibson's return from the hospital he was back to work. He began making calls and started writing, but he paced himself, taking everything "s-l-o-w-l-y."

In the ensuing weeks, Gibson's work progressed at a slow but steady pace. He grew tired easily. The month of July was marked by coughing fits and hernia problems. He got little sleep for the cough would wake him at night. On Wednesday, July 13, he had been kept up the previous night with coughing fits and constipation, so he saw his doctor in the morning. The doctor immediately sent Gibson to Benedictine Hospital. Litzka drove him over and he was admitted. People at the hospital recognized him. He wrote: "Other people recognized me — tho't it was great, my making the *Freeman* on Monday & The Benedictine on Wednesday.... [*sic*]" The hospital had Gibson on a diet of liquid foods, allowing him to eat more solid foods on Friday. By Saturday he felt that he was better and could leave, yet his doctor insisted he stay. Litzka agreed that the finances were in order and that he should stay. On Sunday Gibson "told Bruno [his roommate] that we'd see him ... I said good-bye to other inmates—" On this day, Gibson continued: "Home again & glad!!! But still wondering what if I'd stayed! I'd like to plan it. & try it." Gibson took some pills to ease his cough at home, yet by August 6 the pills didn't seem to be working, "So Litzka phoned Lew's [the doctor's] emergency number —*and*—" The following day he completed the sentence: "Single room stay at hospital until Aug 13."

Upon the advice of a dietician, Gibson began eating well and doing well. He napped frequently and got to work gradually. By September 13 he was "Up & at'em — felt 10 to 20 yrs younger — let's say '10' so I have the 'spirit of 76'—" In October Gibson had acquired a fever and found himself back in the hospital. It was a minor infection, "if anything," Gibson wrote. But while in the hospital his son Robert and family came to visit him and Gibson got to meet his great-grandchildren.

In December Gibson went to the eye doctor to find that his cataracts were getting gradually worse. The chills that had brought him to the hospital the last time continued to haunt him, yet Gibson attempted to exorcise them himself with extra clothes and blankets. In 1984 his appetite was dwindling, along with his weight. In January he weighed 200 lbs, yet by April he was down to 186. Gibson's eyes continued to bother him and would tire quickly when he was reading, which made work more difficult. In June 1984 he wrote:

> On Thurs, June 14, I woke with shifting abdominal pains, so I called Lew, who got me to the hospital where Dr. Wang (Chinese surgeon) checked me & said operation was needed — regardless of "anesthetic risk" which we had purposely avoided during

several years ... [*sic*] so on 14th I had the op — never even realized I'd had an anesthetic — just was wondering when it would begin — only to find it had been done. Instead of a flip-flop "truss" that I'd been wearing night & day — I now had a solid bandage for 4 or 5 days — keeping me in fine shape ... didn't do any walking for a while. So felt somewhat shaky when I finally got into action. Ate sparingly for a while — then Dr. Wang switched me from solid to light bandage & I became more active ... end of week ... bandage itself was removed.... Made gradual walks out in hall with nurse — but no long strolls like last year. Litzka handled letters & other data — Losing weight day by day!!! ...Everything nice & comfy but monotonous.

Gibson's weight decreased even further to 161 pounds which he was afraid was too low. When he returned home Litzka was having a problem with a cough too. Gibson wrote on June 24, "Litzka & I are settling down ... in our Palais des Invalades [*sic*]."

On August 16, 1984, Gibson was back in the hospital with pneumonia. While in the hospital, Litzka brought over the Americana project which Gibson and she finished and sent out to the publisher who received it on the 23rd. Gibson's weight had now dropped to 156 pounds. At home he worked slowly and crawled back into his usual phone routines.

On October 17, 1984, Gibson awoke with chest pressure and Dr. Lew Neporent sent him back into the hospital for tests. Gibson was hooked to a heart monitor and his lungs were also scanned. By October 21st, he was reporting having bad chills, and at 1 A.M. on that date he was switched to the intensive care unit, where he "had two nurses on instant call by tapping a bell. I was wired, piped & otherwise equipped, with a big screen flashing 'heart figures' alongside of the crib. I termed it my 'Dow Jones report'...." After a few days Gibson was moved out of the intensive care unit. On October 29th he wrote, "it's very relaxing with *nothing* to worry over." Amazingly here lies Gibson, struggling with his health at 85 years old, yet he keeps his sense of humor. His mind is still that of a child even though his body is giving out on him. On Halloween Gibson reported the following:

Walter Gibson sits in front of his typewriter in his eighties, his productive mind still creating after all those years. Photograph by Robert Gibson.

Parade! ...It was staged by Metro Life. They had a "costume lunch" & then paraded thru the hospital, peering into our rooms with weird faces — about 40 of them. On their way out, I slid into a gown, put on an oxygen mask & joined them. Nurses had a big laugh....

Gibson returned home on November 2nd.

Despite his declining health in the early eighties, Gibson busily worked on his memoirs in 1983. His writing schedule remained continuous and hectic as always; he was working on a number of projects all at once. One day he reported that he worked on a project all day and then quit in the evening, only to wake up at 3 in the morning to finish it by 6 A.M. In 1984 his writing continued at odd hours, which was similar to his style in the early years. He worked diligently on many projects, yet many were getting difficult. His memoirs were getting "too complex" yet he still struggled through them day after day. The work piled up, and it angered him that he could not keep up with it.

In 1984 Gibson was having difficulty writing. He reverted to dictating many projects, including his memoirs. He thought his memoirs were important, for his publisher kept requesting them, but he found other projects to take precedence. By December 21, 1984, though, the overwork was taking its toll. Gibson wrote: "Trying to catch up with things is becoming very difficult — Must find a way to make work easier for both Litzka & myself."

Gibson's writing continued and his magic continued; he often performed when he gave lectures, and always demonstrated his manipulations to friends. In 1977 a reporter wrote:

> After almost seven decades of trial and error, Gibson has, as you might expect, gotten his act together. Cards disappear and then reappear across the room; a yolk comes out of an eggshell where a cloth had just been stuffed, and torn paper is made whole at the magician's command. For the most part, the tricks are no more unusual than those people are used to seeing, but Gibson's performance is flawless and smooth, and that is what impresses people.[24]

Business, business, business. On May 10, 1983, Gibson wrote: "Another call re Anne Bonney [book for a movie] — all sorts of questions — who's my lawyer? My agent? In 60 yrs. of writing I've dealt with both but never had one in a full sense. Anyway, I named Mike Todd & Nat Sobel."

Projects piled up. Gibson didn't know what to do. He admitted to a close friend, William Rauscher, one evening: "'I don't know whether to turn left or right.... And I had a tiff with Litzka and I don't think I'm going to get my cocoa tonight at 3 A.M.'"[25] His body was old, but Gibson's mind stayed young.

In the 1970s, Will Murray observed Gibson:

> He projects, rather, the image of a prosperous and lately retired banker who, after a long career, is at leisure and looking forward to spending time with his grandchildren. He is a bit rotund; his hair is a crisp, unshadowed white; his voice is deep and slightly hoarse; and, though 79, he is strikingly vital. But his hands give him away; they are never still. These are the hands of a man whose energies and abilities are boundless and will not rest. The same hands that used to emerge bloodied after a daylong stint at the typewriter, are still nimble enough to perform dazzling feats of magic. The truth is that Walter Gibson is more than a legend. He is a legend who, in turn, has created a legend — the legend of the Shadow.[26]

A publicity shot of Gibson, copies of which he often signed for friends. This particular photograph is signed: "To Bob Lewis 'The Shadow Knows' says Walter B. Gibson."— Chicago May 25, 1974. From the collection of William V. Rauscher.

Will Murray commissioned Gibson to write what would become the final Shadow novel. Due to Gibson's poor health, Murray did not put a deadline on this project. Murray waited and waited for this novel with no result. He finally was forced to impose a deadline, and Gibson delivered the manuscript on that exact day. Being a newspaper man, deadlines were important to Gibson and he needed them, yet the work soon became nearly overwhelming. Will Murray truly enjoyed Gibson's company and conversation. "Walter was a joy to know. Friendly, direct, he was the only person I ever met who could talk about himself for hours on end and not seem egotistical or boring."[27] Many can attest to the truthfulness of that statement.

William Rauscher recalls that "Walter had a sense of urgency about getting things done. Accomplishment took precedence. He was dominated by the need to be productive."[28] He continues, "The real Walter was a day-to-day man of accomplishment. He was a man who lived in a world of inner visual situations that could be emptied by a written word. The practical side of Walter was a man who did not function in making repairs, building, cooking or thinking about where he put his coat. He once said, 'I do not hammer nails. I can not put up storm windows. If I mess up my hands, I am in real trouble. They have to be able to write and to type.'"[29] Rauscher provided the following quote from Gibson: "'I live in positives. Time does not mean anything to me. I can be awake and still think I am talking with Houdini. It is all so real to me.'"[30] Rauscher goes on: "In 1984 he said, 'Eighty years ago I walked up the steps to class in Chestnut Hill Academy. You know what I want to do, Bill? I want to walk up those steps again and into that same classroom and say, "Boys, here I am after 80 years, back again." Oh, Bill, there is so much I want to do.'"[31] It seems to be the Gibson family way to live a long life of vitality. Upon visiting his elderly sister, Gibson was confronted with the question, "'Well, Walter, when are you going to get a haircut?'" "They spoke in a youthful way," remembers Rauscher who accompanied Gibson on this visit.[32]

Gibson's life writing the Shadow soon turned into shadows itself as his eyesight continually declined. At one time Will Murray observed Gibson signing his signature of the double x combining Walter Gibson and Maxwell Grant in one signature.

As he wrote he lost his place and was unable to complete the signature.[33] It was very difficult for Gibson to give into the physical ills of his body. His mind still ran fast and furious with ideas, yet he physically could not keep up with them. There was so much Gibson still wanted to do when he was well into his eighties:

> "I have to start a magazine." "I have to go to New York to see some people at Doubleday." "I should write the Blackstone story." "I have to get my nephew, Wendel, to take me to the Peddie School reunion." "Litzka and I have to do something about the Raymond stuff." "They want me to speak in Chicago." And then, "My hands won't type." "My eyes are going." "I can't go upstairs." "I have never known such frustration as not being able to do something." "I don't need a nurse, I need a secretary."[34]

On November 7, 1985, Gibson suffered a second stroke and was hospitalized at Benedictine. His first stroke occurred in 1978 and left him shaky for a while, but he recovered nonetheless. Yet this stroke was more severe. It took away Gibson's vision and rendered him speechless. Friends report that despite such discomfort he was still quite alert.

Walter Gibson's jolly spirit and child-like charm departed this world on a Friday, December 6, 1985, at 5 A.M.: appropriately enough, St. Nicholas Day. He died at Benedictine Hospital in Kingston, New York. Rauscher states that "St. Nicholas Day, December 6, was a memorable day for Walter to have left this world. He was a kind of St. Nicholas in that he was somewhat childlike, generous, great company, conservative, sharing, and easy to love. Walter is a person many will miss and always remember. He was a wonderful friend."[35] He once told William Rauscher: "'Bill, I would like to live to be 100 years old so Willard Scott could mention it on the Today Show, but then again, I think I might like to go out on Halley's Comet like Mark Twain.'"[36]

With no more light, even the shadow fades to obscurity.

Afterword

Rauscher remembers that "Gibson once said he could offer $10,000 for anyone who would do a complete bibliography and they would never collect, because even he couldn't remember everything he had written."[1] Despite Gibson's long literary career, he left the world as he entered it: penniless. Even well into his seventies, Gibson would often do projects for little or no money with the thought that they would lead to good contacts in the future. Saving money was out of the question, for that meant one did not have confidence in one's ability to be productive. During the Depression, Gibson was making around $20,000 a year, which must be equivalent to at least a quarter of a million dollars, speculates Robert Gibson. If he had invested one or two thousand dollars a year "in almost any Goddamn stock that existed," protested Robert, "by his 80s [he] would have certainly been worth a couple of million dollars."[2]

Will Murray remembered Gibson:

> I thought Walter would live to be a hundred years old. At least. Why not? He deserved it. He had a lot of plans. He was always talking new projects. He could have lived off reprints of his old material forever if he got them all back in print. But he wanted to write new stuff, too.[3]

Murray remembers that Gibson, in his final months, was obsessed with writing a new Shadow novel. He was thrilled about the pending movie project that would bring the Shadow to a new generation. He began to dig through his old notes. A Shadow novel would be perfect now, for Gibson could not do much research due to his failing eyesight. Murray reported that Gibson considered doing a fifth Shiwan Khan novel or possibly pitting another villain like the Cobra or the Python against the Shadow. With no publisher interest in the project, Gibson began writing. He pounded away at the keys and waded through his memories. He only completed a couple of chapters. He could not see the keys to type well, which rendered the manuscript nearly unreadable. Will Murray added that we do not need another Shadow novel, but rather "what the world really needs is another Walter B. Gibson."[4]

Between Gibson's frantic attempts to complete a Shadow novel he also dove into his memoirs. Yet he never completed them before he died. He had turned to video-tape to finish his memoirs, having recorded what Litzka called a "wonderful tape" the night prior to his stroke.

The day he died Gibson was cremated. Murray wrote that there was "no funeral, no wake, no last chance to say goodbye."[5] He is buried in Block D, Section 2, Lot 110, Montrepose Cemetery, Kingston, New York. A memorial service was held in Gibson's memory at St. John's Episcopal Church at 207 Albany Avenue in Kingston, New York, on Saturday, January 11, 1986. The service began at 2 o'clock in the afternoon and was conducted by the Reverend Canon William V. Rauscher, rector of Christ Episcopal Church in Woodbury, New Jersey, and the Reverend Canon Robert J. Lewis, associate of St. Mary's Church, chaplain and lecturer of St. Mary's Hall-Doane Academy in Burlington, New Jersey. The memorial presentations were given

by: William W. Wilson, fraternity brother and classmate of the class of 1920 of Colgate University; Ferris Mack, retired senior editor of Doubleday & Co.; and John Nanovic, retired editor of Street & Smith publications. Robert Gibson recalls Nanovic speaking about how typical authors present their manuscripts: carefully packaged in a box and often walked in personally. Not so with Walter Gibson. Robert remembers Nanovic saying:

"I would receive, in the general mail, a box, that maybe it was an old laundry box, and it had a pile of papers that had all been thrown in there. They weren't even in proper order: Some of them were upside-down. It was thrown in there like it was a trash basket," he said. That was the way he would get the Shadow manuscripts. He said there was no author he ever knew of it was as though, "Christ, I'm done with this get the Goddamn thing out of here!"[6]

The Gibson gravesite in Montrepose Cemetery, Kingston, New York, Block D, Section 2, Lot 110. Photograph by William V. Rauscher.

Following the presentations and after a brief organ interlude where organist Deborah Bright played "Now Thank We All Our God" by J. S. Bach, the presentations continued with Father Cyprian, O.F.M. of the Capuchin Friary in Garrison, New York, and chaplain of the Society of American Magicians; John Henry Grossman, M.D., magic historian and president of the Magic Collectors Association of America, and Morris N. Young, M.D., literary associate and co-author of Gibson. Prayers of commendation followed along with the blessing and finally a postlude: "For All the Saints" by R. Vaughan Williams. The more than 125 friends and family members from around the country who attended the service all remembered the "remarkable interest" Gibson took in every person he met and every thing he did. "But mostly," reported R.J. Kelly in the *Freeman* on January 12, 1986, "his friends remember Gibson as a storyteller whose remarkable memory for long-past details flowed in the pages of a manuscript, over a cocktail or on the telephone."[7] The memorial card at the service read as follows:

In Loving Memory of
Walter B. Gibson
Man of Letters and Literature
September 12, 1897
December 6, 1985

Twenty-third Psalm

The Lord is my shepherd; I shall not want. He maketh me to lie down in green pastures: He leadeth me beside the still waters. He restoreth my soul; He leadeth me in the paths of righteousness for His name's sake. Yea, though I walk through the valley of the shadow of death, I will fear no evil; for thou art with me; thy rod and thy staff they comfort me. Thou preparest a table before me in the presence of mine enemies; thou anointest my head with oil; my cup runneth over. Surely goodness and mercy shall follow me all the days of my life; and I will dwell in the house of the Lord forever.

Gibson was survived by his wife Litzka, his son, Dr. Robert W. Gibson, three grandchildren, and two great-grandchildren.

The Shadow movie finally opened on July 1, 1994. It was a Universal Pictures production with a rating of PG-13 due to language, sensuality and violence. Twelve years in the making, *The Shadow* was directed by Russell Mulcahy (*Highlander*) and produced by Martin Bregman, Willi Baer and Michael S. Bregman. It cost a reported $45 million yet did not receive many rave reviews. Many compared it to the Batman movies calling it a "lavish *Batman* wanna-be..."[8] and a "limp jump onto the 'Batman' bandwagon" when in reality, ironically, the Shadow character was the inspiration for the creation of Batman. One critic wrote:

"The Shadow" shows what can happen when you overdress pulp. You wind up with something gorgeous and suffocated, bejeweled trash floundering in its own over-splendid stuffings.... The people who made "The Shadow", despite superficial fealty to their source — the Walter Gibson pulp magazine novels, radio programs and movie serials— don't show much feel for what makes pulp classics work: the speed and cheapness, the fact that the pulps were churned out so swiftly that most self-censorship blocks go down and the stories serve up raw symbolism, raw super-ego, raw emotions.[9]

Producer Martin Bregman wanted the right scriptwriter for the job. David Koepp, who worked on writing the screenplay for *Jurassic Park*, was hired to write the script. He drew out the characters from the radio programs and the pulp magazines. The cast includes Alec Baldwin as Lamont Cranston and the Shadow, John Lone as Shiwan Khan, Penelope Ann Miller as Margot Lane, Peter Boyle as Moe Shrevnitz, Ian McKellen as Reinhardt Lane, Tim Curry as Farley Claymore, and Jonathan Winters as Police Commissioner Wainwright Barth.[10]

Alec Baldwin, at age 36, played the dual role of the Shadow and Lamont Cranston receiving a reported $2 million for the role. Baldwin explained that he enjoyed making the movie and would do a sequel of it if desired. Baldwin took the role of the Shadow because, as he said, "'I wanted to do a movie you can bring kids to. I think that's an obligation today.... [*sic*] My wife [Kim Basinger] to this day has had such a tremendous response from kids who saw *Batman*.'"[11] Baldwin reflected on the premise of the movie and stated that *The Shadow* "'had to be played for laughs.... [*sic*] the one hope we had to distinguish it from other superhero things was to make it funnier.'"[12] Sadly this contributed to the movie's downfall. The Shadow was never a funny character, or in many funny situations. The movie itself gave this author the impression of the recent *Dick Tracy* movie starring Warren Beatty. In *The Shadow* there was a touch of fantasy, and unreality that Gibson never put into his stories. Gibson created this character and his exploits to all be within the realm of reality. The Shadow *is* real and should be captured this way on film. The Shadow has such a glorious potential for television and movies if he were only treated properly, basing him on Gibson's Shadow. As Gibson once said, "'Because of my heavy use of magic and visual illusion, the novels are *ideally* suited for movies or television.'"[13] There are two hundred and eighty some scripts just waiting for the right eyes to envision their full potential on the big screen.

Just prior to the movie's unveiling, Robert hired, on Litzka's behalf, some attorneys who were experts on copyright law. Robert had understood that often when publishing houses contracted out for an author to do some writing for them, the rights could revert back to the author. The attorneys were enthusiastic about researching into the case about the actual creator of the Shadow. They worked diligently and ultimately found that Walter Gibson had filed a suit himself. Robert assumes that his father must have been desperate for money at the time for he had settled the suit for $20,000, relinquishing all rights to the Shadow. Robert had spent thousands in attorney fees to unearth this bitter truth. Yet Robert's attorneys felt it was not right that after writing 283 novels developing the character of the Shadow that Walter Gibson could not claim he was the creator. The attorneys pursued the producers of the movie, free of charge, insisting that they acknowledge Gibson as the creator. At the end of the movie they credit Gibson as the creator of the Shadow.

The release of the Shadow movie was followed by the flooding of the market with over 100 Shadow products, from toys, to trading cards, to T-shirts. That same year *The Shadow* radio program was still heard on 115 stations around the country.[14] The Shadow lives again, and shall continue to haunt the hearts of villains for years to come.

After Gibson's death, a strong connection to the history of the golden years of magic had passed. Litzka remained devoted to Raymond and Gibson's memories, and still hoped that the Raymond collection would be displayed in a museum. Her love of these magical men drove Litzka into a slight paranoia when it came to their possessions. She had devoted her life to their memories and wanted these moments to live on. She did begin to take bids from collectors for the equipment, yet none was ever high enough for her to agree to part with these crates full of memories of her past. There were many more bids through the years, including a bid for select items by David Copperfield for $125,000, yet Litzka wanted the collection to remain together and was asking $250,000. One collaboration of collectors, David Baldwin, Henry Muller and Sidney Radner, greatly intrigued Litzka. They offered $225,000 for, what was now being called, the Raymond/Gibson collection. Muller wanted to add this collection to his Houdini collection housed in the Houdini Museum in Niagara Falls, Canada. Swept away by the actualization of her museum dreams, Litzka agreed to the price.

Plans changed and the Raymond/Gibson collection never made it to the museum. Rather Muller and Radner chose to combine some of the Houdini collection with the Raymond/Gibson one to sell it at auction, yet such a dream literally went up in smoke when a fire on April 30, 1995, destroyed much of the Houdini collection. The grand auction that the two had planned was scaled down and they received approximately $32,000 for the pulp magazines and $50,000 for the Raymond lithographs.[15]

The two held a second auction on November 15, 1999, in Los Angeles at Butterfield & Butterfield; it was presented as the "Houdini Magical Hall of Fame and Other Magic Memorabilia." The auction, featuring the remaining two-thirds of the museum that was not damaged in the 1995 fire, displayed lots of the illusions from the Raymond show and Raymond's personal papers, as well as many rare books and magazines from Walter Gibson's personal library and his own personal papers and collections of posters and magic. Not all of the lots from Gibson's estate were magical. There were also a number of personal photographs and even a complete collection of the Shadow in forty-four bound volumes.[16]

At one time Gibson said to Rauscher, "'Bill, some day when they clean out this house, they will find things they never knew existed.'"[17] This was certainly true, for in March 1996, an auctioneer named Russ Carlson paid Litzka $2,500 to simply remove the incidentals from the house. Only some miscellaneous books, papers and furniture remained, so Litzka quickly accepted this offer. The auctioneer, along with Jay Werbalowsky of JMW Auction Service, packaged and sold the contents of the house on April 16, 1996, in Kingston, New York. Over 700 lots of Gibson material encompassing three hotel ballrooms were auctioned to bidders. Seven copies of *The*

Gibson's pine writing desk, along with the typewriter and photograph of a youthful Gibson, sold for $4,510 at an auction in Kingston, New York, held by JMW Auction Service on April 16, 1996. The solid oak swivel chair that Gibson used with the desk sold separately for $385. Photograph by Gene Utz. Copyright 1997 Maine Antique Digest.

Shadow Comics sold for $1,540. A lot which featured Gibson's pine wood desk that a carpenter had built for him during the construction of his cabin in Gray, Maine, the desk he used to write the Shadow on, was up for bid along with an 8 × 10 photograph of Gibson in his younger days, and the typewriter that occupied the desk when it was removed from the Eddyville home. The bidding started out "with a reluctant $100 bid." Slowly the bids increased to the selling price of a dramatic $4,510. Radio scripts were sold; one 1934 Shadow script sold for $2,200. Some lots held stacks of 15 to 40 magazines featuring Gibson's writings and sold from $44 to as high as $187 per lot. Two 1930 Shadow Movies Club pins, originally given away with a charge of 10 cents for postage, were sold for $2,420. Some Raymond items also sold at the auction. For example, ten sheets of Raymond's sheet music sold for $852.50; a 20 foot by 30 foot black silk backdrop, embroidered in an Oriental design, raised $660. In addition magazines and books collected for personal and research purposes all sold. The auction brought the auctioneer in excess of $54,000; Litzka received nothing else from the auction except for the $2,500 she sold the items to the auctioneer for. Rauscher states that "The physical remains of Raymond's and Gibson's life work had finally been awakened from a long sleep and were now in the hands of several people. These possessions had been like a bank account that earned no interest for the owners, who unfortunately died without funds. If their value had been appreciated

Frank Hamilton commemorates the magical life of Walter B. Gibson. Paper and ink illustration by Frank Hamilton.

and exploited, they could have earned more than Raymond and Gibson ever imagined."[18]

Litzka adored the Eddyville home in which she and Gibson had built a life together. She did not want to leave it, yet age was taking its toll on her and she eventually retired to the Hudson Valley Senior Citizens Home in Kingston. After suffering a fall, she moved to the Kingston Hospital, eventually moving into a nursing home, Ferncliff, outside of Kingston. Litzka's good friend Gertrude Reer, who had power of attorney, requested that Litzka move closer to her. Litzka moved to the Golden Hill Infirmary in Kingston.

Litzka died on May 11, 1996. The Reverend Canon William V. Rauscher conducted her memorial service on May 25. Twenty-three of her friends and family were in attendance. She is buried in Montrepose Cemetery in Kingston, New York, with two of her loves: China Boy and Walter B. Gibson. The Eddyville house sold that summer.

Throughout Gibson's life he had an obsession: an obsession to be productive. He sought neither fortune nor fame, but the genuine feeling of accomplishment and to leave something for the world. He left plenty. Friends will always remember his timeless stories; their conversations being preserved in the mind forever. Gibson has waltzed in and out of the shadows for many generations, and now he remains in the light, casting a glorious shadow onto his past. On January 1, 1918, at 1 A.M., Gibson concluded the foreword to his diary as such:

> And may my hopes; my ambitions; my reputation; my career, be remembered among those — for better or — for worse.

They will be remembered for better. The Shadow knows!

Appendix I

Alfred Gibson's Account of the Lincoln Conspiracy Trials

In the late 1920s, Walter Gibson's father, Alfred Gibson, was noted to be the last surviving person who was present during the Lincoln conspiracy trials. As a result of such a noteworthy position he wrote out his memories of the occasion. In the *Evening Public Ledger* of Philadelphia, on October 7, 1927, and in the article "The Lincoln Conspirators" of April 24, 1928, Alfred Gibson recounts in detail his experiences with the trial:

> President Lincoln was shot by John Wilkes Booth on the night of Good Friday, April 14, 1865, during the performance of Tom Taylor's play, 'Our American Cousin,' given as a benefit to Miss Laura Keene, who had appeared about 1,000 times in the character of Florence Trenchard.
>
> When the shot was fired some lines had just left the lips of Harry Hawk, who was playing the part of Asa Trenchard. The celebrated actors, Joseph Jefferson and the elder Sothern, had both played in this piece with Miss Keene, but were not in her company at Washington.
>
> This was five days after Lee surrendered and exactly four years from the time our flag had been hauled down from Fort Sumter. The tragedy occurred in Ford's Theatre, which was never a place of amusement thereafter, finally being purchased and used by the Government.
>
> Booth fled into Virginia and was overtaken south of the Rappahannock River, where he was shot by Sergeant Boston Corbett during the attempt to capture him. There had been a previous plan to kidnap the President and take him to Richmond, which failed.

General Wallace on Trial Board

The eight prisoners who were in the abduction conspiracy plot to assassinate several heads of the Government were tried by a military commission of nine officers, one of them being Major General Lew Wallace, who afterward wrote

161

'The Fair God,' 'Ben Hur' and 'The Prince of India.' The proceedings were recorded by Benn Pitman, of shorthand fame.

When not yet sixteen I enlisted as a fifer in the 215th Pennsylvania Infantry, but soon after my regiment reached the army in Virginia, at the suggestion of Lieutenant Colonel Jones, who knew my father in Norristown, I applied for and obtained a clerkship at the headquarters of the Third Division, Ninth Army Corps, commanded by Major General John F. Hartranft, also from Norristown and afterward Governor of Pennsylvania. Soon after the assassination of Lincoln, General Hartranft was ordered to report to General Hancock, another Norristown man, at Washington, to take command of the military prison in the old penitentiary building on the arsenal grounds. There the conspirators were confined and there the trial took place.

General Hartranft took me with him in an army wagon to Alexandria, thence by boat to Washington, to act as his clerk at the prison. Four sergeants, acting as turnkeys, gave me daily accounts of all that transpired with the prisoners. I kept a record of those facts and wrote a report every morning for General Hartranft to sign and forward to general Hancock.

A clerk was necessary, but there was so little to do that I had to devise stunts for amusement. Sometimes I would pitch quoits with the prisoners when they were allowed to take exercise in the prison yard. Then I played the fife, annoying the general's staff officers so much that he frequently gave me passes to go out and see the sights of Washington.

After the trial commenced I found much to interest me in the courtroom. Testimony began May 12 and ended June 14. After arguments of counsel the commission deliberated and pronounced sentences June 30, the trial lasting seven weeks. President Johnson gave his approval July 5, eight being convicted. Four were hanged on July 7. Mrs. Surratt, Payne, Atzerodt and Herold were all hanged at one time, standing in a row on two trap doors. Arnold O'Laughlin, Dr. Mudd and Spangler were sentenced to a fort on the Dry Tortugas, an island off the coast of Florida, the first three for life and Spangler for six years.

Spangler was a sceneshifter at Ford's Theatre and failed to carry out his instructions to throw the audience in darkness by turning out the lights at the fatal moment. He arranged the door of Lincoln's box for the entrance of Booth and aided the latter to escape through the rear of the theatre.

Dr. Mudd was shown to be in the conspiracy, and Booth, when in flight, went out of his way to the doctor's residence in Virginia, to have his leg set, it being broken when he jumped from President Lincoln's box to the stage.

O'Laughlin was to attack Grant, but General and Mrs. Grant left Washington unexpectedly early that evening to see their children in Burlington, New Jersey. He [O'Laughlin] was a genial individual and showed some affection for me by giving me a pair of gold sleeve buttons just before he was sent to his future residence.

Arnold was out of the city the night of the assassination, but he was prominently connected with Booth and the other conspirators in the abduction plot, having made a confession regarding same.

A yellow fever epidemic broke out at the Dry Tortugas in 1867, during which O'Laughlin died of the disease. Dr. Mudd rendered such efficient service during the emergency that the officers recommended his pardon, which was granted in 1869. Arnold and Spangler also were pardoned the same year.

Herold, only twenty-three years old, spent much of his time with Booth, somewhat like an errand boy, took part in the flight and was captured with Booth when the latter was shot. Booth was buried under one of the lower ground floor cells of the penitentiary building at the arsenal. In February, 1869, he was reinterred in Baltimore by his brother, Edwin Booth, who never played in Washington after the tragedy and did not reappear on the stage anywhere for nearly a year, when he was received with unstinted applause.

Atzerodt was delegated to kill Vice President Johnson, but made a mess of the job. I was in front of the scaffold at the execution, only ten feet away from Atzerodt, and heard him mumble, "Shentlemens, take ware." Evidently he meant to imply, "You here can see my ending, so, gentlemen, beware."

Dropped Vials in Coffins

When the four bodies were cut down it devolved upon me to place hermetically sealed small glass vials I had prepared, containing the name of each, into the proper coffins. Several years later, when relatives obtained the bodies, I read in the newspapers that identifications was made possible through the discovery of these vials. Annie Surratt, daughter of the convicted woman, came to the prison, and after bidding her mother farewell was taken to my room on the third floor just outside the prison door, and lay sobbing on the bed. Had she looked out the window of my room she could have seen the execution. Some years later I heard of her living on Cherry Street in Philadelphia.

Occasionally some one speaks of hanging an innocent woman, but those on the spot had no doubt of Mrs. Surratt's guilt. Her house was shown to be the meeting place of the conspirators, led by Booth and her son, John H Surratt. Payne, in hiding for three days after stabbing Secretary Seward, was captured while entering this house without knowing it to be in the possession of Government officers. He was disguised as a laborer with a pick on his shoulder and, when questioned, said Mrs. Surratt had sent for him to see about digging a gutter.

It was brought out at the trial that Mrs. Surratt went to a tavern in Surrattsville, twelve miles south of Washington, owned and formerly kept by her, but leased in 1864 to John M. Lloyd, and left Booth's field glasses on the afternoon of the murder with Lloyd, telling him to have them ready that night, some whisky and two carbines that had been left on a previous occasion by John H. Surratt, Herold and Atzerodt. Booth and Herold, while escaping on horseback from Washington, called that night and received the field glasses, whisky and carbines from Lloyd. And it was shown that Booth furnished the money to hire the horse and buggy Mrs. Surratt used that afternoon.

Surratt Jury Disagreed

John H. Surratt, co-master of ceremonies with Booth, was giving directions to the conspirators on Good Friday and fled that night for Canada. About June, 1866, he was located as a papal zouave in Italy, arrested, escaped and recaptured in Egypt. He was placed on trial June 10, 1867, in a civil court in Washington. The jury could not agree and he was finally discharged June 22, 1868.

Ordered Grant to Stop Smoking

General Grant returned hurriedly to Washington the morning after the assassination. He was a witness at the trial of the eight conspirators and, while waiting to be called, sometimes came out of the stuffy courtroom to walk in the corridor, upon which the door of my room opened.

On one occasion he lit a pipe and it became the duty of the 16-year-old clerk from Philadelphia to jauntily saunter up to the ex-tanner of Galena who had commanded a million men, and politely call his attention to a "no smoking" notice that General Hartranft had instructed the youth to place on the wall. Explaining to him that it was dangerous to smoke in the Arsenal, he emptied his pipe, put it in his pocket, and indulged in the sedative weed elsewhere during his attendance at the military court.

Many of the events of my nearly four months' sojourn in Washington appeared to me at the time to be merely everyday, matter-of-fact occurrences, but now they are listened to with interest, after the lapse of more than sixty years, by people of today.

I never saw my regiment again after leaving the Army of the Potomac in that wagon. When the penitentiary job ended General Hartranft arranged for me to go to the headquarters of General Augur, who was in command of the city. The regiment was mustered out at Fort Delaware early in August, 1865, and I received my honorable discharge and extra clerkship pin money a few days later at Washington.

Yearning for knowledge, I was accorded the unusual privilege of re-entering the Central High School, where I started in 1862, finishing in 1867.

Appendix II

Gibson Diary Extract, 1919

In his 1919 diary, under the heading of "Plans for 1919," Gibson writes, "When I record certain experiences, I will pick some of the best, and describe them in detail, imitating as nearly as possible the style of a romance, or of a novel." And here in full is one of his experiences at a séance. Gibson would later attend many more séances, often with Houdini, always with a watchful eye to what was really happening. For years after Houdini's death, Gibson would attend the annual October 31st séance to attempt to make contact with the deceased escape artist.

The Seance

The following account is a record of the Seance which I attended on September 4th [1919]. In it I will try to give exact details and show the methods by which the medium gained her information. My companions at the Seance were ... Paul, who has had considerable experience at such meetings, knows of many fraudulent cases, and demonstrates a mind reading performance as his hobby. Oscar Meyer (Ed Loraine) who is an ardent magical enthusiast; Mr. John Dittman of San Antonio, Texas, and ex-professional magician, who knew and now knows all the great magicians since & including Alexander Herrmann & Buatier deKolta, who has attended seances of the most elite sort, who performs anti-spiritualist's phenomena of the Falking [sic] Hand, Sealed Message variety; and myself.

I arrived at the Seance slightly late. Paul & Ditman were there already. Everyone present had laid an article on the table along with $.50, which the medium said was merely a fee taken to exclude a low class of curiosity seekers, and not as a means of profit. But as 30 people attended the meeting, one could not help but think that $15.00 a night would be a very profitable return for her work if she chose to use it as such. She said nothing about donating the sum to charity, which she might well have done, since it was not a profit. But I digress.

I cannot take time, trouble, nor space to tell of everything that happened. She picked up an article belonging to a young lady present and at once conjured up a "spirit," who carried her back one — two — three — four- weeks, to the early part of August. Turning to the girl she said, "Did not some trouble come into your

165

household at that time?"—"No"—"Now tell me, is there not a young man, with whom you are closely acquainted, somewhat taller and darker than yourself, who calls on you frequently?"—"Well, yes, he *is* rather dark."—"Ah! and did you not disagree with him — not exactly disagree but have some doubts regarding certain matters which he desired to undertake?"—"Well-er-yes, we did have some trouble"—"There! Why did you not tell me that at once! You see I was right!"— and so she went on to exaggerate the difficulties and give the girl advice.

Now to one at all acquainted with the ways of mediums, this was very convincing —convincing of the fact that no spirits were involved. For everyone has trouble of some sort, and every young girl has a beau. And the medium took advantage of this latter fact more than once. Twice — or maybe three times— when talking with a girl, she "ran in" a young man — a very safe venture.

To another girl she asked —"Have you not a delicate little child in your family?"—"Well, no— she's not delicate." (Thus the medium knew the child was a girl.) "I do not mean sickly — I mean not over-strong."—"No, she's quite strong."—"But is she not troubled at times with some trouble here"— designating her throat etc., thus taking in throat trouble, heart trouble, lung trouble, etc.—"Yes— she has a cold now." Then the medium smiled a "know-it-all" grin [and] explained how she was a seer & could tell anything and all the old ladies looked as tho' they were murmuring, "Wonderful!"

To a girl decidedly Irish, "I seem to see an old lady — across great waters, who calls for you. Have you any relative of the sort who has passed into the spirit world?" It was 10 to 1 with the odds on the medium. The girl said, "Yes." With one of the girls a little child was said to have died. The girl knew of no such child. The medium said that such a child had lived and never had a name — died shortly after birth. If it were not a public seance, she would prove it. But, all of these girls had been to her seance before, and if she was not just taking a chance —for the girl had admitted that she had "sneaked out" to come to the seance, and therefore the medium knew she would not bring the matter up at home — I feel sure that the medium knew the girl's name and had looked up birth records.

In the course of the evening, the medium committed one notable "bull". A lady passed up her "marker" to the table, along with that of another lady. "But no!" exclaimed the medium. "Don't do that, or you and not the owner will receive the reading. Let her pass up her own article herself." Then later in the seance, when she went off the track in the course of a reading, she said, looking at the ring which she held, and which was evidently an heirloom, "Has not some one worn this before you?"—"Yes," was the reply. "Oh, that will never do for she will receive the reading and not you!"

In other words the spirits were quite particular. For early in the evening they would only give their reading to the person who *passed* in the "marker," and later in the seance, the person who passed it in had nothing to do with it, but the owner would receive the message!

Early in the evening she said to a girl —"You will go home, and some one will say —'Oh she's been to the Fortune Teller's.' No greater insult could be offered me if some one slapped me in the face. I am not a fortuneteller. My mission is spiritual unfoldment!"

She also commented on the unfair way in which her rent had been raised — how she disliked people who took advantage of a person and thought they were "green" and easily taken in. And she smiled sweetly.

A young man near us was "unsettled" in his affairs but he should keep ahead, and all would come out well. After his reading, she asked for a question. She had done this with all the others, but none of them had one — except one very ambiguous question. He asked, "Will I have to make a trip to the middle West in the near future?"— Quick as a flash, she said —"Yes, you will, but you know you will already," and then she talked on that trip, and sidetracked to some other "advice." From the way he asked the question, however, it seemed evident that he was considering such a trip, but she talked fast to keep him from denying it, in case she should be wrong.

She had previously inquired if we four were all strangers and never there before — we said "yes." She replied she was anxious to see us, for she knew that a thought was coming from some one of us — or more — saying, "I wonder if there is anything in this?" She said, "Thoughts are things!" But of course no[t] one of us had any such thought in mind, altho' Mr. D. was wondering if by some telepathic means she might divulge the secret of our mission, for he (D.) thinks that the mediums may in some cases have latent telepathic powers.

She said once, "Some one in the room wants to move." But no one responded. As a number of people were uncomfortably seated, this was a good chance in her favor, but she missed out, and passed the matter aside.

When she came to D. she was at her best. "I see a short man, who has recently passed into the spirit world. Have you any such relative?"—"No"—"No such a relative who has passed beyond?"—"*Not recently.*"—"No relative at all?"— "*No male relative.*" Quite a natural conversation, but note — in it she found that a male relative *was* deceased —*not recently.* And that a female relative was deceased *rather recently.* At once the male relative disappeared and the medium was upset by the condition of a woman who was alive, but not well. Did he not have such an acquaintance? As Mr. D. told me later, nearly every man is well acquainted with one particular woman. The medium hastened to explain that this "condition" was unknown to him, being just a little trouble or worn out feeling. Mr. D. admitted such an acquaintance, but did not know that she was ill. The medium hastened to explain that the lady was not sick in bed — just a trifle "out of sorts."

Then she came through with her trump card. She described a lady with gray hair who had "passed beyond," and in her description, *described D.* Of course the description would fit a near relative, and the near relative had died, as she had previously found out. Then she spoke of a man, and again described him; this was the male relative who had died *not recently.* Then she spoke of a little child, and "felt around" so that if she missed her guess, she could work it out right. Nearly every family has a little child who is deceased, especially since the paralysis and flu epidemics. It happened that D. had such a child in his family. Of course she made a lot out of her success in describing his deceased relations.

Then he "had trouble in business." Nowadays everyone has. He admitted some difficulties had arisen, but he had several businesses. She "seemed to hear machinery." He said that was his manufactory. Then she tried to describe a man under him, short, and light in complexion. His manager, he said, was short but dark. So she connected trouble up with some vague party, and as he *had* had trouble with his manager, he gave her a lead, which she followed well.

But his question —"Is it advisable for me to keep certain Texas properties?"

He meant manufacturing plants etc. which it was advisable for him to keep thinking he lived *here* and not suspecting his residence in Texas, she thought he had Oil well stock, so prevalent nowadays. But seeing a chance for a private seance, she offered to tell him regarding his properties if he would let her hold a letter from there; and she offered to arrange a private seance.

With Mayer, she got into trouble. He was not over-careful to lead her on, so she got to his question as quickly as possible. She had of course harped on his uncertainty. So he asked her which of two business undertakings he should take up. (Booking agency, or stage.) She said, "I see you moving in one of these out of the city." (But if she had said permanently settled she could have stuck it as well.) "Yes—to some extent," said Meyer. So she told him to take up that work. But she had not hit anything good or spectacular with him, so she tried another scheme of action:

"Some one named William is calling," she said—"Does anyone know a William?" Usually a safe bet, but no one responded. Picking up some keys, she asked the owner if he recognized William. But no result. After vain trials, something "told her" that the influence was not his, so she dropped the keys. Now I know a William K. with whom I was once very familiar, but absence, and our desires and pursuits being different, we no longer are intimate, but nothing has ever come between us—simply a divergence of our channels. So I said I once knew a William very well, and explained that conditions had to some extent separated our acquaintance.

"Ah—one who has passed into the beyond?"—"Oh, no."—"I see one whom conditions—or better, unfortunate circumstances have caused to lose his former friendly relationship with you." And so she went on, supposing a friendship broken by a quarrel, and advising a renewal, and telling of a gray haired man, who was saddened by the occurrence. (The gray haired man was evidently calculated to be a deceased grandfather; she talked as tho' the party in question had "passed beyond," but did not definitely say so, hoping that I would recognize him. But as both my grandfathers died long before I was born, she missed her guess that time.) She told how so far I had shown an aptitude for business—but I had never yet been in any business. Then she told of the possibilities of the fall and winter. My plans *are* at present unsettled, but so they are with most young men of my type. Then, after I had led her on [the few words here are indecipherable] attention she came to the question. A friend of mine H- M- is at present away in the Navy. He and I never write; we have often been separated; but whenever we meet again our joy is boundless. I asked why "my friend" did not write. Could there be anything that could have caused "my friend" to neglect me so? I so worded my question as to make her think the friend was a girl. But she was too sly for that. Acting upon the success she thought she had had with "William," she told how unfortunate conditions were between my friend and myself. How she saw an outside influence of some one who would position my friend's mind against me—"But you know your friend will return?"—"Yes." "Then your acquaintance can be taken up and differences settled—all will come out well."

I having given her plenty of rope she hung herself when she hit Paul. After calling in an old gray haired lady, whom Paul recognized as his mother, she said—"this lady passed into the beyond?"—"Yes"—"But it was not in Philadelphia"—"Oh, yes!"—"You misunderstand me. I meant she was not born in

Philadelphia, did not live here the early part of her life"—"Oh, no." After remarking on Paul's business ability, she asked for his question. He asked, "Will the group of men with whom I am associated succeed in securing the building they desire for their business venture?" The group of men was our magical club. The business venture a performance at the Little Theatre, which we could have any time we wanted it for $100.

"I see four men (meaning us four) at the head of this undertaking."—"Oh, no."—"Are you certain there are not four men heading this—directly concerned in its success?"—"No, there are about 25."—"Yes, but four are the real heads." (There are Pierce, Paul, and Meyer—3—who are really running the affair)— "No, not four, at the head."—"But you wish to know about your venture?"— "Yes." (as 25 men were concerned, she at once scented a big affair.)—"Well, you will have a hard time (rents are high, buildings scarce) but you will finally obtain your building. But you will pay a price, a great price, far more than you wish or expected to pay. You will be successful, etc. etc." She entirely missed the point, talking about a big business, elaborating conditions, and getting things wrong generally.

Meyer and I could not restrain ourselves entirely during the last part of Paul's "reading," and the medium got kind of peeved, so we quieted down. But after leaving that room, I was convinced as before in the saying that, "one is born each minute."

Notes

Chapter 1

1. Robert Gibson, M.D., personal interview with author, 22 August 1998.
2. Kate Douglas Wiggin, *My Garden of Memory — An Autobiography* (Boston: Houghton Mifflin Company, 1923).
3. Jim Haviland, "Revival of The Shadow," *MaineLife* (December 1981): 18–20.
4. Wendel W. Gibson interview.
5. Wendel W. Gibson interview.

Chapter 3

1. "Walter B. Gibson '20 — from poker in the dorm and magic in the classroom to the Shadow and Harry Houdini," *The Colgate Scene* (September 1975).
2. "Walter B. Gibson '20."
3. J. Randolph Cox, *Man of Magic and Mystery: A Guide to the Work of Walter B. Gibson* (Metuchen, NJ: The Scarecrow Press, 1988), pp. 8–9,192.
4. "Hocus Pocus Talks to Walter B. Gibson," *Hocus Pocus*, 3, 1 (January–March 1981): 16–23, p. 19.
5. "Hocus Pocus Talks to Walter B. Gibson," p. 19.
6. "Hocus Pocus Talks to Walter B. Gibson," p. 18.
7. "He Is The Shadow," Rutland *Daily Herald*, 3 November 1983: 7, 14.
8. "Time Stands Still for Author," *Philadelphia Inquirer*, 29 February 1976: 2H.
9. "Time Stands Still for Author."
10. "He Is the Shadow."
11. Robert Gibson, personal interview with author, 22 August 1998.
12. J. Randolph Cox, pp. 5, 191.
13. J. Randolph Cox, pp. 8, 192–193.
14. "Hocus Pocus Talks to Walter B. Gibson," p. 20.
15. Walter B. Gibson, "Memorial" (of Burling Hull), 22 November 1982.
16. "Hocus Pocus Talks to Walter B. Gibson."

Chapter 4

1. Walter Gibson, *The Master Magicians* (New York: Doubleday, 1966), pp. 139–141.
2. Walter Gibson, *The Master Magicians*, p. 161.
3. Walter Gibson, *The Master Magicians*, p. 143.

4. Walter Gibson, *The Master Magicians*, p. 145.

5. "Thurston the Great Magician," program (Pittsburgh: Edward J. Murray, 1927).

6. "Thurston the Great Magician."

7. "Thurston the Great Magician."

8. "Thurston the Great Magician."

9. "Hocus Pocus Talks to Walter B. Gibson," Part II, *Hocus Pocus*, 3, 2 (April – May 1981): 19–23.

10. Programs, radio.

11. Walter Gibson, *The Master Magicians*, p. 147.

12. Programs, radio.

13. *J. Randolph Cox, Man of Magic and Mystery: A Guide to the Work of Walter B. Gibson* (Metuchen, NJ: The Scarecrow Press, 1988), p. 15.

14. "Hocus Pocus Talks To Walter B. Gibson," *Hocus Pocus*, 3, 1 (January – March 1981): 16–23.

15. Walter B. Gibson, "$31,000 Magic Challenge," *Houdini's Magic Magazine*, 1, 1 (August 1977): 18–22, 92.

16. Walter Gibson, *The Master Magicians*, p. 159.

17. Walter Gibson, *The Master Magicians,* p. 132.

18. "Thurston the Great Magician."

19. Walter Gibson, *The Master Magicians*, pp. 133–134.

20. "Hocus Pocus Talks To Walter B. Gibson," p. 21.

21. Walter B. Gibson, personal letter to Jane Thurston, 1 April 1982.

22. Walter B. Gibson, personal letter to Jane Thurston.

23. "Hocus Pocus Talks to Walter B. Gibson."

24. Walter Gibson, *The Master Magicians*, pp. 134–136.

25. Walter Gibson, *The Master Magicians,* pp. 154.

26. Walter Gibson, *The Master Magicians,* pp. 158–159.

27. Walter Gibson, *The Master Magicians,* p. 157.

28. "Hocus Pocus Talks to Walter B. Gibson."

29. "Hocus Pocus Talks to Walter B. Gibson," Part II.

30. Walter Gibson, *The Master Magicians,* p. 159.

31. Walter B. Gibson, interview, 1980.

32. Walter Gibson, *The Master Magicians,* p. 160

33. Walter Gibson, *The Master Magicians,* p. 154

34. "Magician's Trick Turns City Into Bank," *Reading Times*, 9 September 1978: 11, 30.

Chapter 5

1. Walter B. Gibson, "$31,000 Magic Challenge," *Houdini's Magic Magazine*, 1, 1 (August 1977): 18–22, 92.

2. Bernard A. Drew, ed. , "Walter Gibson's Magicians," *Attic Revivals* (1982): 1–8.

3. "Hocus Pocus Talks to Walter B. Gibson," *Hocus Pocus*, 3, 1 (January–March 1981): 16–23.

4. Bernard A. Drew.

5. Walter B. Gibson, *The Original Houdini Scrapbook*, (New York: Sterling Publishing, 1976).

6. Walter B. Gibson, *The Original Houdini Scrapbook*.

7. Walter B. Gibson, *The Original Houdini Scrapbook*.

8. Walter B. Gibson, *The Original Houdini Scrapbook*.

9. Walter B. Gibson, *The Original Houdini Scrapbook*.

10. Walter B. Gibson, *The Original Houdini Scrapbook*.

11. Walter B. Gibson, *The Original Houdini Scrapbook*.

12. "Hocus Pocus Talks to Walter B. Gibson."

13. John Fleischer, "Plywood, Pads, and Prestidigitation!— A Profile of Wendel Gibson," (*FizBin* January–March 1996): 7–9.

14. J. Randolph Cox, *Man of Magic and Mystery: A Guide to the Work of Walter B. Gibson* (Metuchen, NJ: The Scarecrow Press, 1988).

15. "Magician's Trick Turns City Into Bank," *Reading Times*, 9 September 1978: 11–30.

Chapter 6

1. Morris N. Young, M. D., "Shadowing 'The Shadow,'" *Magic Sounds*: 5.

2. Anthony Tollin, "The Shadow—The Making of a Legend," *The Shadow Chronicles* (Carrollton, GA: GAA Corporation Inc. , 1996).

3. Walter B. Gibson, interview, 1980.

4. J. Randolph Cox, Man *of Magic and Mystery: A Guide to the Work of Walter B. Gibson* (Metuchen, NJ: The Scarecrow Press, Inc., 1988), pp. 109–110.

5. Bernard A. Drew, ed., "Walter Gibson's Magicians," *Attic Revivals* (1982): 1, 8.

6. Bernard A. Drew, ed., "Walter Gibson's Magicians."

7. Will Murray, "Walter B. Gibson—Casting a Giant Shadow," *Starlog*, 9, 105 (April 1986): 59–62.

8. Walter B. Gibson, interview, 1980.

9. Will Murray, "Walter B. Gibson—Casting a Giant Shadow."

10. "Hocus Pocus Talks to Walter B. Gibson," *Hocus Pocus*, 3, 1 (January–March 1981): 16–23.

11. Anthony Tollin, pp. 10–11.

12. Wayne Robinson, "Who Is Walter B. Gibson? The Shadow Knows," *Discover— The Sunday Bulletin* (August 6, 1978): 6–9, 18–19.

13. Wayne Robinson, pp. 6, 8.

14. William Gildea, "The Shadow—The Crime Fighter Lives on in Walter Gibson's 282 Novels," *Washington Post* (May 13, 1978): C1, C3.

15. "Walter Gibson—The Man Behind The Shadow," *MAGIC Magazine*, 3, 11 (November 1976): 20–21, 24–25.

16. Anthony Tollin.

17. Bernard A. Drew, ed., "Walter Gibson's Magicians."

18. "He is The Shadow," *Rutland Daily Herald*, 3 November 1983: 7, 14.

19. Bernard A. Drew, ed., "Walter Gibson's Magicians."

20. Will Murray, "Walter B. Gibson—Casting a Giant Shadow."

21. Anthony Tollin, p. 12.

22. "'The Shadow' Knows His Creator to Return to Orlando Scene," *Sentinel Star*, 1977.

23. "Crime Pays Off," *Milwaukee Journal*, 1 July 1979: 1, 5.

24. J. Randolph Cox, pp. 22–23.

25. "Dashing off a yarn—Tales of evil lurked in mind of 'Shadow' creator," *Detroit News*, 24 February 1980: 1, 9A.

26. "Crime Pays Off."

27. Wayne Robinson.

28. Walter B. Gibson, "Me and My Shadow—A sentimental glance over my shoulder," *In the Weird Adventures of The Shadow* (New York: Grosset and Dunlap, 1966).

29. William Gildea.

30. "Author knows the 'Shadow's' checkered past," *Chicago Tribune*, 31 March 1982: 1, 8.

31. William Gildea.

32. Jim Haviland, "Revival of the Shadow," *MaineLife*, (December 1981): 18–20.

33. Wayne Robinson, p. 19.

34. Robert Basler, "Who Is Walter B. Gibson? The Shadow Knows," Eddyville, New York, newspaper article.

35. Bernard A. Drew, ed., "Walter Gibson's Magicians."

36. Walter Gibson (The Shadow), "A Million Words a Year for Ten Straight Years," *Writer's Digest* (March 1941): 23–27.

37. Will Murray, "Out of the Shadows—Walter Gibson," *Duende*, 1, 2 (Winter 1976–1977): 33–46, p. 39.

38. Anthony Tollin.

39. "Is He Gibson or Grant? ... Only The Shadow Knows," *Poughkeepsie Journal*, 24 November 1974.

40. "Dashing Off a Yarn...."

41. "'The Shadow' Knows His Creator to Return to Orlando Scene."

42. "Dashing Off a Yarn...."

43. Walter Gibson (The Shadow), "A Million Words a Year...," p. 24.

44. Walter Gibson (The Shadow), "A Million Words a Year...."
45. Will Murray, "Out of the Shadows—Walter Gibson," p. 45.
46. Will Murray, "Out of the Shadows—Walter Gibson."
47. Walter B. Gibson, "Me and My Shadow...."
48. Anthony Tollin.
49. Walter B. Gibson, "Me and My Shadow...."
50. "'The Shadow' Knows His Creator to Return to Orlando Scene."
51. Will Murray, "My friend, Walter Gibson," *Comics Buyer's Guide*, 3 January 1986: 56.
52. William Gildea.
53. Walter Gibson (The Shadow), "A Million Words a Year...," p. 25.
54. "Letters Stump Author of 7,440,000 Words of Thrills," *New York World–Telegram*, 15 May 1937.
55. "Letters Stump Author...."
56. William Gildea.
57. Walter Gibson (The Shadow), "A Million words a Year...," p. 25.
58. "Letters Stump Author...."
59. "Letters Stump Author...."
60. "'The Shadow' Knows His Creator to Return to Orlando Scene."
61. William Gildea.
62. Bernard A. Drew, ed., "Walter Gibson's Magicians."
63. William Gildea.
64. Bernard A. Drew, ed., "Walter Gibson's Magicians."
65. Wendel Gibson, personal interview with author, February 1997.
66. "How did he do it? Only the Shadow knows," *Examiner*, 12 July 1983.
67. "How did he do it...?"
68. Will Murray, "Out of the Shadows—Walter Gibson," p. 37.
69. "Only the 'Shadow' Knows And a Writer in Eddyville," *Sunday Freeman* (Kingston, NY), 28 May 1972: C–10.
70. Robert Basler.
71. Walter Gibson (The Shadow), "A Million Words a Year...."

Chapter 7

1. Walter Gibson, "Me and My Shadow—A sentimental glance over my shoulder," The *Weird Adventures of The Shadow* (New York: Grosset & Dunlap, 1966).
2. Anthony Tollin, "The Shadow—The Making of a Legend," *The Shadow Chronicles* (Carrollton, GA: GAA Corporation, 1996).
3. Anthony Tollin.
4. Bernard A. Drew, "The Turn-ons of Yesteryear," Gallery (December 1979): 61–63.
5. "Dashing off a yarn—An odyssey into the world of pulp writing," *Detroit News*, 24 February 1980: 1, 8A.
6. Robert Basler, "Who Is Walter B. Gibson? The Shadow Knows," Eddyville, NY, newspaper article.
7. Anthony Tollin.
8. Wayne Robinson, "Who Is Walter B. Gibson? The Shadow Knows," *Discover—The Sunday Bulletin* (August 6, 1978): 6–9, 18–19.
9. Will Murray, "Out of the Shadows—Walter Gibson," *Duende*, 1, 2 (Winter 1976–1977): 33–46.
10. Will Murray, "Walter B. Gibson—Casting a Giant Shadow," *Starlog*, 9, 105 (April 1986): 59–62.
11. Rex Miller, "The Strange Creature in Black—Remembering The Shadow," 1992(?).
12. Rex Miller.
13. Anthony Tollin.

14. Will Murray, "Walter B. Gibson — Casting a Giant Shadow."
15. Anthony Tollin.
16. Will Murray, "Walter B. Gibson — Casting a Giant Shadow."
17. Anthony Tollin.
18. Anthony Tollin.
19. Anthony Tollin.
20. "Help From the Shadow's Realm," *Los Angeles Times*, 8 January 1980: 8.
21. Anthony Tollin.
22. Anthony Tollin.
23. Anthony Tollin.
24. Anthony Tollin.
25. Anthony Tollin.
26. "Author knows the 'Shadow's' checkered past," *Chicago Tribune*, 31 March 1982: 1, 8.
27. Anthony Tollin.
28. Rex Miller.
29. Will Murray, "Remembering Walter B. Gibson," *Echoes*, 5 (February 1986): 36–45.
30. Walter B. Gibson, personal papers.
31. Bernard A. Drew, ed., "Walter Gibson's Magicians,"*Attic Revivals* (1982): 1, 8.
32. Bernard A. Drew, "The Turn-ons of Yesteryear."
33. Will Murray, "Out of the Shadows — Walter Gibson."
34. Rex Miller.
35. Will Murray, "Remembering Walter B. Gibson."
36. Bill Blackbeard, "Fore Shadowings," *Xenophile*, 2, 5 (September 1975): 6–7, 59–60.
37. Bill Blackbeard.
38. Will Murray, "Remembering Walter B. Gibson."
39. "Dashing off a yarn — Tales of evil lurked in mind of 'Shadow' creator," *Detroit News*, 24 February 1980: 1, 9A.
40. Will Murray, "Remembering Walter B. Gibson."
41. Bernard A. Drew, "The Turn-ons of Yesteryear."
42. Jim Haviland, "Revival of The Shadow," *MaineLife*, (December 1981): 18–20.
43. "Hocus Pocus Talks to Walter B. Gibson," Part II, *Hocus Pocus*, 3, 2 (April–May 1981): 19–23.
44. Bernard A. Drew, ed., "Walter Gibson's Magicians."
45. Bernard A. Drew, ed., "Walter Gibson's Magicians."
46. Will Murray, "Remembering Walter B. Gibson."
47. J. Randolph Cox, *Man of Magic and Mystery: A Guide to the Work of Walter B. Gibson* (Metuchen, NJ: The Scarecrow Press, 1988).
48. Bernard A. Drew, ed., "Walter Gibson's Magicians."
49. Will Murray, "Out of the Shadows — Walter Gibson."
50. J. Randolph Cox.
51. Will Murray, "Remembering Walter B. Gibson."
52. J. Randolph Cox.
53. J. Randolph Cox.

Chapter 8

1. Anthony Tollin, "The Shadow — The Making of a Legend," The *Shadow Chronicles* (Carrollton, GA: GAA Corporation, 1996).
2. "The Shadow Returns," TEMPO— *The Sunday Freeman*, (April 10, 1977): 4.
3. "The Shadow Returns."
4. Walter B. Gibson, personal diary, 26 July 1973.
5. Otto Penzler, "The Shadow Returns with Some Sweet Fruit for His Prolific Creator," *People Magazine* (24 November 1975): 49.

6. "Dashing off a yarn — Tales of evil lurked in mind of 'Shadow' creator," *Detroit News*, 24 February 1980: 1, 9A.

7. Will Murray, "Out of the Shadows—Walter Gibson," *Duende*, 1, 2 (Winter 1976–1977): 33–46.

8. Will Murray, "Walter B. Gibson — Casting a Giant Shadow," *Starlog*, 9, 105 (April 1986): 59–62.

9. Walter B. Gibson, personal diary, 11 & 31 July 1975.

10. Anthony Tollin.

11. J. Randolph Cox, Man *of Magic and Mystery: A Guide to the Work of Walter B. Gibson* (Metuchen, NJ: The Scarecrow Press, 1988).

12. Will Murray, "Remembering Walter B. Gibson," *Echoes*, 5 February 1986): 36–45.

13. Will Murray, "Remembering Walter B. Gibson."

14. Will Murray, "Out of the Shadows—Walter B. Gibson."

15. Otto Penzler.

16. Will Murray, "Walter B. Gibson — Casting a Giant Shadow."

17. Morris N. Young, M. D. , "At 79 — The Gibson Phenomenon," *Magic Sounds*, 18: 2–3.

18. Walter B. Gibson, *The Original Houdini Scrapbook* (New York: Sterling Publishing, 1976).

19. Walter Gibson, "Me and My Shadow — A sentimental glance over my shoulder," *The Weird Adventures of The Shadow* (New York: Grosset & Dunlap, 1966).

20. Wendel W. Gibson, personal interview with author, February 1997.

21. Robert Gibson, personal interview with author, 22 August 1998.

22. Robert Gibson, personal interview with author, 22 August 1998.

23. Walter Gibson (The Shadow), "A Million Words a Year for Ten Straight Years," *Writer's Digest* (March 1941): 23–27.

24. Robert Gibson, personal interview with author, 22 August 1998.

25. Robert Gibson, personal interview with author, 22 August 1998.

26. Robert Gibson, personal interview with author, 22 August 1998.

27. "The Shadow' Knows His Creator to Return to Orlando Scene," *Sentinel Star*, 1977.

28. Robert Gibson, personal interview with author, 22 August 1998.

29. Jim Haviland, "Revival of The Shadow," *MaineLife* (December 1981): 18–20.

30. Jim Haviland.

31. Bernard A. Drew, ed., "Walter Gibson's Magicians," *Attic Revivals* (1982): 1, 8.

32. Walter Gibson, "Me and My Shadow."

33. Gerald M. Kimball, personal interview with author, 8 July 1997.

34. Wendel W. Gibson, personal interview with author, 26 June 1996.

35. Robert Gibson, personal interview with author, 22 August 1998.

36. Robert Gibson, personal interview with author, 22 August 1998.

37. Robert Gibson, personal interview with author, 22 August 1998.

38. Wendel W. Gibson, personal interview with author, 10 July 1997.

39. Wendel W. Gibson, personal interview with author, 26 June 1996.

40. Wendel W. Gibson, personal interview with author, 26 June 1996.

41. Walter Gibson, "Me and My Shadow."

42. Wendel W. Gibson, personal interview with author, 26 June 1996.

43. Jim Haviland.

44. Robert Basler, "Who Is Walter B. Gibson? The Shadow Knows," Eddyville, NY, newspaper article.

45. Robert Gibson, personal interview with author, 22 August 1998.

46. Wendel W. Gibson, personal interview with author, February 1997.

Chapter 9

1. Robert Gibson, personal interview with author, 22 August 1998.

2. Robert Gibson, personal interview with author, 22 August 1998.

3. Daniel Waldron, *Blackstone — A Magician's Life* (Glenwood, IL: David Meyer Magic Books, 1999).

4. Robert Gibson, personal interview with author, 22 August 1998.

5. Daniel Waldron.

6. Robert Gibson, personal interview with author, 22 August 1998.

7. Joseph Dunninger, *100 Houdini Tricks You Can Do* (Greenwich, CT.: Fawcett Publications, 1954).

8. Harry Blackstone, Jr., et al., The *Blackstone Book of Magic & Illusion* (New York: New Market Press, 1985).

9. J. Randolph Cox, Man *of Magic and Mystery: A Guide to the Work of Walter B. Gibson* (Metuchen, NJ: The Scarecrow Press, 1988).

10. J. Randolph Cox.

11. J. Randolph Cox.

12. Harry Blackstone, Jr.

13. "Hocus Pocus Talks to Walter B. Gibson," Part II, *Hocus*, 3, 2 (April–May 1981): 19–23.

14. Harry Blackstone, Jr.

15. Morris N. Young, M. D., "At 79 — The Gibson Phenomenon," *Magic Sounds*: 2–3.

16. Wendel W. Gibson, personal interviews with author, February 1997 and 10 July 1997.

17. Harry Blackstone, Jr.

18. Bernard A. Drew, ed., "Walter Gibson's Magicians," *Attic Revivals* (1982): 1, 8.

19. Bernard A. Drew, ed., "Walter Gibson's Magicians."

20. "Magician's Trick Turns City Into Bank," *Reading Times*, 9 September 1978: 11, 30.

21. John Fleischer, *FizBin*, 2, 2 (April–June 1997): 8–10.

22. "Hocus Pocus Talks to Walter B. Gibson," Part II.

23. "Hocus Pocus Talks to Walter B. Gibson," Part II.

24. "Hocus Pocus Talks to Walter B. Gibson," Part II.

25. "Is He Gibson or Grant? ... Only The Shadow Knows," *Poughkeepsie Journal*, 24 November 1974.

26. William V. Rauscher, "Walter B. Gibson —1897–1985. Man of Letters and Literature," monograph, 1986.

Chapter 10

1. "Who knows what magic lurks in the hearts of men?" *Fort Worth Star-Telegram*, 3 September 1978: 24A.

2. Will Murray, "Remembering Walter B. Gibson," *Echoes,* 5 (February 1986): 36–45.

3. J. Randolph Cox, Man *of Magic and Mystery: A Guide to the Work of Walter B. Gibson* (Metuchen, NJ: The Scarecrow Press, 1988).

4. J. Randolph Cox.

5. J. Randolph Cox.

6. Morris N. Young, M. D. , "At 79 — The Gibson Phenomenon," *Magic Sounds*: 2–3.

7. Walter B. Gibson, "Harry Houdini: Magician or Psychic," *Beyond Reality*, December 1972: 16+.

8. Walter B. Gibson, "$31,000 Magic Challenge," *Houdini's Magic Magazine*, 1, 1 (August 1977): 18–22, 92.

9. Harry Houdini, personal letter to Dr. W. J. Crawford, 24 June 1920.

10. Hans Holzer, *Yankee Ghosts* (New York: Bobbs-Merrill Company, 1966), pp. 55–59.

11. Hans Holzer.

12. Hans Holzer.

13. Hans Holzer.

14. Will Murray, "Out of the Shadows— Walter Gibson," *Duende*, 1, 2 (Winter 1976–1977): 33–46.

15. Will Murray, "Out of the Shadows— Walter Gibson."

16. Joseph Dunninger, *100 Houdini Tricks You Can Do* (Greenwich, CT: Fawcett Publications, 1954).

17. Walter B. Gibson, personal papers.

18. J. Randolph Cox.

19. Walter B. Gibson, personal papers.

20. Walter B. Gibson, personal papers.

21. "Is He Gibson or Grant? ... Only The Shadow Knows," *Poughkeepsie Journal*, 24 November 1974.

22. "Time stands still for author," *Philadelphia Inquirer*, 29 February 1976: 2H.

23. "Who knows what magic lurks in the hearts of men?"

24. "Time stands still for author."

25. William V. Rauscher, "Walter B. Gibson—1897–1985. Man of Letters and Literature," monograph, 1986.

26. "Time stands still for author."

27. "Comic Strip Foretold Atom Bomb 3 Yrs. Ago," 1945 newspaper article.

28. "Memories that will not fade," *Freeman*, 22 November 1983: 1, 5.

Chapter 11

1. William V. Rauscher, The *Great Raymond — Entertainer of Kings — King of Entertainers* (Short Hills, NJ: David M. Baldwin, 1996).

2. William V. Rauscher.

3. William V. Rauscher.

4. Walter Gibson, *The Master Magicians* (New York: Doubleday, 1966).

5. Walter Gibson, *The Master Magicians*.

6. Walter Gibson, *The Master Magicians*.

7. Walter Gibson, *The Master Magicians*.

8. Walter Gibson, *The Master Magicians*.

9. Walter Gibson, *The Master Magicians*.

10. M. S. Mahendra, "Maurice F. Raymond," *The Linking Ring*, September 1940: 528–529.

11. William V. Rauscher.

12. William V. Rauscher.

13. "Crime Pays Off," *Milwaukee Journal*, 1 July 1979: 1, 5.

14. William V. Rauscher.

15. Wendel W. Gibson, personal interview with author, February 1997.

16. Walter B. Gibson, personal diary, 5 April 1977.

17. Walter Gibson, *The Master Magicians*.

18. Wendel W. Gibson, personal interview with author, February 1997.

19. "'China Boy' Keeps up with the News," *Boston Globe*, 7 October 1954.

20. J. Randolph Cox, *Man of Magic and Mystery: A Guide to the Work of Walter B. Gibson* (Metuchen, NJ: The Scarecrow Press, 1988).

21. Wayne Robinson, "Who is Walter B. Gibson? The Shadow Knows," *Discover — The Sunday Bulletin*, August 6, 1978: 6–9, 18–19.

22. Frank Gruber, "Walter Gibson," *Xenophile*, 2, 5 (September 1975): 5.

23. "He Is The Shadow," *Rutland Daily Herald*, 3 November 1983: 7, 14.

24. Will Murray, "Remembering Walter B. Gibson," *Echoes*, 5 (February 1986): 36–45.

25. Robert Gibson, personal interview with author, 22 August 1998.

26. *Then & Now*, Bulletin of the D & H Canal Historical Society, 3, 3 (December 1972).

27. Robert Basler, "Who Is Walter B. Gibson? The Shadow Knows," Eddyville, NY, newspaper article.

28. "Is He Gibson or Grant? ... Only The Shadow Knows," *Poughkeepsie Journal*, 24 November 1974.

29. "Is He Gibson or Grant?..."

30. William V. Rauscher.

31. Robert Basler.

32. Morris N. Young, M. D. , "At 79 — The Gibson Phenomenon," *Magic Sounds*: 2–3.

33. Walter B. Gibson, personal diary, 24 January 1975.

34. William V. Rauscher.

35. Walter B. Gibson, personal diary, 27 January 1974.

36. Walter B. Gibson, personal diary, 30 November 1979.

37. Walter B. Gibson, *The Original Houdini Scrapbook* (New York: Sterling Publishing, 1976).

38. Bill Larsen, "Eleventh Annual Academy of Magical Arts Awards Show," *Genii*, 43, 4 (April 1979): 266–271.

Chapter 12

1. "The Shadow Knows," *Hartford Courant*, 24 October 1978: W31.

2. "Is He Gibson or Grant? ... Only The Shadow Knows," *Poughkeepsie Journal*, 24 November 1974.

3. "Crime Pays Off," *Milwaukee Journal*, 1 July 1979: 1, 5.

4. "Time stands still for author," *Philadelphia Inquirer*, 29 February 1976: 2H.

5. "Is He Gibson or Grant?..."

6. Wendel W. Gibson, personal interview with author, 20 April 1997.

7. Robert Gibson, personal interview with author, 22 August 1998.

8. Stuart Matranga, "Superhero Screenwriters," *Comics Scene*, 2 (March): 32–33; 36–37.

9. Will Murray, "Walter B. Gibson — Casting a Giant Shadow," *Starlog*, 9, 105 (April 1986): 59–62.

10. Will Murray, "Walter B. Gibson — Casting a Giant Shadow."

11. Will Murray, "Walter B. Gibson — Casting a Giant Shadow."

12. "Is He Gibson or Grant?..."

13. Will Murray, "Walter B. Gibson — Casting a Giant Shadow."

14. David Kelly, "Who knows what evil lurks in the hearts of men? The Shadow Knows ... and so will Reagan in 1988," *National Examiner*, 22, 9 (February 26, 1985): 2.

15. Will Murray, "Remembering Walter B. Gibson," *Echoes*, 5 (February 1986): 36–45.

16. *Hiking Along History: Delaware & Hudson Canal* (Ellenville, NY: Rondout Valley Publishing, 1971).

17. *Then & Now*, bulletin of D & H Canal Historical Society, 3, 3 (December 1972).

18. *Hiking Along History.*

19. *Then & Now.*

20. Rob Borsellino, "The Shadow Returns," TEMPO— *Sunday Freeman* (April 10, 1977): 4.

21. *Yon Clarion Bell*, (Hamilton, NY: Mu chapter of Delta Kappa Epsilon at Colgate University, January 1978).

22. "DKE? The Shadow Knows," *Colgate Maroon*.

23. Rob Borsellino.

24. William V. Rauscher, personal interview with author, 13 June 1998.

25. Will Murray, "Out of the Shadows— Walter Gibson," *Duende*, 1, 2 (Winter 1976–1977): 33–46.

26. Will Murray, "My friend, Walter Gibson," *Comics Buyer's Guide*, 3 January 1986: 56.

27. William V. Rauscher, *Walter B. Gibson — 1897–1985. Man of Letters and Literature* monograph (1986).

28. William V. Rauscher, *Walter B. Gibson — 1897–1985. Man of Letters and Literature.*

29. William V. Rauscher, *Walter B. Gibson — 1897–1985. Man of Letters and Literature.*

30. William V. Rauscher, *Walter B. Gibson — 1897–1985. Man of Letters and Literature.*

31. William V. Rauscher, *Walter B. Gibson — 1897–1985. Man of Letters and Literature.*

32. Will Murray, "Remembering Walter B. Gibson."

33. William V. Rauscher, *The Great Raymond — Entertainer of Kings — King of Entertainers* (Short Hills, NJ: David M. Baldwin, 1996).

34. William V. Rauscher, *The Great Raymond.*

35. William V. Rauscher, *Walter B. Gibson — 1897–1985. Man of Letters and Literature.*

Afterword

1. William V. Rauscher, *The Great Raymond — Entertainer of Kings — King of Entertainers* (Short Hills, NJ: David M. Baldwin, 1996).
2. Robert Gibson, personal interview with author, 22 August 1998.
3. Will Murray, "Remembering Walter B. Gibson," *Echoes,* 5 (February 1986): 36–45.
4. Will Murray, "Remembering Walter B. Gibson."
5. Will Murray, "Remembering Walter B. Gibson."
6. Robert Gibson, personal interview with author, 22 August 1998.
7. R.J. Kelly, "Friends recall Walter Gibson," *Freeman*, 12 January 1986: 5.
8. "Upfront Alec Baldwin — He doesn't live life in Hollywood's 'Shadow.' What lurks in his heart? Not stardom," *USA Today*, 1 July 1994: 1D, 2D.
9. "All Style, No Substance — Sumptuous sets can't hide flat plot of 'The Shadow,'" *Chicago Tribune*, 1 July 1994.
10. "All Style, No Substance...."
11. "Upfront Alec Baldwin...."
12. "Upfront Alec Baldwin...."
13. Will Murray, "Walter B. Gibson — Casting a Giant Shadow," *Starlog*, 9, 105 (April 1986): 59–62.
14. "Who's Behind That Fedora," *USA Today*, 1 July 1994: 7D.
15. William V. Rauscher, *The Great Raymond*.
16. "Houdini Magical Hall of Fame," *Butterfield & Butterfield*, 15 November 1999.
17. William V. Rauscher, *The Great Raymond*.
18. William V. Rauscher, *The Great Raymond*.

Bibliography

Books

Benner, Helen Frances, M.A. *Kate Douglas Wiggin's Country of Childhood*. University of Maine Studies, second series, No. 71. Orono: University Press, 1956.

Blackstone, Harry Jr., et al. *The Blackstone Book of Magic & Illusion*. New York: New Market Press, 1985.

Cox, J. Randolph. *Man of Magic and Mystery: A Guide to the Work of Walter B. Gibson*. Metuchen, NJ: The Scarecrow Press, Inc., 1988.

Dunninger, Joseph. *100 Houdini Tricks You Can Do*. Greenwich: Fawcett Publications, Inc., 1954.

Gibson, Walter B. *The Bunco Book*. Holyoke: Sidney H. Radner, 1946.

_____. *The Master Magicians*. New York: Doubleday & Company, Inc., 1966.

_____. "Me and My Shadow—A sentimental glance over my shoulder." *The Weird Adventures of The Shadow*. New York: Grosset and Dunlap, 1966.

_____. *The Original Houdini Scrapbook*. New York: Sterling Publishing Co., Inc., 1976.

Hiking Along History: Delaware & Hudson Canal. Ellenville: Rondout Valley Publishing, 1971.

Holzer, Hans. "The Ghost of Gay Street," *Yankee Ghosts*. New York: Bobbs-Merrill Company, Inc., 1966. p. 55–59.

Rauscher, William V. *The Great Raymond — Entertainer of Kings — King of Entertainers*. Short Hills: David M. Baldwin, 1996.

_____. *The Houdini Code Mystery*. Pasadena: Mike Caveny's Magic Words, 2000.

_____. "Walter B. Gibson—1897–1985. Man of Letters and Literature." Monograph, 1986.

Silverman, Kenneth. *Houdini!!!— The Career of Ehrich Weiss*. New York: Harper Collins Publishers, Inc., 1996.

Tollin, Anthony. *The Shadow — The Making of a Legend*. Carrollton: GAA Corporation Inc., 1996.

"Thurston the Great Magician." Program. Pittsburgh: Edward J. Murray, 1927.

Vogel, Robert M. *Roebling's Delaware & Hudson Canal Aqueducts*. Smithsonian Studies in History and Technology 10. Washington: Smithsonian, 1971.

Waldron, Daniel. *Blackstone — A Magician's Life*. Glenwood: David Meyer Magic Books, 1999.

Wiggin, Kate Douglas. *My Garden of Memory — An Autobiography*. Boston: Houghton Mifflin Company, 1923.

Magazine Articles

The Antique Trader Weekly, (21 July 1993): 89, 91–93.

Bennett, Stan, ed. "Walter Gibson — The Man Behind The Shadow." *The MAGIC Magazine*, 3, 11 (November 1976): 20–21, 24–25.

Blackbeard, Bill. "Fore Shadowings." *Xenophile*, 2, 5 (September 1975): 6–7, 59–60.

Borsellino, Rob. "The Shadow Returns." *TEMPO — The Sunday Freeman*, (April 10, 1977): 4.

Cramer, Stuart. "In Person — Raymond." *Magicol Magazine*, (August 1993).

"Danny O'Neil to take over 'Batman,' 'Detective Comics.'" *The Comics Buyer's Guide*, (10 January 1986): 1.

Drew, Bernard A. "The Turn-ons of Yesteryear." *Gallery*, (December 1979): 61–63.

_____, ed. "Walter Gibson's Magicians." *Attic Revivals* (1982): 1+8.

Fellows of Ellsworth's, (March 1978).

Fleischer, John. "Plywood, Pads, and Prestidigitation! — A Profile of Wendel Gibson." *FizBin*, (January–March 1996): 7–9.

_____. *FizBin*, 2, 2 (April — June 1997): 8–10.

Gibson, Walter B. "$31,000 Magic Challenge." *Houdini's Magic Magazine*, 1, 1 (August 1977): 18–22, 92.

_____. "GABBATHA." *The Conjurors' Magazine*, 5, 1 (March 1949): 15–18.

_____. "Harry Houdini: Magician or Psychic." *Beyond Reality*, (December 1972): 16+.

_____. "The Indian Rope Trick." *The MAGIC Magazine*, (March 1975): 30–31.

_____. "Kellar." *The MAGIC Magazine*, (March 1975): 22+.

_____ (The Shadow). "A Million Words a Year for Ten Straight Years." *Writer's Digest*, (March 1941): 23–27.

Gruber, Frank. "Walter Gibson." *Xenophile*, 2, 5 (September 1975): 5.

Haviland, Jim. "Revival of The Shadow." *MaineLife*, (December 1981): 18–20.

"Hocus Pocus Talks to Walter B. Gibson." *Hocus Pocus*, 3, 1 (January — March 1981): 16–23.

"Hocus Pocus Talks to Walter B. Gibson." Part II. *Hocus Pocus*, 3, 2 (April — May 1981): 19–23.

Jones, Lloyd E. "The Amazing Walter B. Gibson." *Genii Magazine*, (January 1970): 239.

Kelly, David. "Who knows what evil lurks in the hearts of men? The Shadow Knows ... and so will Reagan in 1988." *National Examiner*, 22, 9 (February 26, 1985): 2.

Larsen, Bill. "Eleventh Annual Academy of Magical Arts Awards Show." *Genii*, 43, 4 (April 1979): 266–271.

Mahendra, M. S. "Maurice F. Raymond." *The Linking Ring*. September 1940: 528–529.

_____. "Maurice F. Raymond." *The Linking Ring*. October 1940: 605–607.

_____. "Maurice F. Raymond." *The Linking Ring*. December 1940: 756–760.

Matranga, Stuart. "Superhero Screenwriters." *Comics Scene*, 2 (March): 32–33; 36–37.

Miller, Rex. "The Strange Creature in Black — Remembering The Shadow."

Murray, Will. "My friend, Walter Gibson." *The Comics Buyer's Guide*. (3 January 1986): 56.

_____. "Out of the Shadows — Walter Gibson." *Duende*, 1, 2 (Winter 1976–1977): 33–46.

_____. "Remembering Walter B. Gibson," *Echoes*, 5 (February 1986): 36–45.

_____. "Walter B. Gibson — Casting a Giant Shadow." *Starlog*, 9, 105 (April 1986): 59–62.

"Norgil the Magician." *Publishers Weekly*, (10 October 1977).

Penzler, Otto. "The Shadow Returns with Some Sweet Fruit for His Prolific Creator." *People Magazine*, (24 November 1975): 49.

Prideaux, Tom. "How It Was in the Happy Days of Humbug." Review of *The Master Magicians*, by Walter Gibson. *Life*, (30 September 1966).

Robinson, Wayne. "Who is Walter B. Gibson? The Shadow Knows." *Discover — The Sunday Bulletin*. (August 6, 1978): 6–9, 18–19.

"The Shadow Returns." *TEMPO — The Sunday Freeman*, (April 10, 1977): 4.

Then & Now Bulletin — D & H Canal Historical Society, 3, 3 (December 1972).

Vermont News Guide, 18, 44 (7 November 1978): 2.

"Walter Gibson — The Man Behind The Shadow." *The MAGIC Magazine*, 3, 11 (November 1976): 20–21, 24–25.

"Walter B. Gibson '20 — from poker in the dorm and magic in the classroom to The Shadow and Harry Houdini." *The Colgate Scene*, (September 1975).

Yon Clarion Bell. Mu chapter of Delta Kappa Epsilon at Colgate University, (January 1978).

Young, Morris N., MD. "At 79 — The Gibson Phenomenon." *Magic Sounds*: 2–3.

_____. "Shadowing 'The Shadow'" *Magic Sounds*: 5.

Newspaper Articles

Basler, Robert. "Who Is Walter B. Gibson? The Shadow Knows." Eddyville, NY.

Buffum, Richard. "Help From the Shadow's Realm." *Los Angeles Times*. 8 January 1980: 8.

Chamberlain, Charles. "A Conversation with 'The Shadow.'" *Nashua Telegraph*. 25 October 1978: 26.

"'China Boy' Keeps up with the News." *Boston Globe*. 7 October 1954.

Clifton, Lewis. "How did he do it? Only the Shadow knows." *Examiner*. 12 July 1983.

Datko, Karen. "Magician's Trick Turns City Into Bank." *Reading Times*. 9 September 1978: 11 & 30.

Dawson, Bob. "DKE? The Shadow Knows." *The Colgate Maroon*.

Detjen, Jim. "Is He Gibson or Grant? ... Only The Shadow Knows." *N.Y. Poughkeepsie Journal*. 24 November 1974.

Dunn, William. "Dashing off a yarn — An odyssey into the world of pulp writing." *The Detroit News*. 24 February 1980: 1 & 8A.

_____. "Dashing off a yarn — Tales of evil lurked in mind of 'Shadow' creator." *The Detroit News*. 24 February 1980: 1 & 9A.

Ehrenburg, Ann. "Who knows what magic lurks in the hearts of men?" *Fort Worth Star — Telegram*. 3 September 1978: 24A.

Engle, William. "Letters Stump Author of 7,440,000 Words of Thrills." *The New York World-Telegram*. 15 May 1937.

Gilbert, Justin. "Comic Strip Foretold Atom Bomb 3 Yrs. Ago." 1945.

Gildea, William. "The Shadow — The Crime Fighter Lives on in Walter Gibson's 282 Novels." *Washington Post*. 13 May 1978: C1 & C3.

Hayes, Ed. "'The Shadow' Knows His Creator to Return to Orlando Scene." *Sentinel Star*. 1977.

Holmes, Mycroft. "The 'Shadow' returns." *The Boston Globe*. 24 July 1975: 13.

Horowitz, Mikhail. "Memories that will not fade." *The Freeman*. 22 November 1983: 1 & 5.

Huff, Claire. "Time stands still for author." *Philadelphia Inquirer*. 29 February 1976: 2H.

"Just among our shelves." *Cleveland Club Life*: 22.

Kelly, R. J. "Friends recall Walter Gibson." *The Freeman*. 12 January 1986: 5.

_____. "Magician Gibson dead, created 'The Shadow.'" *The Freeman*. 6 December 1985: 1 & 5.

La Francis, Mark. "Psychics Aim to Rouse Houdini." *Transcript Telegram*. 30 October 1982: 21.

Mulvaney, Lynn. "Disputed D & H Towpath.... A Significant Victory." *The Sunday Freeman*. 3 December 1972: 3.

"Only the 'Shadow' Knows and a Writer in Eddyville." *The Sunday Freeman*. 28 May 1972: C-10.

Price, Megan. "He is The Shadow." *Rutland Daily Herald*. 3 November 1983: 7 & 14.

"Revisiting Bygone Characters." *Philadelphia Inquirer*. 17 August 1984: 2.

The Rondout Valley Times. 29 March 1973: 1.

Saxon, Wolfgang. "Walter B. Gibson, the Creator of 'The Shadow', Dead at 88." *The New York Times*. 7 December 1985.

"Séance Seeks 'Word' from Houdini." *The Daily Freeman*. 31 October 1979: 1.

"The Shadow Knows." *The Hartford Courant*. 24 October 1978: W31.

"Studebaker—'The Great Raymond.'" *Chicago Daily News*. 9 March 1913.

Terry, Clifford. "Author knows the 'Shadow's' checkered past." *Chicago Tribune*. 31 March 1982: 1 & 8.

"Upfront Alec Baldwin—He Doesn't Live Life in Hollywood's 'Shadow.' What Lurks in His Heart? Not Stardom." *USA Today*. 1 July 1994: 1D & 2D.

Utz, Gene. "The Shadow's Resurrection." *Maine Antique Digest*. July 1996: 12D—14D.

"Walter B. Gibson." *Chestnut Hill Local*. 26 December 1985: 23.

Walters, Ray. "Paperbacks: New and Noteworthy—Paperback Talk." *The New York Times—Book Review*. 29 July 1979.

Wells, Robert W. "Crime Pays Off." *Milwaukee Journal*. 1 July 1979: 1 & 5.

"Who is Walt Gibson? 'The Shadow' knows." *Boston Herald American*. 24 October 1978: 36.

Wilmington, Michael. "All style, no substance—sumptuous sets can't hide flat plot of 'The Shadow.'" *Chicago Tribune*. 1 July 1994.

Wloszczyna, Susan. "Who's Behind That Fedora." *USA Today*. 1 July 1994: 7D.

Other Sources

Figner, Libby. Personal letter to author. 10 August 1998.

Gibson, Robert. Personal interview. 22 August 1998.

Gibson, Walter B. Interview. 1980.

_____. Lecture on 27 October 1973. Audiocassette. B. J. Hickman, 1999

_____. Personal diary. Keewaydin Log Book (Part I & II). 1913.

_____. Personal diary: 1908, 1913, 1914, 1916, 1917, 1918, 1919, 1920, 1921, 1973, 1974, 1975, 1976, 1977, 1979, 1980, 1981, 1982, 1983, 1984.

_____. Personal letter to Jane Thurston. 1 April 1982.

_____. Personal papers.

_____. "Memorial"—of Burling Hull. 22 November 1982.

Gibson, Wendel W. Personal interview: 26 June 1996, February 1997, 20 April 1997, 10 July 1997.

Grossman, John Henry. Personal letter to David Goodsell. 17 April 1986.

Houdini, Harry. Personal letter to Dr. W. J. Crawford. 24 June 1920.

Kimball, Gerald M. Personal interview. 8 July 1997.

Morey, Jim. Personal interview. 14 July 1997.

Press Release. "Memorial Service for Walter B. Gibson."

Rauscher, William V. Personal interview. 13 June 1998.

Reer, Gertrude. Personal interview. 10 August 1998.

Index

185